On the Very Edge

On the Very EDGE

Bidentities in Michelle Cliff's Fiction

Ian Kinane

University Press of Mississippi / Jackson

The University Press of Mississippi is the scholarly publishing agency of the Mississippi Institutions of Higher Learning: Alcorn State University, Delta State University, Jackson State University, Mississippi State University, Mississippi University for Women, Mississippi Valley State University, University of Mississippi, and University of Southern Mississippi.

www.upress.state.ms.us

The University Press of Mississippi is a member of the Association of University Presses.

Any discriminatory or derogatory language or hate speech regarding race, ethnicity, religion, sex, gender, class, national origin, age, or disability that has been retained or appears in elided form is in no way an endorsement of the use of such language outside a scholarly context.

Copyright © 2025 by University Press of Mississippi
All rights reserved
Manufactured in the United States of America

∞

Library of Congress Cataloging-in-Publication Data

Names: Kinane, Ian, author.
Title: On the very edge : bidentities in Michelle Cliff's fiction / Ian Kinane.
Description: Jackson : University Press of Mississippi, 2025. | Includes bibliographical references and index.
Identifiers: LCCN 2024036152 (print) | LCCN 2024036153 (ebook) | ISBN 9781496855145 (hardback) | ISBN 9781496855152 (trade paperback) | ISBN 9781496855169 (epub) | ISBN 9781496855176 (epub) | ISBN 9781496855183 (pdf) | ISBN 9781496855190 (pdf)
Subjects: LCSH: Cliff, Michelle—Criticism and interpretation. | Identity (Psychology) in literature. | Bisexuality in literature. | Biculturalism in literature. | Racially mixed people in literature. | LCGFT: Literary criticism.
Classification: LCC PR9265.9.C55 Z696 2025 (print) | LCC PR9265.9.C55 (ebook) | DDC 813/.54—dc23/eng/20240913
LC record available at https://lccn.loc.gov/2024036152
LC ebook record available at https://lccn.loc.gov/2024036153

British Library Cataloging-in-Publication Data available

To Melanie, for Michelle

Contents

Acknowledgments ix

"The Bifurcated Female":
An Introduction in Fragments 3

1. "Split into Two Parts":
Michelle Cliff's Double Consciousness 35

2. "The Third Division":
Michelle Cliff's Killing Ambivalence 59

3. "A Place for In-Betweens":
Michelle Cliff's Liminality 79

4. "Ways into Their Own Bodies":
Michelle Cliff's Queer Transactions 100

"Like the Bisexuality I Clung To":
Some Concluding Thoughts 122

Notes 127

Bibliography 137

Index 149

Acknowledgments

With great thanks to my former supervisor, Melanie Otto, in whose class on "African and Caribbean Literature" I first discovered Michelle Cliff.

To my colleagues Clare McManus, Lara Thorpe, and Jess Gray for their ever-steady steer on this project.

To past students Claire MacDiarmid, Gabrielle Nash, and Paige Carlson, whose own dissertations and assessment work paved the way for my thinking around this project.

To Mary Heath and Corley Longmire at University Press of Mississippi for their enthusiastic support, to Debbie Burke for her assiduous edits, and to the two anonymous reviewers for their insightful comments—whose names, in all likelihood, are to be found somewhere in the pages of this book.

And my greatest thanks, as ever, to Elizabeth Parker, who taught me how to live in the gray.

On the Very Edge

"The Bifurcated Female"

An Introduction in Fragments

Michelle Cliff's 1987 novel, *No Telephone to Heaven*, opens with something of an ironic promise. As the open-backed truck transporting the revolutionaries and their assortment of guns, rifles, and grenades wends its way upward through Cockpit Country in Jamaica, the novel's protagonist, Clare Savage, muses on the credulity of the American tourist trade and the propensity of the "white kids high on dope" (1996, 6) to stupefy themselves with Jamaican ganja, thus making it easier for Clare and her fellow revolutionaries to pilfer from them supplies of clothing and money. Clare reflects with mock pity on these so-called "sleepy-headed kids," the "poor little Americans," with their expectations of lives of sun-kissed tropical redolence and exotic ease, drawn to Jamaica's shores by the promise that has been advertised to them of "JAMAICA, A WORLD OF CULTURE WITHOUT BOUNDARIES." Within the broad political framework of Jamaican's neoimperial touristic practices, the promise of a "boundary-less Jamaica enables tourists . . . to inscribe themselves onto the island" and to "indulge their fantasies [as these poor little Americans are seemingly encouraged to do] by imaginatively writing themselves onto the scene" (Beriault, 662). As Fiona R. Barnes notes, "like so many so-called 'Third World' countries, [Cliff's Jamaica] has become the 'exotic' raw cultural material upon which the jaded palates of the First World feed" (23). Moreover, the irony of such a promise is all the more evident when we consider the fact that "[t]he Jamaica in Cliff's narrative is neither without boundaries nor allowed to coexist alongside its American mythology" (Gourdine, 45). Indeed, the very title of Cliff's novel, *No Telephone to Heaven*, centralizes the significance of conceptual boundaries and the bifurcation throughout the narrative of the physical and metaphysical realms: as Carmen Birkle notes, "[i]t seems that for Cliff and her female characters, there is 'no telephone to heaven,' no direct line to wholeness and happiness" (73). The title itself draws attention to the inherent and paradoxical split between the material world (telephone) and the transcendental or extramundane spiritual plane (heaven). As this book will evidence, Cliff's writings may be said to be concerned almost entirely with boundaries: with interrogating binary divisions, remapping conceptual borderlines, and figuratively rerouting Cliff's own—and by extension her readers'—considerations of boundaried identities across intersectional markers of race, gender, and sexuality.

Contrary to William Tell Gifford's claim that "[m]ost of Cliff's characters, and to some extent, her narrators, are radically free in constructing their own worldviews" whose "futures are open and [for whom] contingency surrounds them on all sides" (7), boundaries and borderlines—limiting, constraining, suppressing—actually abound in Cliff's writings, in both her fiction and in her creative nonfiction. For Jennifer Thorington Springer, Cliff's writings are specifically about "the dangers of ignoring boundaries" (56), which are often presented as "unchangeable and static" (51), while for Yi-Peng Lai, Cliff's work is concerned with the "borders between individual and nation, between domesticity and nature, and between homed and unhomed" (45). Isabel Hoving argues that boundaries and borders within Cliff's writing constitute "space[s] of the unspeakable," spatio-conceptual interstices "between living and dead, real life and shadowlife, present and past" (2001, 258), which Cliff occupies to redress (or perhaps readdress) those, like her, who occupy such interstices: those who exist on the borderlines of race, gender, and sexuality. Prominent Cliff scholar Kaisa Ilmonen also notes that Cliff's "borderline characters provide numerous examples of . . . the ambivalent positionings" necessary for Cliff to navigate the "rigid boundaries of her social environment" in Jamaica, the borders of which are often "violently policed" (2017, 93, 210). Indeed, as Cliff herself confesses in the poem "Within the Veil," published in her collection of autobiographical prose and poetry, *The Land of Look Behind* (1985), borders and boundaries are conceived of in essential terms as part of her racialized and gendered upbringing as a biracial Jamaican child: "Don't overstep your boundaries, girl!"—Cliff writes—"Act like you have a little sense / Was the lesson mama taught me / To live surrounded by a whiteman's fence" (1985, 90).

Gifford's above claim notwithstanding, though, in many ways, Cliff's oeuvre is about the emotional processional work involved in forging one's subjectivity along those borderlines of race and culture and along the boundaried fault lines of gender and sexual identity markers. Overstepping boundaries is precisely what Cliff does, both in her writing and in her being. Born in 1946, Michelle Cliff was a light-skinned Jamaican Creole with African and English heritage—that is to say, the mixed-race descendant of European and African intermarriage in the Caribbean. Complicating her racio-cultural status, Cliff moved with her parents from Jamaica to New York and back again during her adolescence and during the period in which Jamaica's nationalist agitation was at its highest. In her adolescence, Cliff returned to New York to earn a degree in European history, after which she enrolled in the Warburg Institute in London to undertake a PhD in comparative approaches to the Italian Renaissance. Cliff later worked as an editor for *Life* magazine in London and New York, where she connected with authors and critics of the women's movement, including the poet Adrienne Rich, who became her life partner. From a young age, Cliff's self-conception as a bisexual also ran up against traditional, boundaried, gendered expectations for Jamaican women, while her status as biracial and bicultural further confused her understanding of self during a politically tumultuous threshold in Jamaica's social and cultural history.

Cliff's first major book was *Claiming an Identity They Taught Me to Despise* (1980), a collection of poetry and prose fiction, the focus of which was "interracial prejudice" that enumerated "both the advantages gained by being light-skinned in a colorist society and the ways in which light-skinned blacks are taught to collaborate with the masters" (Barnes et al., 2). In 1984, Cliff published her first novel, *Abeng*, about Clare Savage, the fair-skinned biracial daughter of a Jamaican Maroon and the proud descendant of British plantocrats. Of *Abeng*, Lizabeth Paravisini-Gebert notes that "Clare's desire to reconcile the two sides of her ancestry is the focal point of her search for identity in the text" (40), a theme that, as we shall see, will become pervasive throughout Cliff's writing life. *Claiming an Identity They Taught Me to Despise* was followed in 1985 by another collection of poetry and prose fiction, the aforementioned *The Land of Look Behind*, and in 1987, *No Telephone to Heaven*, the sequel (of sorts) to *Abeng*. Having immigrated to the United States, Cliff's 1990 short story collection, *Bodies of Water*, addressed "her familiar topics of race relations, gender oppression, and imperialism" (41). This was followed by two further novels, *Free Enterprise* (1993) and *Into the Interior* (2010), as well as two more short story collections, *The Store of a Million Items* (1998) and *Everything Is Now* (2009), a compendium of new and collected stories. In summarizing Cliff's literary contribution, Isabel Hoving has noted that "Cliff called herself a political novelist, and this *double orientation* characterizes her work throughout" (2011, 27; my emphasis). As a *bi*cultural, *bi*racial, *bi*sexual woman of Jamaican American heritage, then, who lived between Jamaica and the United States, and whose fair skin meant that she was often perceived to be white, the frequently binaried nature of Cliff's writings represent something of a corollary to her duolocation as a subject: her "double orientation." As Lilleth Trewick notes, Cliff's "fragmented, liminal subject operat[es] in between [the] various polarities" (11) of traditional identity markers: Jamaican and North American (and British); Black and white; homosexual and heterosexual. Trewick further argues that Cliff's ethos as a postcolonial, feminist writer is reflected in her subjectivity: "[Cliff] starts by identifying herself as a Jamaican, but later realizes . . . her bi-racial status in Jamaica, her outside position as a migrant in America, as well as her lesbianism." (Though it must be acknowledged that Cliff does note in *The Land of Look Behind* that "Jamaica is who I am. No matter how far I travel—how deep the ambivalence I feel about ever returning. And Jamaica is a place in which we/they/I connect and disconnect—change place" [1985, 76]). Trewick also asserts that "[a]ccepting her fragmented identity, and finding strength in her liminal status, will provide the necessary foundation for [Cliff] to enact resistance" (11), as we shall see throughout the various chapters below. As this study will illustrate, Cliff's critics are particularly invested in the process of (often erroneously) labeling, categorizing, and identifying both Cliff and her characters, many of whom occupy precisely the fragmented, liminal status Trewick outlines, and as such, resist such efforts to be labeled, categorized, or identified according to traditional binaried assumptions.

Nowhere is this more evident, perhaps, than in the controversy surrounding Cliff's status as a writer of Caribbean fiction. However, in order to address this controversy, it becomes necessary for me to contextualize Cliff within the continuum of Caribbean writing at large. What follows is very much a whistlestop tour of Caribbean literary and critical history and one that is not meant, by any means, to be taken as definitive. Rather, my intention with the below is to identify major points of intersection between Caribbean literary history, in particular, and the critical ideation and thematic concerns at the heart of Cliff's writing. In so doing, my purpose is to illustrate how Cliff's work might be viewed (rightly) as having emerged from the overarching traditions of Caribbean writing before going on to explore the ways in which certain critics have problematized this inclusion. It is also worth underlining the fact that to speak of a "Caribbean literary history" or of "Caribbean writing" is itself something of a misnomer; as Louis James reminds us, the Caribbean Basin is "fragmented into Islands . . . there is no common language, its countries have inherited English . . . modified into Creole forms which are different within each area" (2). Moreover, the Caribbean territories are scattered across two thousand miles of ocean, from Guyana on the South American mainland to Barbados in the Atlantic Ocean (3); and Caribbean literatures appear in "at least four imperial languages and a number of local languages" (Dalleo, 1). While Rudyard Alcocer argues that "[a]ny attempt to speak of the Caribbean in theoretically abstract or holistic terms is potentially a risky project because each of the islands in the region has . . . a distinct history, ethnic make-up and economy" (6), J. Michael Dash believes that the (assumed) heterogenous nature of the Caribbean Basin "has become the methodological ground that facilitates recent attempts to establish theoretical models of the Caribbean" (6–7).

A number of scholars and cultural critics have attempted to provide theoretical models for discussing a unifying Caribbean identity while also paying respect to the heterogeneity of different islands and cultural contexts in the Basin. Paul Gilroy, for one, offers a conception of the Caribbean as part of the "Black Atlantic," the title of his eponymous 1993 book that identifies the slavery ship as the central metaphor of foundational Caribbean identity that draws together and connects the combined cultural heritage of imperialism across England, North America, and Africa, while another, Antonio Benítez-Rojo, in his seminal 1992 book *The Repeating Island*, argues that the heterogeneity and discontinuity of the Caribbean as a whole can be unified by the shared historical influence of plantation culture across the region. It is the disparity of the Caribbean region as a whole that led Benítez-Rojo to declare the Caribbean the "ultimate meta-archipelago" with the "spiral chaos of the Milky Way" (1, 5). Moreover, we must also contend with the somewhat prejudicial assumption that, for many in the Anglophone West, Caribbean literature was not considered to have "existed" until approximately the mid-twentieth century—another factor in assessing the complicated heritage of Michelle Cliff's inclusion within the canon of Caribbean writers, for, as we shall see, much of her writing derives from and extends some of those earliest traditions of the pre-twentieth-century period.

Prior to the "boom" years of the 1950s, the Caribbean was said to have been, in A. J. Seymour's words, "literarily asleep" (83). Indeed, in his article on "Discovering Literature in Trinidad," C. L. R. James notes that he did not "know much about West Indian Literature in the 1930s—there wasn't much to know" (1969, 73), while Arthur Derrick proclaimed that "[t]here seems to have been little worthy of serious consideration written before 1940 in the British West Indies" (73). Nevertheless, as David Dabydeen and Nana Wilson-Tagoe point out, the development of Caribbean writing "from the derivative and imitative poetry of the eighteenth and nineteenth centuries, from the often unconscious rejection of the West Indian experience in the early prose fiction, towards the social awareness and cultural consciousness of the mid-twentieth century is an indication of a literary trend steeped in the historical development of the West Indies itself" (13).[1]

In terms of definitional understandings, so-called "West Indian" literatures are those that usually have a "West Indian setting and contain fictional characters and situations whose social correlates are immediately recognizable as West Indian" (Ramchand 1970, 3); or, as Dabydeen and Wilson-Tagoe assert, literature "written by people from the West Indies . . . [concerning] subjects relevant to West Indian history and culture" (9). Much like Alison Donnell and Sarah Lawson Welsh, my preferred term—and that which I will use throughout—is "Caribbean literature," which is "more suggestive of a literature freed from the (re-)centring tendencies of a colonial and Commonwealth framework" (5; see Cummings 2012, 1–2). This is in preference to the various neologisms coined by critics, such as Rosamond King's "Cariglobal" (2014, 2) or Donnell's "Anglocreole" (2006, 9), the latter of which is used as inclusive of literatures written in Creole languages of the English-speaking Caribbean region in addition to those of Standard English. Caribbean literature, then, I take to be *any* work authored by inhabitants and/or immigrants of the Caribbean—that is, those former British islands in the Caribbean, the Greater and Lesser Antilles, as well as the Bahamas, Guyana on the South American mainland, and the coastal zones of Central America. The earliest of these works, according to Kenneth Ramchand, is *Becka's Buckra Baby* (1903), written by Jamaica's first poet laureate Tom Redcam, the nom de plume of Thomas Henry MacDermott (1970, 3)—though Ramchand himself also takes Herbert de Lisser's *Jane's Career: A Story of Jamaica* (1913) as the starting point for his *Introduction to the Study of West Indian Literature* (1976). (It should be noted, however, that *The History of Mary Prince, A West Indian Slave, Related by Herself* (1831), the first autobiography published by a Black woman recounting her enslavement in Bermuda, does predate Redcam.) Like Michelle Cliff, Redcam was a (white) Creole whose prolific work as an editor propelled his own literary career. Redcam's stewardship of the *Jamaica Times* and, in particular, *The All Jamaica Library*, a (failed) serial publication of Jamaican literature, illustrates his desire to give voice to a national Jamaican literature. Moreover, in 1909, Redcam published *One Brown Girl and ¼*. Much like Cliff's later novel *No Telephone to Heaven*, Redcam's novel is about a young woman who returns to Jamaica after undertaking her education in England and who, like Cliff's semi-autobiographical protagonist Clare Savage, struggles with the sense of alienation she feels from her Jamaican cultural and ethnic identity.

Another prominent early Caribbean writer, Herbert de Lisser, also a white Creole Jamaican (with African and Portuguese heritage), was a contemporary of Redcam's (indeed, had been encouraged by him in his own literary aspirations) and, in addition to his editorship of *The Jamaica Gleaner*, the national newspaper of Jamaica, a librarian and journalist. De Lisser's first novel, *Jane's Career: A Story of Jamaica*, is distinguished as the first published work that contains a Black Caribbean protagonist (Sani, 15) and the first in which the figure of the peasant is "given full status as a human person" (Ramchand 1971, xiv). The thematic links of *Jane's Career* to another of Cliff's novels (her first, *Abeng*) are evident in both authors' focus on the village life of their early-age protagonists: that of Jane's years in domestic apprenticeship during the burgeoning Jamaican protests against British colonialism in de Lisser's novel and Clare's school-age reflections on race, class, and inequality in Cliff's. Indeed, Cliff also seems to share de Lisser's propensity for narrative analepsis: much like Cliff's *Free Enterprise*, which recounts, in part, the historical friendship between African American entrepreneur Mary Ellen Pleasant and the white abolitionist John Brown, whose raid on Harpers Ferry was largely financed by Pleasant, de Lisser's final novel, *The Arawak Girl* (1958), is concerned with similar historicizing of the past—in this case, the socioeconomic contexts of the Indigenous Arawak people in the wake of Christopher Columbus's arrival to the Americas in 1492. However, unlike Cliff, whose work engages very much with the problematic heritage of colonialism and the fragmentation of Creole identities in postimperial nation-states, both Redcam and de Lisser's work served as apologist narratives, glorifying Britain and "emphasis[ing] white culture as the panacea for achievement" (Sani, 16). Adrianne Baytop notes that these earliest writings were the "well trained foster offspring of conventional pre-twentieth-century British literature" (32). Indeed, as Donnell and Lawson Welsh also observe, "[t]he fact that the majority of writing from this period is by Creoles (whose work tends to celebrate Caribbean culture and geography within the context of colonialism) has undoubtably affected both the quality and quantity of critical responses to literature before 1930" (22).

In response to this issue, as part of Caribbean literature's "precocious [rebellion] against British literary precedence" (Baytop, 33), a number of journals and periodicals emerged that focused on the social and political realities of "Caribbean-ness," particularly in the Trinidadian context: between 1931 and 1933, C. L. R. James and Alfred H. Mendes published *Trinidad*, a magazine of stories, poetry, and essays, and Albert Gomes spearheaded publication of *The Beacon*, a similar such magazine ("Grand Mixture," 9). A while later, in 1937, *Public Opinion* appeared, a political weekly staffed by a number of culturally significant women: Edna Manley, wife of Jamaica's first prime minister; poet Una Marson; and women's rights campaigner Amy Bailey. C. L. R. James's first (and only) novel, *Minty Alley* (1936), was not only the first novel by a Black Carib to be published in England, but it can also be credited as establishing—along with Mendes's *Pitch Lake* (1934)—the broader trend toward social realist "barrackyard fiction" representing the working class as literary subjects in Caribbean writing (Donnell and Welsh,

24)—a trend that Michelle Cliff would readily pick up. Also like Cliff, poet and novelist Claude McKay was an early Caribbean *émigré* who was born in Jamaica and who traveled to the United States and Britain: his writings in *Home to Harlem* (1928) and *Banjo* (1929), in particular, foster a sense of McKay's dislocation as a culturally dual subject that Cliff would later emulate. His novel *Banana Bottom* (1933), the story of Bita Plant, the so-called "first West Indian heroine" (Sani, 21)—and according to Louis James, the "first major West Indian novel" (4)—is about the repatriation to Jamaica of the protagonist after several years of university education in England, in much the same vein as Clare Savage's ruminations on cultural dualism in Cliff's *No Telephone to Heaven*, a novel that follows an almost identical narrative structure. As such, between them, C. L. R. James, Mendes, and especially McKay can be said to move Caribbean writing away from the apologist, colonialist offerings of Redcam and de Lisser and more toward the "realities" of island life engaged in their respective struggles for national identity that can be found in much of Cliff's writing.

With the advent of the 1940s, new literary periodicals—such as *Bim* (1942) in Barbados, *Focus* (1943) in Jamaica, *Kyk-Over-Al* (1945) in Guyana, and the *Caribbean Quarterly* (1949) in Jamaica—engendered yet further engagement with the intellectual heritage of the Caribbean, providing more avenues for writers to dialogue with one another—though it must be said that much writing from this period has been inaccessible due to the material difficulties of locating texts that were not archived or preserved (see Donnell and Lawson Welsh, 12). This period—what Adrianne Baytop terms the so-called "second period of development" (33) in Caribbean writing—is characterized by those writers and poets who were the precursors of contemporary Caribbean writing as it came to be more popularly understood in the mid-twentieth century.

It was during the 1950s and 1960s that Caribbean writing was considered to have reached its zenith with the publication of works by a group of writers writing largely from positions of self-imposed exile from the Caribbean. As Donnell and Lawson Welsh note, the "Caribbean canon has been traditionally dominated by a number of seminal works from the 1950s and 1960s, the period when Caribbean literature 'boomed' in the metropolitan motherland, London" (5), while Susheila Nasta argues that "it was London that created the possibility, in many cases, of a bridge between the past . . . and the present, which posited a strong need to establish West Indian 'cultural pedigree'" (80). The most significant Caribbean literary and cultural texts around this period were produced in exile and include C. L. R. James's *The Black Jacobins* (1938), Aimé Césaire's *Cahier* (1939), Frantz Fanon's *Black Skin, White Masks* (1952), George Lamming's *In the Castle of my Skin* (1953)—which Bruce King identifies as the first Caribbean "classic" (4)—and *The Pleasures of Exile* (1960), and V. S. Naipaul's *A House of Mr. Biswas* (1961)—which C. L. R. James himself called "the finest study ever produced in the West Indies . . . of a minority" (1967, 75). Other prominent "boom" writers were Edgar Mittelholzer, whose early novels *A Morning at the Office* (1950) and *Shadows Move Among Them* (1951), in particular, explore the roots of prejudice in fear and loneliness, and whose fascination with myth and superstition would also be echoed in Cliff's own early writing, as well as Sam Selvon, whose early works, *A Brighter Sun* (1952) and its sequel, *Turn Again, Tiger* (1958), examine a young Indian couple's sense of dislocation as they adjust from rural to urban living (a theme that plagues the young Clare Savage as she moves between her parents' and grandparents' homes in Cliff's *Abeng*), and whose *magnum opus*, *The Lonely Londoners* (1956), illustrates the pathos of West Indian immigrant life in the London metropolis in many of the same ways as Cliff's *No Telephone to Heaven*. George Lamming's second novel, *The Emigrants* (1980), has become somewhat synecdochal with discussions of West Indian immigrants' experiences in England, while Roger Mais's novels *The Hills Were Joyful Together* (1953) and *Brother Man* (1954) are social realist works focused on the impoverished underclass of the Jamaican slums—again, much like Cliff's Clare Savage duology. V. S. Naipaul's often absurdist early fiction in *The Mystic Masseur* (1957) and *The Suffrage of Elvira* (1958) satirizes wealth and political power structures among the Caribbean's East Indian communities, while Wilson Harris's early novels *Palace of the Peacock* (1960) and *The Far Journey of Oudin* (1961) deal with the legacy of slavery under various repressive sociopolitical orders. Of course, the poetry of Nobel Laureate Derek Walcott—whose major works of this period include *Green Night* (1962), *Selected Poems* (1964), and *The Castaway and Other Poems* (1965), and whose epic *Omeros* (1990) has been described as "shift[ing] the heartland of cultural enquiry to an unmistakable Caribbean milieu" (Balderston and Gonzalez, xix)—and Edward Kamau Brathwaite—whose best work is largely considered to be the *New World Trilogy* comprised of *Rights of Passage* (1967), *Masks* (1968), and *Islands* (1969)—also mark definitive contributions to this era.

It must not go without notice that all of the aforementioned works are authored by male writers. Indeed, it is not hard for the casual reader to misconceive of Caribbean literary culture as a predominantly male purview when critics such as Glenn O. Phillips list "Michael Anthony, Edward Ricardo Braithwaite, Jan Carew, Austin Clark, George Lamming, Edgar Mittelholzer, Vidiadhar S. Naipaul, Andrew Salkey, Herbert de Lisser, and Claude McKay"—that is, not a single female author—as "reflect[ing] the socioeconomic struggles of Caribbean peoples from (the lowlands of)

Guyana to (the mountains of) Jamaica" (177), or when Kenneth Ramchand lists only one work by a female author (Jean Rhys's *Wide Sargasso Sea* [1966]) in his entire *Introduction to the Study of West Indian Literature* (1976), or when Bruce King does the same in his collection on *West Indian Literature* (1979), or when Selwyn Cudjoe declares the first International Conference on Women Writers of the English-Speaking Caribbean that took place in Wellesley College, Massachusetts, in 1988, as "the founding event of Caribbean women's writing" (5). On the contrary, as Carole Boyce Davies and Elaine Savory Fido assert, "[o]ut of this [perceived] voicelessness and absence, contemporary Caribbean women writers [were] beginning some bold steps to creative expression" (2). Although Evelyn O'Callaghan has argued that it remained for much of this period "difficult to identify a female [Caribbean] literary tradition" (1987, 9), the first steps to uncovering a "tradition" of women's writing, according to Donnell and Lawson Welsh, actually necessitates overcoming the denial that such a "tradition" might have existed in the first place (236). Indeed, Joan Anim-Addo has argued that "[w]hether [Caribbean] literature is read through critical frames that privilege postcolonialism, cultural nationalism, feminism, formalism or any other theoretical stance, it is undeniably and overwhelmingly a literature shaped by experiences of gender" (xi–xii).

With respect to women writers in the Caribbean, the history of women's writing cannot be said to either begin or end with Jean Rhys, though Rhys's *Wide Sargasso Sea* "certainly brought the subject of West Indian women into ... sharp focus" (Agbor, 156) and has become something of a metonym within the Anglo-European worldview for Caribbean women's writing at large—while Rhys herself is "usually the one Creole and woman writer to be admitted into the canon alongside ... male writers" (Donnell and Lawson Welsh, 6). Rhys's immediate contemporaries include Merle Hodge, whose 1970 novel *Crick Crack, Monkey* is distinguished as the first major work of fiction to be published by a Black Caribbean woman; Joan Riley, whose debut novel *The Unbelonging* (1985) was the first Afro-Caribbean–authored account of Black people in England; Jean Buffong, whose 1992 novel *Under the Silk Cotton Tree* details the importance of interconnectedness and migration to everyday Caribbean lives; Amryl Johnson, whose poetry and travel writing are largely autobiographical meditations on diaspora and on the violence she encountered as an emigrant to Britain; and Beryl Gilroy, who is distinguished not only as a prolific writer but as the first Black headteacher in London. It was on account of the burgeoning proliferation of Caribbean women's writing that the first International Conference on Women Writers of the English-Speaking Caribbean took place, focusing on "Caribbean women who had published poetry and fiction in English and who up to that moment had scarcely been recognized as a group" (Greene, 532). At the subsequent conference, held in Trinidad in 1990, delegates concluded that "[women's] literature is essentially different from that of Caribbean males (and of women outside the Caribbean)," and that "although race, class, identity . . . were commonalities, women experienced all of these in a way different from the way men experienced them" (533).

From the 1970s onward, a more sustained interest was paid to female Caribbean writing as a tradition unto itself. Significant publications of this period include *Guyana Drums* (1972), an anthology of women's poetry, a *Savacou* special issue on writing by Caribbean women in 1977, and Pamela Mordecai and Melvyn Morris's anthology *Jamaica Woman* (1980) (see Donnell and Lawson Welsh, 235). The 1970s onward saw an explosion of Caribbean women's writing and a concomitant critical interest in the literature by Erna Brodber, Olive Senior, Maryse Condé, Simone Schwarz-Bart, Rosario Ferré, Astrid Roemer, and Nancy Morejón—as well as writers and thinkers of Caribbean descent such as Audre Lorde, June Jordan, and Barbara Christian—as women who "offered new ways of understanding literary subjectivities, new concerns with mother-daughter relationships and with the politics of domestic and intimate encounters, as well as different literary voices and styles" (Cummings and Donnell, 5). Ronald Cummings and Alison Donnell further point out that the proliferation of Caribbean women's writing was supported by the advent of feminist publishing houses (such as Virago, The Women's Press, and Sister Vision Press) that afforded the "pronounced rebalancing of literary attention from men to women" (6)— though as Pamela Mordecai and Betty Wilson point out, "[t]he interesting question is . . . whether these women had been writing much before that time and therefore whether what appears to be a sudden literary blossoming may not . . . be a flowering of publishing interest consequent on the Women's Movement and the improved economic status of women" (xi). This publishing trend continued into the 1980s with the proliferation of writing by poets Lorna Goodison and Jean "Binta" Breeze, as well as Jamaica Kincaid—whose novels, short fiction, essays, and creative nonfiction shone a light on Caribbean women's experiences and lives—and Grace Nichols, whose first collection of poetry, *I Is a Long-Memoried Woman* (1983) won the Commonwealth Prize for Literature and has been described as a project of "reconstructing and re/membering of (black) Caribbean women's histories" (Donnell and Lawson Welsh, 294). In 1990, Pamela Mordecai and Betty Wilson's anthology on pan-Caribbean women's writing, *Her True Name*, was published to "recuperate a self-determined identity" for Caribbean women writers—though as

Donnell and Lawson Welsh point out, "these proposals for a common agenda for Caribbean women's writing and a single 'true' identity are constraining frameworks which cannot accommodate the diversity of interests and styles represented in the writings collected" (357). Mordecai and Wilson themselves acknowledge such shortcomings: "[W]e have omitted . . . at least as many women writers as we have included . . . in the face of poor documentation and archival work that seems at its best biased" (x).

The first collection of critical essays on Caribbean women's writings appeared in 1990 with the publication of Carole Boyce Davies and Elaine Savory Fido's anthology *Out of the Kumbla: Caribbean Women and Literature*, a collection that actively engages with the absence of women writers and scholars from the Caribbean literary canon and revitalized the discourse of Caribbean feminist literature and criticism. Boyce Davies and Savory Fido identify a number of important critical phases in the development of Caribbean feminist literary discourse that have tended to move away from the parameters of earlier works informed by colonial literary heritage. These include Lloyd Brown's full-length study of African women writers and poets in *West Indian Poetry* (1978); Maryse Condé's *Parole des Femmes* (*Women's Voices*) (1979); the cross-cultural discussion of Black women in Filomina Steady's *The Black Women Cross Culturally* (1981); the 1985 conference on Black women writers in the diaspora at the University of Michigan; the 1985 special issue of the *Bulletin of Eastern Caribbean Affairs* on "The Female Presence in Caribbean Literature"; Yvette E. Miller and Charles Tatum's *Latin American Women Writers* (1977); Mineke Schipper's collection *Unheard Words. Women and Literature in Africa, the Arab World, Asia, the Caribbean and Latin America* (1985); Kirsten Holt Peterson and Anna Rutherford's *A Double Colonization: Colonial and Post-Colonial Women's Writing* (1986); and Darryl Dance's *Fifty Caribbean Writers* (1986) (see Boyce Davies and Savory Fido, 11–16).

In spite of the gendered, geographical, linguistic, and sociocultural disparities of life across the Caribbean Basin as a whole, it is, as Dabydeen and Wilson-Tagoe remind us, "still possible to talk in general terms of a Western Indian literature of English expression" on account of the shared history of "colonisation, displacement, slavery, indenture, emancipation and nationalism [that] has shaped most West Indian environments" (1987, 921). As Adrianne Baytop notes, the "micro-international composition" of the Caribbean "tends to obscure the argument for an existing Caribbean cultural norm," much of which ascribes "British imperialistic traditions as the common and dominant denominator" (29). Baytop further argues that Caribbean literary sensibilities derive from the nature of Caribbean peoples—that is, both the inherent characteristics of its inhabitants as well as its environmental ecosystems; she suggests that the "celebrative" nature of the Caribbean people "underscores the literary style, substance, and tone" of Caribbean literature and that the "tropical environment, itself an emotionally charged atmosphere, sets the tenor of a specialized aesthetics" (30). Caribbean writing—and Michelle Cliff's literary output, more specifically—is marked by its "dramatics, music, and mysticism," its optimism, and its animated language and rich vocal cadences. In addition, Bruce King identifies the following characteristics as endemic to Caribbean writing of the mid to late twentieth century, all of which are applicable to Cliff's writings: the (re)creation of myths of the past, the use of local color and a focus on peasant livelihoods, an emphasis on community, nation, and race, and the modification of Standard English as a literary language, as well as themes such as identity, historical injustices, imprisonment, social order, the discovery of folk tradition, and the foundation of a new society (7). To this, María Teresa Babín notes that further "common threads" of Caribbean literary culture of this period—which, again, dovetail with Cliff's writings—are "Black power agitation, radical movements and intellectual pursuits, regional pride, national consciousness and the search for identity, [and] the struggle to shed the protective mantle of colonialism" (69), while Alison Donnell asserts that "the paradigms of Caribbean literary criticism have become normalised around a cluster of issues"—particularly "the concept of women as doubly colonised and the marginalisation of sexuality and homosexuality"—with much of her critical focus paid to the many "exclusions, eclipses, and eschewals" embedded within Caribbean literatures and discourses (5, 7).

Principal themes of pan-Caribbean literary culture, as Dabydeen and Wilson-Tagoe identify them within key texts, include anti-imperialism, nationalism, and the political move for independence in the poetry of Claude McKay, George Campbell, and Martin Carter, the historical novels of V. S. Reid, Samuel Selvon, and Roger Mais, and meditations on freedom and resistance in George Lamming's *Of Age and Innocence* (1958), *Season of Adventure* (1960), *Water with Berries* (1971), and *Natives of My Person* (1972), and V. S. Naipaul's *A House for Mr. Biswas* and *The Mimic Men* (1966). The treatment of race and ethnicity is the focus of V. S. Reid's *The Leopard* (1958), Derek Walcott's plays *Ti-Jean and His Brothers* (1958) and *Dream on Monkey Mountain* (1967), Wilson Harris's novels *Palace of the Peacock*, *The Secret Ladder* (1963), and *Heartland* (1964), and the works of Naipaul, Selvon, Lamming, and Edgar Mittelholzer, more broadly. Childhood and the experiences of the child are central to George Lamming's *In the Castle of My Skin*, V. S. Naipaul's *Miguel Street* (1959), Michael Anthony's *The Year in San Fernando* (1965) and *Green Days by the River* (1967), and

Merle Hodge's *Crick Crack, Monkey*. Other predominant themes include the treatment of women in Jean Rhys's *Wide Sargasso Sea*, Erna Brodber's *Jane and Louisa Will Soon Come Home* (1980), Zee Edgell's *Beka Lamb* (1982), Grace Nichols's *I Is a Long-Memoried Woman*, and Olive Senior's *Lightning and Other Stories* (1986); migration in Paule Marshal's *Brown Girl, Brown Stories* (1959), Edward Kamau Brathwaite's "The Emigrant" (1967), Linton Kwesi Johnson's *Dread Beat and Blood* (1975), Samuel Selvon's *The Lonely Londoners*, and George Lamming's *The Emigrants*; and carnival and calypso in V. S. Naipaul's *Miguel Street*, Edward Kamau Brathwaite's *Islands*, Hodge's *Crick Crack, Monkey*, and Earl Lovelace's *The Dragon Can't Dance* (1979) (see Dabydeen and Wilson-Tagoe).

So where does Michell Cliff fit within this complex and varied heritage? In their *Anthology of Women's Writing from the Caribbean*, Pamela Mordecai and Betty Wilson contend that Cliff is "[t]he only one of the recently published Caribbean writers who does not affirm at least aspects of being in the Caribbean place" (xvii). They argue that Cliff's literary consciousness is more traditionally Francophone than it is Anglophone; that she is "'white'—or as light-skinned as makes, to the larger world, little difference"; that her work promotes those values of the Euro-American metropole and not her island home; and that "[o]ne of the prices she has paid is a compromised authenticity in some aspects of her rendering of the Creole." As Joanne Chassot notes, it is also not unimportant that "Mordecai and Wilson's introductory remarks on Cliff make no mention of her sexuality" (2018, 161). In addition to her biraciality and her biculturality, Cliff's bisexuality has often been erased in critical considerations of her work. Not only do Mordecai and Wilson "invisibilise" Cliff's sexuality—to borrow a term from Chassot—by making no mention of it at all, but it may be said that, in the critical discourse surrounding Cliff, her sexuality is doubly invisibilized: if her sexuality is mentioned at all, she is most frequently referred to as a lesbian (see Trewick 11, quoted above). Isabel Hoving, for one, is adamant that, for Cliff, "sexuality is thematized as *lesbian* sexuality" (2001, 239), a comment which makes little allowance for the more complex exploration of bisexual desire in Cliff's fiction—particularly in the relationship, in *No Telephone to Heaven*, between Clare Savage and her friend and sometime lover Harry/Harriet. Thus, not only do Mordecai and Wilson call into question the potential erasure of Cliff as a whole from the discourse of Caribbean women's writing on the grounds of her interstitial racial and cultural identity, but they also succeed in erasing from the discourse another of Cliff's important identity markers: her sexuality. Chassot argues that "Mordecai and Wilson conjure the ghost of Cliff in order to better affirm the coherence and authority of the community of

Caribbean women writers their anthology constitutes" (2018, 162). Moreover, she contends that Mordecai and Wilson's treatment of Cliff (the erasure of her sexuality; their dismissal of her Jamaican cultural authenticity) is "profoundly at odds with the stated purpose of their anthology, which is to give Caribbean women writers a visibility they have long been denied."[2]

By way of a response, Cliff herself has countered the claims of cultural illegitimacy made by Mordecai and Wilson, centering her rebuttal on the editors' designation of her so-called whiteness. Cliff notes that

> [Mordecai and Wilson] say something to the effect that I am light enough that I might as well be white, which is not true. It's one thing to look x and to feel y, rather than to look x and feel x, and that's part of the difficulty being light-skinned: some people assume you have a white outlook just because you look white. You're met immediately on that level. But it varies a great deal. (qtd. in Schwartz 1993, 607)

Cliff often seeks (not without a certain defensiveness) to contextualize for appraising critics her connections to Afro-Caribbean cultural and racial histories, "giving several biographical examples of her difficulties in creating and maintaining relationships with white people," as well as "discussing her historical novel *Free Enterprise* in relation to the example it gives of a successful interracial friendship" (Machado Sáez, 85). *Free Enterprise*—the subtitle of which is "A Novel of Mary Ellen Pleasant"—illustrates through reportage the fast friendship between African American entrepreneur Pleasant and the white abolitionist John Brown, whose raid on Harpers Ferry was largely financed by Pleasant. When Pleasant died in 1904, her gravestone was engraved with the words, "She was a friend of John Brown." But despite Cliff's passionate rebuttals, the contestations of racial authenticity leveled by Mordecai and Wilson have long plagued the reception history of Cliff's work in the Caribbean context.

Isabel Hoving points out that a number of Cliff's critics "considered her early efforts to claim a Jamaican identity as failed, because of her feminism, her light skin color, her US residency and the assumed elite complexity of her writing" (2011, 31), all of which led to considerable debate concerning the ambivalence of Caribbean writers. As Françoise Lionnet has noted, it is on account of her perceived whiteness and her cultural indeterminacy that Cliff's treatment as a Jamaican author is so uncomfortable; she is viewed "like many other West Indian female intellectuals, as an expatriate, and is accused of exhibiting a feminism colored by Euro-American ideology" (325). Similar to Lionnet, Izabella Penier has argued that Cliff "honors the anachronistic tradition of essentialism" and that, aside from the issues of her racial and cultural authenticity raised by Mordecai and Wilson, her writings are flawed "because of her championing of essentialized female identities" (165). Penier's concern with Cliff is the quality and style of her writings, of which she is more scathing than most. She contends that "[Cliff's] novels not only enhance pretty hackneyed clichés and binary oppositions about the colonial encounter and its legacy but also lead to bewildering and paradoxical conjectures about Jamaican culture and the national identity of Jamaican women." Furthermore, Penier challenges the essentialist gender premises of Cliff's reliance on the "affirmation of matriliny," which, she argues, is "typical for female authors of African descent, and [their] not-so-typical elision of motherhood" (166), and which, she contends, is to be found in Cliff's fiction, particularly *Abeng* and *No Telephone to Heaven*.

Sally O'Driscoll argues that, while Cliff's status as a Jamaican expatriate is not called into question, it is only in attempting to define who or what the Caribbean writer *is* that Cliff becomes problematic: she contends that, as a "very light-skinned woman who identifies herself as black, a product of the Jamaican upper class (she came from a family of landowning plantocrats), an expatriate (who has lived in Europe and the United States since 1975), a lesbian, a feminist, and an academic," Cliff "stands at the point of connection—or rupture—between two major non-congruent constructions of identity: third-world postcolonialist and first-world postmodern" (56). As O'Driscoll further contends, the authority of Cliff's identity, as a bicultural, biracial, and bisexual woman, is a "central issue for a writer who straddles first world and third world, colonizer and colonized, the postmodern and the postcolonial—the word 'postcolonial' itself being a symbol of disagreement between the two worlds" (56). Suzanne Bost is another critic who has addressed the contingent relationship between biracial fluidity and postmodernism; she notes that, like the postmodern subject, "[b]iracial figures have always possessed decentered identities forced upon them by the historical circumstances, politics, and racial dynamics of their times" (675). Bost argues that Cliff's work, "while retaining roots in Jamaican culture, also moves fluidly from the Caribbean to Europe to the United States, crossing not only oceans but also borders of identity and history" (679), much like the postmodern novel. Or, as William Tell Gifford puts it, Cliff is "a living crossroads of several layers of 'social surroundings' (European, African, Carib, modernist, postmodernist, lesbian)" (8). Indeed, Joanne Chassot encapsulates the conflict around Cliff's cultural and racial legitimacy quite succinctly when she notes that "[a]s a Jamaican who lived most of her life in the United States, a lightskinned woman who identified herself as Afro-Caribbean, a nonheterosexual writer whose work was long surprisingly seldom analysed from a queer perspective, Cliff does not fall easily into any one category" (2018, 152). Most damningly, Chassot asserts that "the apparent discrepancy between what Cliff is and what she considers herself to be suggests that Cliff is not what she claims to be, and claims to be what she is not—in other words that she is trying to pass as a nonwhite, or at least a mixed-race, writer" (2018, 160). This position coheres with Belinda Edmondson's assertion that Cliff's "discovery of a black identity is a foreign fashion that she has appropriated," that her writings "emanate from an American feminist sensibility," and that she is "not truly part of an Afrocentric Caribbean discourse" (1993, 181–82).

Cliff's categorical indeterminacy, however, far from a cause of disturbance for her, is one that she embraces for personal and political ends. In her very being, Cliff elides boundaries and transgresses sociocultural borders, antagonizing traditional identity markers and disrupting categorical conventions. As Chassot has noted, Cliff "was not comfortable with clear-cut categories, especially when they were imposed on her." As Cliff writes in *The Land of Look Behind*, "This is who I am. I am not what you allow me to be. Whatever you decide me to be" (1985, 70). It is for this reason that Cliff views Creolization—a consequence of miscegenation vis-à-vis the blurring of traditional racial and cultural divisions—as "a natural part of cultural evolution . . . stemming from the mixtures of different groups of people" (Hyatt, 5). For Cliff, as a biracial Jamaican American woman, her very existence is contingent upon the transgression of (not just) racial fault lines; she exists on the margins of traditional racial—and cultural and sexual—delineations. While a number of Cliff's critics and detractors denounce the fact that Cliff, in Lilleth Trewick's words, "enjoys the lifestyle of the White middle class while she seeks acceptance from the Black underclass," Trewick herself argues for a reconsideration of Cliff's liminality: the fact that Cliff exists "in between her Blackness and Whiteness and may never fully occupy one position or the other" (13).

It is not just Trewick who sees both the resistant and redemptive power of liminal subjectivity; Cliff herself embraces interstitiality—that is, her occupation of in-between spaces along the boundaried fault lines of racial, cultural, and sexual identity markers—as fundamental not only to her identity but as the very essence of her literary politics. In an interview published in the *Kenyon Review* in 1993, interviewer Judith Raiskin inquires of Cliff as to whether the "double-voiced discourse" (1993, 58) of Cliff's *créolité* is achievable on the level of literary form. To this, Cliff responds by acknowledging that, having grown up in the Caribbean, she is "of at least two voices," the consequence of which for her, as a Caribbean writer, is that "[y]ou can be much more experimental, you can mix styles up, you don't have to be linear, you don't have to be dichotomous" (qtd. in Raiskin 1993, 58). Thus, Cliff's categorical indeterminacy as an interstitial subject, her racial and cultural créolité, becomes formalized through her writings, as her work "elaborates the sources and implications of a creolized . . . identity" (Rody, 152). Although Cliff's hybrid status (as *bi*racial; as *bi*cultural; as *bi*sexual) initially proved afflicting to her burgeoning self-determination, her later writings reprioritize and celebrate this hybridity—caught, as she saw it in her youth, between the interstices of race and culture: a "white cockroach" in Jamaica. In *The Land of Look Behind*, Cliff recalls this term as one of a number of pejorative labels that were affixed to her at a young age. In attempting to conceive of herself as "the sister of Bertha Rochester," the fictional "mad woman in the attic" of Charlotte Brontë's *Jane Eyre* (1847), later reimagined in Jean Rhys's *Wide Sargasso Sea*, and who was, herself, Creole, Cliff alludes to her own kind as "the remainders of slavery": "white cockroaches" and "white" (1985, 41), both disparaging terms for light-skinned Jamaicans. Belinda Edmondson argues that such designations are "evidence of the [Black Caribbean's] perception that the white woman creole share[s] the status of the working class as a marginalized outcast" (1993, 182), a view that is consistent with Kaisa Ilmonen's assertion that "the white Creole is in many ways [seen to be] culturally 'black'" (2002, 116). Another term that recurs throughout Cliff's writing is "Aristocoon"—a portmanteau of "aristocrat" and "coon" (an offensive slur for a Black person)—which, Claudia Buonaiuto argues, "shows Cliff's ironic eye and her ability to play with words, as she retraces the history of British colonialism on [Jamaica]" (127). Indeed, for Cliff, the interrelated conceits of "split" subjectivity and, in particular, fragmented identity operate as a sort of leitmotif throughout the entirety of her life and literary oeuvre.

In her autobiographical creative writing in *The Land of Look Behind*, Cliff confesses to coming from "a fragmented people"; she argues that "my struggle to get wholeness from fragmentation while working within fragmentation, producing work which may find its strength in its depiction of fragments through form as well as content, is similar to the experience of other writers whose origins are in countries defined by colonialism" (1985, 14–15). Indeed, Elizabeth Wilson argues that Cliff's "search for wholeness is, and has been, a recurring theme in Caribbean fiction" at large (2). Cliff's writing and her life both are products of—and a search for—wholeness or completeness through fragmentation, and fragmentation represents a key condition of her existence that finds expression through her literary form. Cliff herself problematizes the concept of wholeness, calling into question the degree to which her own quest is paradoxical. She notes that

[t]o write a complete Caribbean woman, or man for that matter, demands of us retracing the African past of ourselves, reclaiming as our own, and as our subject, a history sunk under the sea, or scattered as potash in the canefields, or gone to bush, or trapped in a class system notable for its rigidity and absolute dependence on color stratification. Or a past bleached from our minds. It means finding the art forms of those of our ancestors and speaking in the patois forbidden us. It means realizing our knowledge will always be wanting. It means also, I think, mixing in the forms taught us by the oppressor, undermining his language and co-opting his style and turning it to our purpose. (qtd. in Barnes et al., 3)

Implicit within the politics of Cliff's literary fragmentation and her will to some form of wholeness is the elision of boundaries: the traversal of traditional fault lines or markers of race, culture, and sexuality. As I mentioned above, Cliff's Jamaica is not so much "A WORLD . . . WITHOUT BOUNDARIES" (1996, 6); however, her writings open up the possibility of a world wherein traditional binary divisions can—and must—be challenged and where conceptual boundaries are remade. It is through her writings that Cliff contravenes those lessons learned in childhood not to "overstep [her] boundaries" (1985, 90); that is to say, her writings become precisely the means by which Cliff traverses the boundaries that have marked and contained her in order to unify the fragmentary shards of her selfhood.

Even a rudimentary survey of Cliff's fiction and creative nonfiction turns up (almost everywhere) evidence of these kinds of fragmented boundaries and instances of boundary elision. As Eva María Méndez Blázquez notes, a number of Cliff's literary characters traverse altogether the boundaries of race, class, gender, and sexuality (12). We find, for instance, examples of racial boundary elision in the so-called "Girl from Martinique," the circus worker at the center of the short story "Burning Bush," from Cliff's 1990 collection *Bodies of Water*: she is a biracial woman who whitewashes her body (thereby camouflaging her Blackness) in order to further exoticize herself for circus audiences. Perhaps ironically, Cliff's narrator emphasizes the ludic nature of this woman's racial interplay: the Girl from Martinique is described as "*parti*-colored" and as a "*checkerboard* of a woman" (1991a, 76; my emphasis), terms which not only communicate to the reader the stark (literally black and white) visual dynamics of this interplay, but that also underline the girl's augmented act of passing as an act of play or a game. Indeed, as Suzanne Bost notes, the Girl from Martinique reimagines her biracialism as a "constructed, self-chosen artifice. If it is merely painted on, it can be washed off" (684). The childishness perhaps hinted at through the nature of play here is literalized when the Girl from Martinique gives birth to a light-skinned baby, whose skin, her mother hopes, will darken with age.

We also find instances of playful racial and gender boundary elision in the attempts by the biracial heroine of *Free Enterprise*, Annie Christmas, to deny her European ancestry by applying Liquid Blackener to her light skin and crossdressing (or playing dress-up) as a man to participate in a revolt of enslaved peoples. And like Annie, the titular Mary Ellen Pleasant (after whom the novel is subtitled), also light-skinned, passes in a number of roles throughout the narrative, including as Mammy, a blacksmith, and as a house servant—although Elena Machado Sáez argues that, for the numerous roles and guises that Pleasant adopts throughout *Free Enterprise*, one that is not often given much critical attention is her identity as a queer subject (110). As Suzanne Bost notes, Cliff's traversal of racial and gender boundaries in *Free Enterprise* "empower[s] her characters and enable[s] them to construct fluid identities"; she argues that the characters' "protean power to transform themselves enable them to belong as insiders in many different racial, cultural, and class-based milieus" (684). We also see fragmentation in the description by the unnamed narrator of *Into the Interior*, Cliff's fourth and final novel, of the idiosyncratic twins, Elizabeth and Isabel: "Orlando at each end of existence, they seemed, the bifurcated female" (2010, 84). Not only might we say that, in their twinship, Elizabeth and Isabel can be seen to represent a monozygotic fragmentation, the division and splitting of their mother's fertilized egg into two separate embryos, but, as the narrator muses omnisciently, Isabel's sexuality, too, is couched in terms of a certain cleaved divarication, for "[y]ears of self-abuse with an industrial-strength vibrator had distended Isabel's labia to such an extent that there was a swishing, flapping sound when she walked. Her very own Hottentot apron."

Clare Savage—the protagonist of the so-called "Clare Savage" duology, *Abeng* and *No Telephone to Heaven*, semiautobiographical, fictionalized accounts of Cliff's early life in Jamaica—perhaps best represents in toto Cliff's "fragmented self yearning for wholeness" (Agosto, 104). Irene Nicácio Lacerda has argued that *No Telephone to Heaven* is Cliff's most deeply autobiographical work. While it is true that this novel illustrates Cliff's "strong criticism towards colonialism through a rewriting of her people's history and, consequently, a recovery of their filiations, which is also hers" (2), Cliff herself has claimed that the events recounted in *Abeng* are far closer to her own life than those of *No Telephone to Heaven*: "Emotionally, [*Abeng*] is an autobiography . . . I was a girl similar to Clare and have spent most of my life and most of my work exploring my identity as a light-skinned Jamaican, the privilege and the damage that comes from that identity" (qtd. in Grimes, n.p.). It is through Clare that Cliff's writings mostly "disregard . . . the boundaries between racial, class, and gender division." Clare is the ultimate "split character" (Eldmair, 39). Like Cliff, she is a light-skinned biracial Jamaican who is "torn between the conflicting worlds of her racially mixed family" (Penier, 168). Clare's father, Boy Savage, passes as white and loudly proclaims his British ancestry, while Clare's mother, Kitty, is of a darker complexion and has a deep and abiding love for Jamaica. Also like Cliff, Clare "struggles to find a place of her own" (Hashimoto, 85) within the transatlantic social and cultural contexts of her upbringing. Cliff and Clare are both "mixed-race characters . . . culturally as well as racially hybridized" (Kilinski, 155). Cliff recalls the ways in which she was able to "pass" for white and so benefited from the many privileges of whiteness: as her mother tells her in her youth, "[y]ou're lucky you look the way you do . . . you could get any man. Anyone says anything to you, tell them your father's white" (1980, 47). Cliff also reflects that "[t]hose of us who were light-skinned, straight-haired, etc., were given to believe that we could actually attain whiteness" because of the assumption that "[t]he light-skinned person imitates the oppressor [and] becomes an oppressor in fact" (1985, 72–73). (See also Robinson-Walcott, 96.) Finally, like Cliff, Clare's sexuality is shown to be fluid. Thus, both Cliff and her quasiautobiographical avatar Clare are not only "split into two parts" (Cliff 1995, 119) or "split between two worlds" (Johannmeyer, 1) along the lines of "simple" racial classification; rather, this "splitting" is a condition of their shared hybridized identities, a consequence of the duolocation of their subject positions as a whole: split, bifurcated, and fragmented along intersecting lines of sexuality and, in particular, race and culture. Anke Johannmeyer expands on this point, noting that "[Clare] is partly African, yet far too light-skinned to be accepted as Black. She is formed from pieces of English culture and African traditions, but the pieces do not fit together and some pieces seem to be missing. Clare thus feels fragmented, and she dedicates her life to achieving wholeness of self. In her search for identity, place has a key role" (1). Jennifer Donahue notes that "Clare faces the struggle of negotiating her place in binaries such as black/white, English/Maroon and city/country" (135), while Kaisa Ilmonen argues that "Clare is still unable to understand or balance her dual consciousness as a Creole, and she feels that she is made up of fragments which she cannot combine" (2002, 117). Nicole Branca takes this a step further, noting in *No Telephone to Heaven* that Clare is "a mixture on more than one level because she not only is both light-skinned and dark-skinned, but also partly Jamaican, American, and British" (35). Finally, Isabel Hoving contends that the "multiplicity of [Cliff's] identity can never be articulated as a whole in one and the same voice," and that the "essence of [her] Caribbeanness is situated in plurality and hybridity" (2001, 245, 247).

For both author and character, it seems, subjectivity is divided across categorical lines that are perceived to be arbitrary and discriminatory; each is aware of the contradictions within themselves: that is, the hypocrisy of the ruling class from whence they come and the privilege afforded them within that context (Agosto, 105, 108). As Suzanne Bost argues, "[w]omen like Clare [and Cliff] use their biracial advantage to benefit the revolution with economic resources and knowledge from two cultures" (686)—a process, according to H. Adlai Murdoch, by which "[their] condition of ethnocultural pluralism in its turn leads to the simultaneity of . . . identity, a liminal form and, indeed, a simulacrum of hybridity through which [their] ongoing subjective tensions are ultimately worked through and cancel themselves out" (33). Thus, Cliff's "bi-ness," and the "bi-ness" of her characters, more generally (Clare in particular) as subjects conditioned by the "multipolar inscriptions" (Murdoch, 33) of their biracialism, their biculturalism, and their bisexuality, function strategically to "subvert singular categories of identity and chart new space for shifting, multiple, feminist subjectivities" (Bost, 686). The "in-between-ness" of their bi identities, then, represents not simply a radical liminality wherein "a person is able to locate him/herself historically and construct an unexcluded identity" (Ilmonen 2002, 115), but rather a nexus of multifragmentary positions through which the subject is not reflected but refracted as continually birfurcated, or split. As Murdoch elaborates, Cliff "forcefully disrupts previously stable identity categories grounded in race, gender, and colonial history to reveal an alternative set of burgeoning identities whose inscription lies 'in-between' those fixed, earlier notions of being and belonging that were the heritage of the colonial encounter" (31). We see this, for example, in the description of Mary Lamb, the matricidal narrator of "Belling the Lamb," a story from Cliff's final collection, *Everything Is Now*, who is described as "[t]he woman estranged from herself; what it is ordained she become. Who resists what she was meant to be" (38). Mary Lamb's multifragmentary nature is borne out by the fact that there are no less than five separate "in-between" subject positions implicit in this particular sentence structure (i.e., "the woman"; "herself"; the she "it is ordained she become"; the she who "resists"; and the she who "she was meant to be"). Indeed, the fragility and brittleness of Mary's subjectivity are evident from the opening line wherein she is described as "[a] woman held together by shoelaces" (36).

Cliff herself acknowledges the fragmentary bifurcation of her own Anglocentric subjectivity, noting that "[a]s a writer, as a human being, I have had to . . . [find] what has been lost to me from the dark side, and what may be hidden, to be dredged from memory and dream" (1985, 13). Not only is Cliff's process of writing—her very being—bifurcated between multiple cultural and racial contexts, but she also suggests that her process of self-recovery, the recovery of her potential "wholeness" as a subject, is one that takes place, paradoxically, along and between the fault lines of multiple, fragmentary, bifurcated subjectivities: that is, on the border between one (light?) side and another ("the dark side"). Cliff also acknowledges here another kind of psycho-spiritual borderwork when she notes that part of her subjectivity may very well be irretrievably lost to her own subconscious—a space of inherent fragmentation, rupture, and division. For Isabel Hoving, Cliff's borderwork, her focus on fragmentation and pluralistic subjectivities, is "tempestuous, innerly contradictory, and replete with gaps and voids," a distinctly painful process on account of what Hoving sees as the "impossibility of putting the plurality into words" (2001, 247, 248). Hoving suggests that Cliff's fragmentary approach to her writing—"the organization of the text as a series of loosely connected fragments separated by blanks" (254)—is an obstacle to expressing her pluralistic identity. For Hoving, Cliff's use of narrative gaps and fragments means that the narrative voice "often remains in the background and has things described and named by others. In this way [Cliff] is able to write a multivoiced discourse . . . and she is still able to suggest her own truth is elsewhere, still somehow unspoken" (2001, 254). Similarly, Marian Aguiar also contends that "[a]lthough Cliff ostensibly celebrates the hybrid, it is obvious that hybrid is ultimately a problematic status for her"(104). However, while Cliff does, at times, acknowledge the dilemmas inherent in existing along the racial and cultural fault lines of her fragmented subjectivity (of her upbringing, Cliff has recalled the effects her light skin had upon the family dynamic, the almost clandestine nature of her being, and the burgeoning split to her consciousness which, it seems, was both afflicting and necessary for her survival [1980, 11]), it is precisely in fragmentation that she finds salvation: "I sink into the sea of fragments. *Alive*" (2009, 52; my emphasis). So concludes the unnamed female narrator of the short story "Crocodilopolis," from the collection *Everything Is Now*, whose forbidden love with another woman has been discovered (during a time when such things were disapproved of) and who must now navigate alone the perils of a bifurcated personal-romantic life as she suppresses her same-sex desire for the sake of social propriety. The final word of the story ("Alive") suggests that fragmentation is a necessary means of survival. Like this unnamed narrator, like Mary Lamb, Clare Savage, and many of Cliff's other literary characters—as well as Cliff herself, of course—fragmentation is a necessary condition of living and a necessary condition of writing—albeit a painful one, as Hoving reminds us.

Contrary to Hoving, a number of critics have also recognized the importance of fragmentation to Cliff. Simon Gikandi propounds that Cliff's fragmentary technique and literary-formal approach actually enables her writing: "First, it allows the writer to recover the colonial repressed.... Second, it enables the writer to inscribe herself in the previously disdained vernacular and use it to challenge the norms of the 'Queen's' English. And finally, it helps to undermine the authority of given discourse through intertextual references and parodic forms that questions the historical totalities that sustain ethnocentrism" (234). For Cliff, Noraida Agosto argues that "fragmentation is essential for the avowal of hybridity, which, in turn, enables connection with marginalized 'others' and creates a solidarity that fosters dignity and agency" (103–4). Martha Addante, too, suggests that the structure of the "Clare Savage" novels, in particular, replicates Clare's psychological fragmentation (144), while Kaisa Ilmonen contends that the "double articulations" of Cliff's writings are "structurally reflected within the narrative technique ... a collection of voices, polyphony" (2017, 58). Indeed, as Ilmonen has also stated elsewhere, "[f]ragmentation ... function[s] as a strategy when creating a new, postcolonial identity" (2002, 115). As Erica L. Johnson notes, this fragmentation allows Cliff to "[measure] the sayable and the unsaid in a language so concise that it is almost violent in its rapid fire" (268). Cliff's borderwork, then, the continual testing of boundary limitations and of her own existence forged in fragmentation, is, as Joanne Chassot has argued, both a condition and a strategy of her resistance to colonial, racial, cultural, and gendered metanarratives, "a source of strength and subversive power against cultural domination" (2009, 2).

Fragmented, too, is the critical history of Cliff's writings. Thematically, race is the focal point of many critical responses to Cliff's work, whether it be the representative politics of race (Edmondson 1993, O'Driscoll 1995) or mixed-race identity formation and racial subjectivity in Jamaica (Lionnet 1992, Bost 1998, Dagbovie 2006, MacDonald-Smyth 2011), while relatively less focus has been paid, on the whole, to queer sexual and gender identities in Cliff's work (Elia 2000, Raiskin 1994, 1996; see also Vella 2013). The "Clare Savage" novels *Abeng* and *No Telephone to Heaven* are a primary focus, but by and large, Cliff's short story collections have all but been ignored. For this reason, Anke Johannmeyer is not quite correct in her claim that "most critics base their articles on [Cliff's] short stories and poems rather than her novels" (6); in fact, most contemporary criticism tends to focus even further on Cliff's early novels rather than on her later novels and short story collections. And while it might not be wholly inaccurate of Johannmeyer to claim that "Cliff's work has attracted comparatively little scholarly attention," this point is a relative one: there has been a plethora of book chapters and articles on various aspects of Cliff's writings, but to date, only three full-length academic monographs dedicated exclusively to her work—and even these do not cover the entirety of Cliff's oeuvre.

As its title suggests, Noraida Agosto's *Michelle Cliff's Novels: Piecing the Tapestry of Memory and History* (1999) examines the interplay between memory and history and the ways in which the alternate histories of Jamaica's enslavement cultures can be gleaned from Cliff's novels. To that end, much of Agosto's argument centers on Cliff's strategies of resistance to pervasive oppressive cultures—such as her implementation of marginalized memories through her characters' use of patois or the role of women's bodies in challenging monolithic metanarratives of received phallogocentric histories. William Tell Gifford's *Narrative and the Nature of Worldview in the Clare Savage Novels of Michelle Cliff* (2002) is much more constrained in its focus (on just two of Cliff's novels, *Abeng* and *No Telephone to Heaven*). Like Agosto, Gifford spends much of his time on Cliff's efforts to rewrite history through her fiction, although for reasons that are never made apparent to the reader, he centers his criticism on the motivational drives of both the protagonist, Clare Savage, and the narrator of the two works in which this character appears, as well as on the ill-defined concept of their "worldview." Gifford's book is mostly summary with relatively little reflective criticism, characterized by a consistent but undeveloped obsession with Lyotard's metanarratives. Much more robust is Kaisa Ilmonen's *Queer Rebellion in the Novels of Michelle Cliff: Intersectionality and Sexual Modernity* (2017), which focuses on the queer aesthetics of Cliff's work. Like Agosto and Gifford, Ilmonen is concerned with Cliff's rewriting of Caribbean histories and female identities in her novels, but unlike her predecessors, Ilmonen argues that those aspects of Cliff's (and, often, her characters') queered gender and sexual identities account for much of the liberatory poetics of her work. Ilmonen argues that the queer counterdiscourses of Cliff's novels render intersecting forms of subordination visible and that an intersectional approach to Cliff's work—one that takes into account multiple axes of identity such as race, culture, sexuality, gender, class, etc.—is necessary for the future direction of Cliff studies. This view adheres with Joanne Chassot, who calls for further study of—but does not herself necessarily expand upon—"[Cliff's] treatment of race, gender, and sexuality intersectionally" (2018, 153). Chassot argues that an intersectional approach to Cliff is paramount due to the "many recurring images, motifs, and themes [that] run throughout her work" and the fact that "each text throws light on the others."

As such, *On the Very Edge: Bidentities in Michelle Cliff's Fiction* builds on Ilmonen and Chassot's proposals, taking an intersectional approach to Cliff's literary canon as a whole. Unlike Agosto, Gifford, and Ilmonen, though, whose respective works focus almost exclusively on Cliff's earlier novels, this book encompasses the entirety of Cliff's oeuvre and will cover the "Clare Savage" duology, *Abeng* and *No Telephone to Heaven*, as well as Cliff's later novels, *Free Enterprise* and *Into the Interior*; her short story collections, *Bodies of Water*, *The Store of a Million Items*, and *Everything Is Now*; and her prose poetry, *Claiming an Identity They Taught Me to Despise* and *The Land of Look Behind*. For the large part, my focus will not be on memory or on Cliff's historiography (Agosto, Gifford), nor am I contending "simply" with the queer sexual and gender aesthetics of Cliff's work (Ilmonen). Rather, I intend to examine various axes of identity across the whole of Cliff's canon, reflecting on the intersectional fault lines of Cliff's fragmentary identity markers: race and ethnicity, culture, and sexuality and gender.

My approach to Cliff's intersectional identities—her characters' biracialisms, biculturalisms, and bisexualities—is very much modeled after Cliff's own mode of literary exploration: like Cliff, whose work is replete with recurring images, motifs, and themes of fragmentation, splitting, and bifurcation, I will employ a bifurcatory critical mode in my intersectional analysis of Cliff's work. That is to say, I take bifurcation *in and of itself* as the analytic mode of my intersectional analysis. I am focusing not simply on bi*racialism*, bi*culturalism*, or bi*sexuality* as fragmentary identity markers; rather, I will examine Cliff's ubiquitous implementation of bifurcatory identities, focusing on spaces and/or states of "bi-ness" as categorical imperatives within her writings. While I am, of course, interested in what Cliff has to say (and how she says it) about race, culture, and sexuality, I am more interested in the quality of bi-ness that underpins and indeed frames Cliff's multipolar conceptions of biracialism, biculturalism, and bisexuality at large. In other words, I intend to examine those aspects of bi-ness that inform her writings on race, culture, and sexuality. So, while critical considerations of race, culture, and sexuality are often the product of my discussions throughout this book, Cliff's bifurcatory aesthetic, the exploratory mode through which she examines her multiple fragmentary identities, is my primary concern here. Indeed, I argue that Cliff's literary works illustrate a new way of thinking with and through bi-ness that reconfigures traditional conceptions of binary identity divisions and formal divisions of categorization.

Furthermore, my approach takes a considered view of Cliff's body of work, exploring a number of thematic "phases" by which she can be said to work through the fragmentary nature of her multipolar identities. Following the approach taken by Evelyn O'Callaghan and Tim Watson in their volume on *Caribbean Literature in Transition* (2), these phases are not to be thought of as strictly chronological; rather, my focus on the phasal nature of Cliff's writing might be thought of partly in terms of a continuum along which Cliff moves at various stages of her experimental writing and the various points of which certainly speak to and, indeed, overlap with one another. As such, I will be discussing a number of Cliff's texts from across disparate time periods in her writing career to underline the fluid and multipolar forms not only of her writing but also of the development of her critical and creative thinking on bi-ness throughout her oeuvre as a whole. That is to say, much like O'Callaghan's approach in her 1993 monograph *Woman Version: Theoretical Approaches to Fiction by Women*, I aim not to construct a singular, chronological model for understanding the development of Cliff's literary form but rather stress the need for "plural and syncretic theoretical approaches which can take account of the multiplicity, complexity, [and] the intersection of apparently conflicting orientations" that are to be found in Cliff's writing (15).

Moreover, my approach to race and ethnicity in Cliff's work is indebted to—indeed, comes out of—the critical heritage of work undertaken on Creole studies. The term "Creole" has its origins in the sixteenth century and was originally used to distinguish between those born in the "Old World" of Europe and the "New World" of the Americas (Stewart, 1) or, more specifically, those Afro-descendants of enslaved peoples born in the Caribbean and not in Africa. From the Spanish *criollo* ("a child, particularly of Europeans, who is born in the New World" [Alcocer, 9]), the term "Creole" refers to those of "predominantly European descent who regard the Caribbean as home" (Donnell and Lawson Welsh, 8). Popularized by the Martinican writer Édouard Glissant, creolization is positioned as "halfway between … two 'pure' extremes" (140); that is to say, Glissant views creolization as an endeavor to "disrupt the unfortunately associated binaries of good/bad and pure/mixed" (Alcocer, 8) usually in racial and cultural terms. More contemporarily, "Creole" has been used to refer to "African-diasporic geographical and historical specificity" (Flores, 27) occurring when "participants select particular elements from incoming or inherited cultures, endow these with meanings different from those they possessed in the original cultures, and then creatively merge these to create new varieties that supersede the prior forms" (Cohen, 369). In much the same way, my bifurcatory approach to Cliff's literary mode is couched in similar such disruptions of binary classification, where I take as my focus the "multi" rather than the "polar" aspect of Cliff's multipolar identity markers. That is to say, I am more concerned with the bifurcated, fragmentary duolocation of Cliff's conceptions of biracialism, biculturalism, and bisexuality rather than the specific polarities of these positional identities between which Cliff attempts to locate herself (e.g., Black *or* white; Jamaican *or* American; heterosexual *or* homosexual).

To that end, I am also borrowing from Fernando Ortiz's conceptualization of Cuban culture (his particular microcosm) as akin to an *ajiaco*, an analogy made in his essay "Los Factores Humanos de la Cubanidid" ("The Human Factors of Cubanness," 1940). Ortiz employs the notion of *ajiaco* (a popular local stew in Cuba) as a metaphor for the "mestizaje de cocinas, mestizaje de razas, mestizaje de culturas. Caldo denso de civilización que borbollea en el fogón del Caribe" ("mestizaje of cuisines, the mestizaje of races, mestizaje of cultures. Dense broth of civilization that bubbles in the kettle of the Caribbean," 169). Ortiz argues that "there has been so much intermixture between such dissimilar races and where their amorous embraces have been so frequent, so complicated, so tolerant, and so indicative of a ... future de-racialization of humanity" (170). He uses the term "transculturation" to refer to the cultural and racial heterogeneity he identified in Cuba, which, he argues, expresses the "extremely complex transmutations of culture" (11) that have taken place in Cuba and across the Caribbean as a whole. For the present study, I expand on Ortiz's notion of the transmuting intermix of racial and cultural identities through my focus on Cliff's intersectional duolocation as a *bi*racial, *bi*cultural, and *bi*sexual woman—that is, located (as Cliff is) across and between multiple polarity markers, themselves often defined in terms of their inherently split or fragmented nature.

While not dissimilar to Ortiz's conception of transculturation or intermixing, the term "hybridity" is one that I adopt as shorthand throughout this study. Originally referring to the cross-fertilization of two distinct species of plant or animal, the term was adapted in the nineteenth century and applied to theories of race (see Young), where it was often employed as part of fearful discourses around miscegenation and racial mixing (see Carvalheiro). More contemporarily, the concept of hybridity has become a cornerstone of postcolonial discourse and its attendant critiques of cultural imperialism, particularly in the work of Homi K. Bhabha, who declared in *The Location of Culture* (1994) that hybridity refers to "the strategic reversal of the process of [colonial] domination through disavowal ... [and] the revaluation of the assumption of colonial identity through the repetition of discriminatory identity effects" (112). In simpler terms, hybridity represents a positional ambivalence (between colonizer and colonized), a doubling or dissembling image of being in two places at once, thus rendering the authority of the colonist no longer readily visible. Caribbean theorists have tended to avoid the term "hybridity" in large part because the Caribbean is already a hybrid region; it is already "an area of mixture and cross-cultural contact" that has experienced multiple generations of miscegenation (Alcocer, 13). However, more broadly, the concept of hybridity has informed debates within postcolonial discourses about "cultural contestation and appropriation and in relation to the concept of the border" (Brah and Coombes, 1). That Cliff's work is concerned almost exclusively with borders, boundaries, and with the intersectional margins of/between race, gender, and sexuality—as well as Cliff's multipolar duolocation as a biracial, bicultural Jamaican American; a figure who has been considered within the critical heritage of Caribbean literary studies as "not affirm[ing] at least aspects of being in the Caribbean place"; whose "authenticity" is considered to have been "compromised" by her proximity to the Francophone, Euro-American metropole (Mordecai and Wilson, xvii); and who embodies the "mixture" and "cross-cultural contact" that Alcocer outlines (13)—the term "hybrid" satisfies, for me, the ambiguous abstraction of Cliff's racio-cultural relationship with/to the Caribbean.

Extending my consideration of racial and cultural bifurcation in Cliff's work to include gender and sexuality, while there has been a broader movement to reconstitute discussions on Caribbean gender and sexuality studies at large, much of which is beyond the specific purview of this book,[3] at the root of my discussion is the commonly held assumption, articulated by Kamala Kempadoo, that "sexual practices and arrangements [within the Caribbean] are held to be operational around a gender binary that firmly attaches the biological to the social, and where heterosexuality is seen as the only form of legitimate sexuality" (9). As part of this so-called "naturalisation" of gender and sexuality hierarchy in the Caribbean, as Elleke Boehmer sees it, "gender informs nationalism and nationalism in its turn consolidates and legitimates itself through a variety of gendered structures" such that "the ideal of nationhood wears a masculine [heterosexual] identity" (6). In addition, as M. Jacqui Alexander makes clear, such "naturalized heterosexuality" has shaped, in particular, the notion of a Black masculinity and nationalism on the islands (1994, 7). The context of my critical discussion of Cliff's treatment of gender and sexuality is one, in part, grounded in the assumptions of heteronormativity reinforced by media culture and political and national metanarratives across the Caribbean Basin; that is, the "dominant, almost, unquestioned, links between sexuality and gender [that] are lodged in a norm of heterosexuality as natural." While such staid assumptions have, of course, been challenged in Caribbean critical discourse by the likes of Gloria Wekker, who has argued for a distinction between the concepts of gender and sexuality, and Timothy S. Chin, who has problematized the "patriarchal and heterosexual ideologies that have resulted in the marginalisation of women and gay men" (129), I will argue, much like Kempadoo, that "the collapse of sex and gender in everyday and academic discourse often elides the existence of persons whose social identities, sexual practices or physical bodies do not adhere or conform to these categories" (9). The common assumption—that "[s]ex folds into gender, and masculinity and femininity are viewed as complements to each other: two parts of a whole"—is something I will address in respect to my discussion of Cliff's challenge throughout her work to not only the monolithic notions of racial and cultural identity but gender and sexual identity as well. It is precisely because of the "[b]inary divisions and absolutes that categorize, rank, and sequence sexualities [and races and cultures]" (Valens, 3) that I will track Cliff's own move away in her writings from traditional conceptions of the Caribbean as a binaried social, cultural, political, racial, and gendered space to a multivalent realization of the Caribbean as a liminal space informed by the politics of bi-ness, whereby "sexuality, alongside race, class, gender and ethnicity, [instead] becomes a constitutive part of making a national community" (Pećić, 1). Indeed, Frantz Fanon advocates as much when he argues in *Black Skin, White Masks* that "[i]f one wants to understand the racial situation . . . considerable importance must be given to sexual phenomena" (123). Much like Alison Donnell, this study will call into question the "dominant matrix of race, ethnicity, gender, class and nation" (181) and will "depart from the trend of exclusively examining either heterosexual or nonheterosexual experiences" and hegemonies (King 2014, 9). As a general note, my use of the word "queer" within the context of alternate sexualities denotes that word's applicability to cross-categorization and the circumventing of rigid classificatory markers altogether.

Thus, in chapter 1, I explore the ways in which bifurcated identity is conceived of by Cliff, herself a bicultural, biracial, and bisexual writer. I will explore the ways in which Cliff's earliest writing "phase" illustrates a preoccupation with inherent contradictions and with the irreconcilable nature of not only linguistic but also racial and cultural identity. As I will demonstrate, the juxtapositions of Cliff's créolité result in a series of imagistic bifurcations within her writing that are made manifest through Cliff's insistence on metaphors of disembodiment and dissociation and that, in turn, condition the proliferation of doubles, reflections, and refractions that appear throughout her early-to-middle work—early signs of Cliff's eventual move toward a multipolar subjectivity. In chapter 2, I examine the means by which Cliff disrupts binary conceptions of identity while she is nevertheless beholden to her biculturalism, her biracialism, and her bisexuality. I will cover Cliff's efforts to come to terms with the apparent "void" of her biracial/bicultural identity by occupying what she terms the "third division." I argue that Cliff's assertion that "[w]e are triangular people, our feet on three islands" (1998, 22) is as much her thesis on identity as it is an expression of her own multilocatedness as a bicultural, biracial subject. Furthermore, I argue that the triangular nature of identity that Cliff posits defies binary logic and represents neither one state of being nor another but a new conceptual location-space for identity. In chapter 3, I address the question of how Cliff reconciles and amalgamates the various factions of her bicultural, biracial, and bisexual identities within a coherent subjectivity. This chapter examines Cliff's occupation of the bi-spatial in-between and the maturing assimilation of her own liminal ethnic, cultural, and gender identities. In this chapter, I argue that Cliff's work undergoes yet another shift: I contend that, in her later work, Cliff moves away from conceiving of the self as indivisibly whole while embracing the fragmentary nature of her various bi identities—which, her writings advocate, lead to a more considered and comprehensive conception of self. Finally, in chapter 4, I engage with the issues of trans identities and the way they are conceived of within the politics of Cliff's work. I will extend the discussion begun in chapter 3 on the nature of transnational and transcultural identities to incorporate a more focused discussion of transcorporeality and the trans-ness of Cliff's contiguous bodies. I argue that Cliff's maturing literary oeuvre is constituted by her and her characters' surrender to the fullness of their own multipolar bifurcation and an embracement of the interracial queer identities that have been belied throughout Cliff's work by the fluid hybridizing of culture, race, gender and sexuality, and class.

1.

"Split into Two Parts"

Michelle Cliff's Double Consciousness

Michelle Cliff's *The Land of Look Behind*, a collection of reflective prose-poetry pieces, is a meditation on Jamaican folkloric traditions and landscape and on the author's own bifurcated sense of identity growing up as a biracial, bicultural Jamaican American. In one fragment, titled "A Visit to the Secret Annex," Cliff's narrator can be seen, in effect, addressing herself, her younger self: "Yes, my girl"—she writes—"I say this to myself. (Because part of me is a girl and part of me is a woman speaking to her)" (1985, 105). Not only does this call to mind the multifragmentary nature of the narrator in "Belling the Lamb" mentioned in the introduction—the so-called "woman estranged from herself" (2009, 38) across no less than five separate interstitial subject positions—but more significantly, it is one of the earliest indications in Cliff's work of the bifurcated form she would adopt throughout much of her later literary practice. Cliff's narrator is very clear about the fragmentary nature of her own self-conception in this piece: "part" of her is a girl, and another "part" of her is a woman. Aside from the temporal disjunction inherent in the sentence structure of the first line ("I was born later" [1985, 104]), as well as the piece's intrinsically self-reflexive quality (addressing one's childhood self), Cliff makes it clear that, if there is a totality of self to be located and/or occupied in adulthood, it is only to be achieved through the celebratory rediscovery of that earlier, unformed self in juvenilia. The eponymous "Land of Look Behind," then, which Cliff's narrator in "A Visit to the Secret Annex" figuratively occupies, may very well be adulthood itself, a spatiotemporal realm characterized by repeated and insistent returns to the past: the childhood over her shoulder, so to speak, upon which the adult is always reflecting from a distance. The part-self of her childhood that Cliff's narrator reflects upon, however, is "suspended" (105), caught not only in the interstice of time—between the reflecting "now" and the reflected "then"—but stultified through the formal fragmentation of the prose poetry itself: short, sharp segmentations of speech that do not so much recuperate memories of childhood as they do deliberately create the impression that that childhood is contingent upon a fragmentary process of recollection, of looking back in pieces. On the level of linguistics, Cliff's prose-poetry is suspensive: broken interchanges of memory, of the past and of the present day; fragments of speech, a series of speech acts in fragments.

Cliff's formal approach to the piece (and to *The Land of Look Behind* as a whole) is best summarized by the narrator of "A Visit to the Annex," who notes at one point that her in-text interchanges are like "hold[ing] a conversation with myself" (106). The narrator's dialogue with herself is more than just reflective rumination, however; it is the communicational mode conditioned by Cliff's own créolité, the linguistic, cultural, and racial heterogeneity of the Caribbean region, and can be traced back to Cliff's earliest writings and reflections on literary practice. In an interview with Meryl F. Schwartz, Cliff herself explains the condition of her créolité in simple terms: "When you come from a poly-glossal culture, which is what Jamaica is, you do speak in several tongues" (qtd. in Schwartz 1993, 609). Writing in the preface to *The Land of Look Behind* in a piece titled "A Journey into Speech," Cliff elaborates: "In my current work-in-progress, a novel, I alternate the King's English with *patois*, not only to show the class background of characters, but to show how Jamaicans operate within a *split consciousness*. It would be as dishonest to write the novel entirely in *patois* as to write entirely in the King's English" (1985, 14; my emphasis). Here, Cliff is discussing her first novel and the first of the Clare Savage stories, *Abeng*. While Françoise Lionnet has argued that Cliff's "split subjectivity" and the "split subjectivity" of some of her narrators is "mirrored accurately in the self-conscious move from English to Creole, since the appropriation of the vernacular sets off the discontinuous and fragmented nature of the postcolonial subject" (327), Kaisa Ilmonen argues, conversely, that, in *Abeng*, Cliff "constantly shifts back and forth from Standard English to Creole speech and using Creole terms, which would be difficult for a non-Jamaican reader to understand without a glossary (which is, however, included at the end of the novel)" (2002, 113). Lionnet suggests that Cliff's inclusion of a glossary of Creole terminology at the back of the book is "tantamount to a gesture of inclusion/exclusion that forces the reader to situate him or herself with regard to his or her particular understanding of Jamaican Creole," the result of which may mean that the American reader (on whom Lionnet focuses) feels "excluded" if they are unaware that the glossary exists (324). However, I see Cliff's créolité not as a stylistic choice or linguistic tool to aid her readers; rather, I take her polyglossia to be an inescapable consequence of her split racial and cultural consciousness deriving from the fragmented biracial and bicultural polarities she has historically occupied. Cliff's duality of speech is not simply, in Lionnet's words, "meant to underscore class and race [or even linguistic] differences"; it is, as Lionnet herself continues, a viable linguistic means by which Cliff "makes manifest the double consciousness of the postcolonial, bilingual, and bicultural writer who lives and writes across the margins of different traditions and cultural universes." Indeed, the "split consciousness" of Cliff's own literary self-conception, the stylistic fragmentations that underpin and that are the very subject of her exploratory prose poetry, are later embodied in Clare Savage, *Abeng*'s protagonist, who is, by her own admission, "split into two parts" (1995, 199). Clare's split discourse, her usage of both Creole and Standard English, is not only an "alternative discourse to the one proposed by Eurocentric Caribbean nationalisms" (Martínez-San Miguel, 152); rather, it is demonstrative of the much greater juxtapositions of racial and cultural identities that exist within Clare—and within Cliff's writings at large.

The central tensions inherent in both Clare's créolité and Cliff's writings, then, and that which I take as the focus of this particular chapter, is summarized by Judith Raiskin as "the shifting between sameness and difference in all relationships, a shifting that moves between defining and deconstructing identity" (1996, 185). That is to say, I will explore the earliest "phase" of what I see to be Cliff's conceptualization of identity relations, examining the ways in which her writings illustrate a preoccupation with inherent contradictions and with the irreconcilable nature of not only linguistic but racial and cultural juxtapositions: créolité writ large across the early canon of Cliff's work. As I will demonstrate, the juxtapositions of Cliff's créolité—her biracialism, her biculturalism—result in a series of imagistic bifurcations within her writing that are made manifest through her insistence on metaphors of (dis)embodiment and (dis)sociation and that, in turn, condition the proliferation of doubles, reflections, and refractions that appear throughout her early-to-middle work.

Irreconcilable Differences: Juxtaposition in Cliff's Early Writings

Clare Savage's assimilation of her multipolar positionality is one that is first born out of the racial, cultural, and socioeconomic juxtapositions of her early upbringing. Clare's early life and her burgeoning self-conception are very much conditioned by the strict bifurcations Cliff constructs in her writings along the fault lines of race, culture, and gender and sexuality. In *Abeng*, much of Clare's earliest meditations on selfhood are determined by her conception of those divisions most readily apparent around her. Indeed, Clare's early childhood is marked by bifurcation and division: she spends the late summer months with her grandmother in the countryside, separated from her parents and her sister, who is sent to another relative elsewhere in town. Clare reminisces that "[t]hese two distinct places [her parents' and her grandmother's homes, the town and the countryside] created the background for the whole of their existence" (1995, 49). This geographical division is played out yet further in her parents' relationship, as these locales "reflected the *separate* needs and desires of [her] two parents" (my emphasis). Clare's mother, Kitty, "came alive only in the bush"; for her, "[t]own was evil," while Clare's father, Boy, "armed himself against" the countryside by "carrying newspapers and books and liquor, and a Swiss watch" to stave off the crushing boredom of the country. Of Jamaica's wider political topography, Clare notes that "[i]n 1958 Jamaica had two rulers: a white Queen and a white governor" (5). As such, even the hegemonic power structure under which Clare operates and through which she is reified as an ideological subject in the first instance is itself bifurcated as a result of the bicameral parliamentary democracy and constitutional monarchy that govern Jamaica. Clare further notes that the religious practices of her family during her early childhood were also couched in terms of an inherently racialized division: "[t]he congregation at John Knox [her father's preferred place of worship] was Black and white—Jamaican and English and American" (7). Furthermore, Clare's observation that the congregation is comprised "[m]ostly of the middle class" suggests another point of (socioeconomic) bifurcation. The congregation is very much drawn from those who inhabit Jamaica's economic fault line: those who are neither wealthy nor poor, neither in one socioeconomic bracket nor the other. Thus, Clare's conception of her early life is, in part, also informed by the juxtaposition of the congregation's admixture of racial and economic subjectivities.

Of her own biracial existence, Clare's racial self-conception is yet a further matter of contradiction. It is not without regret, for example, that she notes of life in Jamaica that "the worst thing to be—especially if you were a girl—was to be dark" (77). As a light-skinned Jamaican who often passes as white and who thus benefits from the privileges afforded to people of that color, Clare recognizes from a young age the positional juxtaposition she occupies. She notes that a certain "unease" with Jamaica's systemic racism occupies the "tiny space in her soul," and she acknowledges the "unfairness and cruelty" of that system while at the same time admitting to herself that "she was glad of the way she looked and [that] she profited by her hair and skin." Indeed, it is not so much her biracialism in and of itself but the irreconcilable contradictions within her young life that *stem* from her biracial condition to which Clare attributes the cause of the "split within herself" (96). In other words, Clare conceives of herself as "split" not simply (or not even) because of her bifurcated racial status, the ramifications of which she cannot be said to apprehend in toto at her young age. Rather, the confusion she feels, her "split" consciousness, largely derives from the cognitive dissonance she experiences in having to conceptualize Zoe (a dark-skinned girl whose mother works as a servant to Clare's maternal grandmother) not as "inhuman" (96), as the light-skinned girls at the school bus stop call her, but as her closest friend. This cognitive dissonance shapes the material practices of Clare's lived reality; she "passes" as white when around the similarly light-skinned town folk of Kingston, but during the summer season, which she spends in the countryside with her grandmother, Zoe is her closest playmate. Clare and Zoe both attend the same school, but whereas Clare is middle-class, Zoe is from an underprivileged background whose ancestors were formerly enslaved (and who were, in all likelihood, owned by Clare's paternal ancestors or their ilk). Thus, Clare's understanding not only of the divisive racialism and classism of the society around her but also her conception of the closest personal relationship in her young life is determined by and through a bifurcatory world vision, or, as William Tell Gifford puts it, Clare and Zoe "not only face differences between middle-class and poor, between urban and rural, but also between light and dark skin" (54).

These differences come to a head later on in the novel when the girls reach the figurative limits of their friendship. As a result of a heated exchange over their social and economic disparity in which Zoe points out the impossibility of continuing their friendship into adulthood, the narrator notes that Clare "felt hurt. By territory, Zoe's division of it, and by Zoe's conclusion that without a doubt their lives would never be close once they reached womanhood. This was not something that had passed between them before. . . . Clare was having trouble taking in all that Zoe said; she didn't want to believe it. She wanted them to be the same" (1995, 118). Here, Zoe's dissolution of their friendship is couched in topological terms: the fracturing of the girls' social relationship is conceived of metaphorically by Clare as a rending of space ("territory"). The racial, social, and cultural divisions that have implicitly underpinned the girls' relationship are now figuratively reconceived by/for Clare as an almost literal act of bifurcation; the "something that had passed between them" is the metaphoric interstice, the rupturing of Clare's psychological *terra firma* and the fragmentation of the girls' shared geospatial connection to one another. To Clare's mind, then, it is not the conditions of their racial, social, or cultural separateness that caused this rupture; it is Zoe herself. William Tell Gifford suggests that "Zoe knows that Clare's view of things is rigidly confined within her lighter-skinned, upper-class society" and that "[f]or the sake of her own survival, Zoe must be alert to values both within her own society and within Clare's" (54). This is, perhaps, one of the reasons why Clare conceives of the rupture of the girls' friendship as specifically Zoe's fault. Clare's ignorance of Zoe's motivations is representative of her ignorance of the racial and sociopolitical conditions that underpin their relationship at large, of which Zoe has a much firmer grasp than Clare, who feels hurt but does not understand what she perceives to be the callousness of her friend's actions. Cliff emphasizes here the fact that the cause of Clare's cognitive dissonance is not simply race or culture or class but a matter of her trying and failing to psychologically repress and reconcile herself to those irreconcilable elements of her *personal* relationship with Zoe, that which she does not necessarily conceive in terms of larger racial and cultural macronarratives.

Clare's burgeoning cognizance of the metanarratives of class, as well as her dawning comprehension of the material consequences of racialist ideologies, in particular, is played out in *Abeng*'s sequel, *No Telephone to Heaven*, a bildungsroman that follows Clare's maturation from young adulthood into adulthood proper. Cliff carries over from *Abeng* the imagistic leitmotifs of bifurcation, expanding further upon her study of Clare's fragmentary consciousness, which takes on a much more pressing anxiety in adolescence as a result of her family's immigration to the United States in the 1960s, where her light-skinned father, Boy, manages to pass for white, while her dark-skinned mother, Kitty, of course, does not. As with the relationship to her childhood friend Zoe in *Abeng*, Cliff suggests that the foundation of Clare's cognitive dissonance in *No Telephone to Heaven* is not a direct consequence of those larger metanarratives of race and class that shape Clare's existence on the whole but of which Clare is only cognizant in part, but rather, as a result of her strained efforts to reconcile herself personally to the split family to which she has been acculturated since childhood. If in *Abeng* Cliff charted the "*separate* needs and desires of [Clare's] two parents" (49; my emphasis again), then in *No Telephone to Heaven*, Clare's psychology is shown to be the product of a family unit rended from itself as a result of the seemingly incontrovertible bifurcation of her parents themselves. As the narrator tells us, Kitty "lived divided" (1996, 75), a comment that speaks not only to Kitty's inability to "pass" or to blend in within New York City as well as her light-skinned husband, but one which, through the juxtaposition of its (almost) visual rhyme, suggests the paradox of her fragmentary existence, a life made unwhole. Moreover, Kitty's "divided life" is perhaps somewhat heavy-handedly literalized in her adoption of the guise of "Mrs. White," the imaginary wife of the proprietor of White's Sanitary

Laundry in New York at which Kitty works and under whose fictitious name Kitty is directed to write and sign notes to customers advising them on the best course of upkeep for their clothes. Thus, Kitty's actual inability to "pass" is ironized through her adoption of the pseudonymous "Mrs. White," the ostensibly all-American (all-white) housewife.

While Kitty's effacement is racially and culturally prescribed, Boy is more adept at self-effacement. Nevertheless, even in those scenes of the novel in which Boy is shown to deliberately conceal from others his racial origins, Cliff elects to underline for the reader the inherently bifurcated nature of his character, never allowing us to set aside our conception of him as a divided subject. In her description of Boy, Cliff's use of the oblique stroke ("mestee/sambo/octoroon/quadroon/creole" [75]) provides a visual illustration and literal underlining of Boy's fragmentation; as it is visually augmented, his portmanteaued, multipolar subjectivity is shown to be (again, literally) bifurcated a number of times over. Boy's wholesale reconfiguration of his own and his family's identity—his exhortation to Clare, for example, that "[y]ou are an American now" (102)[1]—is contrasted with Kitty's embodied *aide-mémoire* for Clare to "never forget who your people are" (103). For Boy, Clare is "too much like [her] mother for [her] own good" (102). In other words, Boy bemoans Clare's tendency to "have more feelings for n-----s" (104) than for her own self-regard as an outsider in the predominantly white New York City. In contrast, Kitty believes that Clare's responsibilities to her racial history far outweigh those she has to herself or to her immediate family. When Kitty implores Clare to fill the "space between who you are and who you will become" (103), she is, in effect, entreating Clare to recognize the fallacy of Boy's fragmentary racial politics and to consider the interstitial contexts of her mixed-race heritage. Thus, Clare's ignorance of the sociopolitical conditions of race during her childhood in *Abeng*, which resulted in the dissolution of her friendship with Zoe and her passive assimilation of Boy's asseveration that "[y]ou're white because you're a Savage. . . . You are my daughter. You're white" (1995, 73), seemingly gives way to Clare's passionate resolve in *No Telephone to Heaven* that "[m]y mother was a n----r. . . . And so am I" (1996, 104).

Boy and Kitty are not the only bifurcated pair within the Savage family. Clare and her younger sister Jennie are also partially estranged from one another as a result of their parents' bifurcatory racial and cultural politics. In *No Telephone to Heaven*, the reader is told that Jennie "[spoke] her mother's language, while Clare spoke her father's adopted tongue. One daughter raised in captivity, the other in the wild" (1996, 104). If Clare is Boy's daughter, then Jennie is very much Kitty's—though Clare's narrative arc across both *Abeng* and especially *No Telephone to Heaven* is very much about her assimilation of her mother's racial-ideological consciousness. As Belinda Edmondson has argued, "Cliff is setting up a dichotomy in the white father/black mother parallel, so that Clare's search for a black identity becomes aligned with a woman-centered, incipiently feminist consciousness" (1993, 188). It is no small wonder, then, that in both *Abeng* and *No Telephone to Heaven*, Clare is shown to vacillate radically between the racialized subject positions occupied by her parents: her light-skinned father, on the one hand, who is descended from Jamaica's former plantocracy, and her dark-skinned mother on the other, whose land and family were subjugated by her father's ancestors, for as Wendy Walters reminds us, "Clare is not only nationally hybrid but also of mixed race and class—her father's ancestors were slave owners" (1998, 219). Veronique Maisier argues that "Clare is trying to make sense of the two worlds in which she lives. . . . *Torn* between her parents" (52; my emphasis). Jocelyn Fenton Stitt employs equally evocative language: she argues that Cliff "*bifurcates* the identities of Clare's Jamaican parents into an inauthentic and racist white father, and a racially mixed mother who honors the country traditions of Jamaica's past" (57; my emphasis). Critics, too, it seems, cannot but employ the language of rupture and division when discussing the outwardly irreconcilable contradictions of Clare's créolité in Cliff's early work. Sidonie Smith argues that Clare's "confounded fragmentation" is a consequence of her father's "fierce allegiance to genealogical pedigree and her mother's haunting remoteness, her palpable autobiographical silence" (48–49),[2] while Yolanda Martínez-San Miguel suggests that Clare's racial "fronterizo" is bisected yet further by the "whitening ideology represented by the father and the Afro-centric identification of her mother" (155). Sophie Croisy goes further, suggesting that Clare's identity is conditioned not by fragmentation, rupture, or division—but by erasure. She argues that Clare is "both witness to the erased traumatic part of her Jamaican past (that is her maroon heritage, a heritage denied to her by her 'white' father) and victim of that erasure as she is unable to know herself and her history until she begins to recuperate her mother's and her maroon people's genealogical memory" (133). Finally, as Zheng Xiuxia concludes, "Clare is posited *between two worlds* as she searches for a coherent identity," while the "dilemma of choosing between white and black heritages results in [her] *split* identity and a lack of sense of belonging" (74, 76; my emphasis). Indeed, Cliff herself has described the sense of unbelonging that she shares with Clare, resulting from her own racial and cultural créolité, as "schizophrenic" (1994a, 275), which is itself a mentality characterized largely by cognitive fragmentation. This splitting is, ultimately, perhaps unsurprising, given Clare's family legacy: her paternal great-great-grandfather, "Justice" Savage, is a white plantocrat who burned hundreds of enslaved people alive the night before they were due to be emancipated. Such is the prejudice among Jamaica's plantocracy toward miscegenation and mixed-race relations. Clare's fragmentary consciousness, then, may be said to be historically conditioned by Justice's fears that "the white seed would be diluted and the race impoverished"; as Cliff makes clear, Justice is shown to think "*along the lines* of Jefferson and Franklin, the founding fathers of a free society of white men" (1995, 38; my emphasis). Justice very much adheres to and reinforces the binaried racial and cultural divisions that those lines bisect, demarcate, and maintain.

Similarly, it is "along the lines" and the bordered fault lines of her racial and cultural divisions that Clare attempts to come to terms with her hybridized, fragmentary subject position. We witness Clare's burgeoning attempts to comprehend those paradoxical racial ideologies she has been schooled in in *No Telephone to Heaven* during the sequence set in the University of London, in which she tries to get to grips with responses to the National Front protest march outside the university calling for "N-----S [to] CLEAR OUT!" (1996, 137). The poster that appears in response on the student bulletin board the day after the demonstration—"WE ARE HERE BECAUSE YOU WERE THERE"—represents a critique in spatial-temporal terms of the binarism inherent in common cultural conceptions of racial discourse. The notion of a geospatial "here" (in this context: London, England, the Empire) and "there" (those colonial outcrops imperialized by Britain) seemingly underlines, in the first instance, Justice Savage's belief that race is a dualistic concept, a staunchly demarcated binary between two "sides" that are diametrically opposed to one another, never to be crossed. However, as the author of the poster intimates, there is nevertheless something of a positional interchange implied between the geospatial "here" and "there" (indeed, the implication is that one is a direct consequence of the other), an understanding Clare will not have until later in the chronology of her life. As William Tell Gifford reminds us, it is not just Justice Savage for whom race is conceived of in strictly binary terms: for the adolescent Clare, too, who was unable to reconcile her relationship with her childhood friend Zoe in *Abeng* on the grounds of race and class, London as the center of Britain's empire also "epitomizes a duality" (36) which reinforces the strictly binaried self-conception of her upbringing. Gifford argues that for Clare, London "represents the colonial empire responsible for yanking her ancestors out of Africa and turning them into slaves in the strange land of Jamaica," but that, simultaneously, it also "symbolizes her ancestors who did the yanking."

It is also worth pointing out, as Gifford does, that Clare's intellectual foray to the heart of Empire "does not magically reconcile her two racial halves" as she initially believes it would. Kaisa Ilmonen echoes many of her critical forebears, mentioned above, when she notes that Clare is "caught between these two ways of living," between the "here" and "there," so to speak: she "cannot position herself in either way," she is "unable to define her relationship to her home country," and she "cannot go beyond the ambivalent nature of her status as a Creole girl who is able to pass as white" (2017, 46). Ultimately, Clare is confronted in London with the realization that, as Noraida Agosto argues, "there are no in-betweens" (116) for her there. Clare's commitment to defining herself in strictly bifurcated racial terms runs up against itself precisely because, in doing so, she attempts to disavow the fragmentation of her subjectivity conditioned by the very hybridity she is unable to embrace. As Agosto argues, Clare's prioritization of race as an essential marker of her subjectivity suggests that "she has absorbed the binary (white/black) conception of race and racial purity held by the dominant discourse" (117).

Clare's assimilation of this dyadic racialist ideology is evident from her childhood musings in *Abeng*, during which she ponders the possibility of a wealthy benefactor who would, she imagines, deliver her from her family's impoverished situation, much like the character of Pip in Charles Dickens's *Great Expectations*, a novel she has read in school.[3] Most significantly, Clare's consideration takes the form of a series of self-directed questions: "Who would she choose were she given the choice: Miss Havisham or Abel Magwitch? She was of both dark and light. Pale and deeply colored. To whom would she turn if she needed assistance? From whom would she expect it? . . . The Black or the white? A choice would be expected of her, she thought" (1995, 36). Once again, Clare's existence is conceptualized as an irreconcilable bisection, a choice to be made between the deeply entrenched binary divisions of race and culture that underlines the bifurcatory aesthetic of Cliff's early imagistic mode. Clare's adolescent assumption that a choice in this matter is necessary for her survival (as either one *wholly* racial subject entity or another) is, of course, a form of protracted and discontinuous self-annihilation, for in choosing one side of this paradigm, Clare would, presumably, have to forego the other. It is for this reason that Suzanne Bost is not quite accurate in her assessment of this moment in Clare's chronology: Clare may very well identify with both Havisham and Magwitch, but she is not yet ready, as Bost asserts, to "[position] herself on both sides of [the] racial and sexual borders" (681). Clare's disinclination to choose, then, is not so much about her *failing* to choose one racial or cultural identity (or "side") over another; rather, it speaks more to her inability at this stage of her life to even conceive of the possibilities inherent in biculturation, a notion that she continues to consider in her move from adolescence to adulthood in *No Telephone to Heaven*.

In that novel, much like her identification with Miss Havisham and Magwitch in *Abeng*, Clare reads Charlotte Brontë's *Jane Eyre* and finds herself unsure of who to identify with. At first, she reasons that she is more like Jane—"Betrayed. Left to wander. Solitary. Motherless" (1996, 116), and white—before the realization dawns on her that she is, in fact, more akin to Bertha Mason: "Captive. Ragôut. Mixture, Confused. Jamaican. Caliban. Carib. Cannibal. Cimarron. *All Bertha. All Clare*" (my emphasis). While this confusion certainly parallels the dualism intrinsic to *Abeng*'s bifurcatory aesthetic and to Clare's life thus far, what is of note here is Clare's assimilation of the encompassing predeterminer "all," a word that suggests wholeness or completeness. This is, of course, ironically paradoxical, since wholeness is what Clare desires but is pointedly incapable of achieving. On the one hand, Clare's identification with Bertha Mason fulfills Kitty's imploration to her daughter in *Abeng* that Clare must "never forget who your people are" (1995, 103); but on the other hand, her embracing of Bertha Mason as an identity marker is a repudiation of her father's exhortation, also in *Abeng*, that "you're white because you're a Savage" (73). Thus, in embracing Bertha Mason, Clare actually sacrifices wholeness itself. The need to choose, Cliff implies, borne of a family rended along the fragmentary lines of race, proves that wholeness for Clare is a paradox, an unattainable end.[4]

That much is evident in Clare's doleful admission in *No Telephone to Heaven* to her boyfriend Bobby, a Black Vietnam War veteran: "You are lucky, Bobby. So lucky . . . to be one and not both" (1996, 153). To be both means to Clare that she must inevitably choose between her bifurcated identities. There is also the insinuation in the novel that Clare and Bobby's potential offspring might be monstrous, as Bobby imagines them as "a little Black baby with no eyes, no mouth, no nose, half a brain, harelip, missing privates, or a double set like some fucking hyena, missing limbs, or limbs twisted beyond anything you might recognise, organs where they are not meant to be, a disharmony of parts" (1996, 156). While Cliff's narrator does make it clear that the reason for any potential aberrations is the chemical poisoning Bobby suffered while on tour in Vietnam, the reader cannot escape the inference that this "monstrosity" might also be a result of yet further miscegenation—that is, the very kind of mixing that defines the contradictory juxtapositions of Clare's already bifurcated existence. Toward the end of *No Telephone to Heaven*, when Clare is interrogated by the leader of the revolutionary paramilitary group she intends to join, in response to the question, "To whom do you owe your allegiance?" Clare's answer—"I have African, English, Carib in me" (189)—illustrates yet further the ultimate irreconcilability of her multipolar, pluralistic subjectivities, split, as she is, into two parts: "white and not white, town and country, scholarship and privilege, Boy and Kitty" (1995, 119). As Zheng Xiuxia notes conclusively, Clare "feel[s] split between two worlds ... torn in the complex intersection of class and race" (58, 60).

"Something to Take Me Out of Myself": Dissociation and Disembodiment

In the preface to *The Land of Look Behind*, Cliff acknowledges her own so-called "journey into speech," a process of trauma she ties intimately to the writing of her graduate dissertation on the Italian Renaissance at the Warburg Institute in London in 1974. In typical ambivalent fashion, Cliff concedes that the experience of writing her dissertation afforded her "an intellectual belief in myself that I had not had before, while at the same time distancing me from who I am, almost rendering me speechless about who I am" (1985, 11). This "distancing" from herself rendered Cliff not only "speechless" but also resulted in a fragmentation of her self-conception, a bifurcation of self that is, in some ways, not tied explicitly to concerns of race and culture but to the intimacies of her own personal existence: "I wondered who she was and where she had come from," Cliff muses in the third person. Here, Cliff's fragmentation is reflected on the level of linguistic paradox, a veritable splitting between the pronouns "I" and "she," both of which, it is made clear, refer to Cliff. In this sentence structure, Cliff's identity is ruptured along the fault lines of subject-participant—that is, the "I" who speaks and observes—and the object of discourse, the "she" who is observed and interpellated within this discourse. Cliff's self-referentiality here constructs a discursive communicational loop in which the subject and object of speech are one and the same: Cliff herself. In effect, Cliff's speech acts "go nowhere," resulting in a veritable silencing of her subjectivity any time she moves to speak (to herself).

Of course, silence is one of the thematic keystones of Cliff's writings and a significant motif throughout her literary work, as a number of critics have pointed out. Kaisa Ilmonen notes that, in her writings,

> [Cliff] must learn to break the silence, find a voice, and come out of the Kumbla, which is a common metaphor in Caribbean women's writing. The Kumbla describes the state of speechlessness, but also invisibility and false safety in its ability to hide and cover.... In Cliff's fiction the Kumbla, being at the same time protective and silencing, is constituted out of passing and invisibility, but also out of colonial language, white mythologies, and heteronormativity. (2017, 12)

Ilmonen further argues that "Cliff's early works such as *Claiming an Identity*, *Abeng*, and *Land of Look Behind*, are more focused on the revealing of the processes of constructing these Kumblas in the colonized Caribbean reality, while her later works are more concerned with the breaking out of the Kumbla" (124). For Isabel Hoving, Cliff's use of silence is a "strategy of representation to tell her stories about silence" (2001, 241) and a way of exemplifying her "deep mistrust of language" (240). Silence, Hoving argues, is linked to passing, hiding, and invisibility: "On the one hand, silence has an ambiguous function in Cliff's writing. She needs it to be able to break her silence. On the other hand, the inability to break her silence in a literal way is not her problem" (242–43). As such, Cliff "experiments with syntax, with prose and poetry, with hampered speech and stuttering to find fuller means of expression" (240).

For Cliff herself, it is clear that silence and speechlessness are intricately bound up with her perceived powerlessness as a biracial, bicultural subject—her voice is rended from her as she herself is rended from a conceptual and totalizing wholeness. Cliff has argued that "[i]t is important to realize the alliance of speechlessness and powerlessness; that the former maintains the latter; that the powerful are dedicated to the investiture of speechlessness on the powerless" (1978, 5). She contends that speechlessness is "implosive, not explosive," and that "it is most effective—most devastating—against the speechless person. It may seem explosive: it may seem to affect those around and those in opposition to the speechless person, but its real effect is against she who will not! cannot speak." Cliff adds that "non-expression implodes into depression" and that "denial of the self is the origin [and] outcome of speechlessness. It is self-annihilation." Cliff further contends that speechlessness is a "self-punishment," "something self-induced to preoccupy in order to preclude growth" (6). One of the reasons Cliff offers for her own speechlessness is the attendant dangers of addressing her queer sexuality openly: "[c]oncealing lesbianism and thereby entering a dual masquerade—passing straight! passing lesbian. The effort of retaining the masks enervates and contributes to speechlessness—to speak might be to reveal" (7).[5] Cliff is adamant that her survival as a subject is contingent upon finding her voice; that is to say, she "seek[s] those modes of thought and articulation which will assure the unity rather than the division of myself" (1978, 9). Such a process, to Cliff's mind, involves "separat[ing] out and eliminat[ing] those elements which split me. Those elements which have divided me into mind/body, straight/lesbian, child/adult. This means nothing more or less than seeking my own language." Cliff's search for self(-expression) is often tied in her autobiographical writings to language itself. In *The Land of Look Behind*, she notes that "[w]hen I began ... to approach myself as a subject, my writing was jagged, nonlinear, almost shorthand" (1985, 12). Here, Cliff's inability to reconcile the dualisms inherent in her existence finds form in the perceived imperfections of her script; in approaching a sense of who she is, Cliff recognizes that this self is a "jagged" and "nonlinear" one, frayed and fragmented. Julie R. Enszer notes that, in addition to Cliff's own published fiction and creative nonfiction, her cocuration (with her partner Adrienne Rich) of the lesbian literary, theory, and art journal, *Sinister Wisdom*, from 1980 to 1984, also afforded "a new language by an array of women writers reaching for unity rather than division of the self" (111). Thus, Cliff's inability to reconcile the seemingly inherent contradictions and juxtapositions of her bifurcated existence, and her powerlessness to speak as the subject and not the interpolated object of her own discourse, finds initial expression, I contend, through her reliance in her literary works on metaphors of dissociation and disembodiment, imagistic representations of her desire to "separate out and eliminate those elements which split [her]." For example, the young Clare Savage undergoes a process of gradual dissociation across the novels *Abeng* and *No Telephone to Heaven*. While the catalyst for this progression is ostensibly her punishment for accidentally shooting her grandmother's bull, Old Joe (after which her grandmother, Miss Mattie, and her parents, Kitty and Boy, refuse to talk to or even address Clare), it is also clear from Cliff's narrative that Clare's inability to reconcile the internal contradictions of her fragmentary and conflicting racial and cultural identities certainly contributes to her dissociation from self. Clare notes that she "had heard herself referred to in the third person so often by now, she almost began to think that [her parents and her grandmother] were talking about someone else" (1995, 147). Clare's sense of her own dissociation is expanded upon yet further in *No Telephone to Heaven* when, in a passage musing on isolation and the loss of her family's tribal culture, she notes that she does "not [feel] much of anything, except a vague dread that she belongs nowhere" (1996, 91). Her inability to psychologically reconcile the strict bifurcations and scattered identity markers of (and within) herself, and to comprehend the possibilities inherent in her own hybridity, result in a certain dislocation and a displacement of Clare's subjectivity: she conceives of herself as "someone else," a "someone else" who exists, paradoxically, in a state of "nowhereness." Indeed, the interrelated themes of displacement and dislocation run through a number of Cliff's early short stories. In "Election Day 1984," for instance, which appears in Cliff's collection *Bodies of Water*, in response to the question "Where you from?" the protagonist replies "New York," following which the narrator offers this insight: "She answers with the place she last was, not the place she is made of. Anyhow, she belongs there no longer. Her voice would not be recognized by her people. They are background" (1991a, 107–8). Here, the protagonist's dislocation, her sense of unbelonging, is topographized as "self" and "place" are metonymized in one. Similarly, in "My Grandmother's Eyes," the first story in Cliff's collection *Everything Is Now*, the homodiegetic narrator is literally a displaced, dislocated personage: "I had no papers, no passport, no birth certificate—nothing to prove my existence" (2009, 8).

Cliff's stylistic progression, then—from her use of the oblique stroke in the description of Boy's multipolarity earlier in *No Telephone to Heaven* ("mestee/sambo/octoroon/quadroon/creole" [1996, 75]), to the declarative full stop used to delineate Clare's seemingly irreconcilable pluralism ("She is white. Black. Female. Lover. Beloved. Daughter. Traveler. Friend. Scholar. Terrorist. Farmer" [91]), what Caroline Rody refers to as Clare's "range of 'crossroads' identities" (163)—represents on the level of form Cliff's desire to "separate out and eliminate those elements which split [her] (1978, 9). The full stops above can be seen to silo each of Clare's identity markers (in contrast to the poetic enjambment of sorts implied by the oblique stroke) and parallels in form the dissociation, rather than "simple" fragmentation, which Clare feels within herself and which Cliff is attempting to express. Thus, when Clare notes toward the end of *No Telephone to Heaven* that she is "looking for something to take me out of myself" (1996, 194), she is not only offering on a literal, textual level her reasons for traveling to London, the metropolis of Empire, she is also expressing as best she can her own positional displacement. In being "taken out of herself" in London, Clare implicitly configures Jamaica as a metonym of selfhood, a *heimlich* space from which she is displaced and through which her metaphysical dissociation is topographized. Arguably, Clare is also looking for a way to escape from herself following her mother's separation from Boy and her departure with Clare's younger sister, Jennie, from the family home in New York. As such, Clare's loss is frequently metaphorized in *No Telephone to Heaven* in terms of displacement and dislocation. The narrator writes that "[a]fter her mother left her, in the days before she started school, Clare remained in the apartment until her father reappeared, abiding by his rule that she was to leave the house on no condition. So she stayed in, keeping house and watching television, *moving within the space of her loss*. But not allowed to be lost because her father said the family would be *reattached. Soon*" (1996, 93; my emphasis). The narrative continues: "No one made a move. September came. Each partner seemed *reconciled to the distance between them*, talking of missing all the while" (97; my emphasis).

What is more, in being "taken out of herself," the topographization of Clare's mental and spiritual dissociation from herself is also couched in terms of images and metaphors of physical (dis)embodiment as her body becomes the site of ex-change upon which this dissociation is materialized. As Lianne Vella notes, "Clare's identity formation is . . . bound up in the body, in how the body stands in for a series of significations, which she must break free from in order to come of age" (153). Thus, when Clare states in *Abeng* that she is "split within herself" (1995, 96), she is not speaking simply in figurative terms; rather, she suffers through a "break between body and mind" and a "disjunction between body and identity" (Vella, 153). It is for these reasons, perhaps, that Lemuel A. Johnson describes *Abeng* as a novel that "(re)calls out of and into connections and disconnections" (120). For Lin Knutson, Clare's "psychic dismemberment and reassembly" is more accurately mirrored in (the title of) Cliff's second novel, *No Telephone to Heaven*, which "reflects the 'disconnection' Caribbean people feel from their own complex history" (277). Knutson explains that the Caribbean people of Cliff's novels "lack a connection to an African past that once supplied them with spiritual and cultural power through vodun rites, tribal guides and gods, as well as female resistance." In *No Telephone to Heaven*, Clare also describes herself as an "albino gorilla" (1996, 91), which suggests that her dissociation as it manifests through and on her body is signified twice over: firstly, in the suggestion that her supposed "decolouration" is congenital and thus inherent, as opposed to social (i.e., the perception that Clare *is* white rather than just *passing* as white); and, secondly, in her apparent transmutation from homo sapiens to primate (although one cannot ignore the problematic implication of devolution intrinsic to this metamorphosis). In Lianne Vella's words, "[Clare's] internal self-identification is black . . . however, her body is seen as white, encoding her in a series of social roles and ideas which she herself is unconnected to" (53), while Amy Woodbury Tease argues that "Clare's body is positioned *not* as the cultural site of reproduction in the novel, but rather as a site of discontinuity, ambiguity, and contradiction" (96; emphasis in original). Melissa R. Stephens seems to agree with this stance in her assertion that Cliff's narrative bodies, more generally, are not so much *lieu de mémoire* as they are sites of creative interaction, sites of "re-orientation for the purposes of cultivating alternative visions of sociality propelled by political heterogeneity, conflict, and collaboration" (301–2).

The topographization of Clare's dissociation is also evident in Jennifer J. Smith's reading of the relationship between bodily physicality and landscape in the Clare Savage novels. Smith argues that "[t]he experience of the land through the body . . . suggests that the body's connection to history and place is limited, as these forces render [Cliff's characters'] bodies sites of death and reproductive loss" (144). For Smith, the image of the body in Cliff's writing is "the agent of violence and simultaneously its victim," and she cites numerous instances of menstruation, miscarriages, hemorrhages, and womb imagery throughout Cliff's oeuvre as evidence of the imbrication of dissociative trauma and the disembodiment and/or dislocation from the female body.[6] Meryl F. Schwartz also notes that bodies in Cliff's writings are "[vulnerable] to dismemberment along established lines of social division" (1996, 289). Cliff herself is very clear on this point. In her autobiographical reflections in *The Land of Look Behind*, Cliff conceives of her own life as "[a] life *cut off*" (1985, 71; my emphasis). Indeed, Cliff frames her personal reflections with images of disembodiment and bodily segmentation: from the "paisley-shawled bodies cut off from the undistinguished heads" (35) to the "split tongues" and "sliced ears" (65). Her description of patriarchal, symbolic culture ("slicers/suterers/invaders/absuers/sterilizers/infibulators/castrators/dividers" [33]) also puts the reader in mind of the oblique stroke she uses in her description of Boy in *No Telephone to Heaven* ("mestee/sambo/octoroon/quadroon/creole" [1996, 75]) as a visual signifier of the fragmentation, splitting, and segmentation that defines much of her worldview. Thus, the figurative language of rupture and division that is used to convey the contradictions inherent in Cliff's multipolar positionality at large is transposed onto the many images found throughout Cliff's work of broken, wounded bodies and torn appendages, ripped and rended from one another. As Noraida Agosto argues, Cliff "reads the body of her female characters and shows that slavery and oppression have been engraved on women's bodies," which, more often than not in Cliff's writings, become "a site of struggle that determines historical events" (8). Amy Woodbury Tease goes one step further and asserts that Cliff's canon as a whole "relies on images of wounds, of wounding, of wounded subjects and landscapes" and that "themes of loss and mourning, of trauma, history, and identity, emerge out of and converge upon images of the wound and wounded bodies in her text[s]" (94). Woodbury Tease argues that the image of the open, bleeding wound is given prominence particularly in *No Telephone to Heaven*, the epigraph for which is taken from Saint Lucian poet Derek Walcott's poem "Laventille" (1965), and that includes the lines "[s]omething inside is laid wide like a wound / some open passage that has cleft the brain" (qtd. in Cliff 1996, vii). Woodbury Tease contends that "materials wounds in [Cliff's writings] are described as gaping holes that are difficult to bear, to explain, and to comprehend" (100). She continues:

> The blood and scars that are produced by the wounds within Cliff's text mark both the landscape of the novel itself and the landscapes of the *bodies* that are present within it, remind the reader of the instability or fractured nature of identity that emerges out of an unspeakable history.

> Thus, the abuse and abduction of land by colonizers is made visible for Cliff by the wounded bodies in her novels. (emphasis in original)

Finally, Woodbury Tease contends that "[f]or Cliff, loss gets articulated *not* in the *closing down* or *suturing* of the past-as-wound but only through a violent *opening up* of the wound that bleeds and stains the landscape an unrecognizable shade of red" (100–101; emphasis in original). Such images are also to be found in the earliest of Cliff's fiction, in *Abeng*, in the description of Justice Savage's brutal mutilation of an enslaved personage whose body is literally rended apart. The narrator notes that Justice "dissected the naked body of the African . . . woman into four parts," and that "[e]ach quadrant of this human body was suspended by rope from a tree at a corner of the property" (1995, 30). Indeed, as Ramchandran Sethuraman argues, Clare's fragmented identity—and the various fragmentary identities present within the Clare Savage novels—is "nowhere more excruciatingly written than on the surface of the body" (273).

It is not just Clare Savage's body—or the bodies within the Clare Savage duology—that are subject to wounding; as Woodbury Tease argues, "Cliff's narrative refuses to limit the image [of the wound] to any one body, allowing the wound to circulate and multiply within her text" (101). The wounding and dismemberment of the Black body can further be seen in Cliff's third novel—the first of her full-length narratives not to focus on the character Clare Savage—*Free Enterprise*. In this novel, the wealthy white abolitionist Alice Hooper hosts a dinner party at which she displays the J. M. W. Turner painting *The Slave Ship*—originally titled *Slavers Throwing Overboard the Dead and Dying, Typho[o]n Coming On*, painted circa 1840. Following an awkward contretemps over dinner, during which Mrs. Hooper attempts to solicit the reaction of the African American abolitionist Mary Ellen Pleasant to the painting, Mrs. Hooper's dreams are shown to be haunted by images of dismembered enslaved peoples from Africa, whose "brown arms and legs on the ocean floor [drift] soundlessly down, barnacled, burnished finally by their intercourse with sand" (1993, 81). As in *Abeng*, the African body is not only one that is fractionated and segmented ("arms and legs") but also distinctly aligned with biological horror. In her dream, Mrs. Hooper "[pushes] aside the arms and legs and ghosts of an ocean floor" (82), suggesting that the Middle Passage is a space of ghostly dissociation and literal disembodiment. The body horror of Cliff's narrative is compounded yet further, much later in the story, when the character of Annie Christmas, a young Jamaican woman with whom Pleasant exchanges epistles, recounts her experience of rape at the hands of the overseers of the Confederate chain gang to which she is attached, who force her for pure sport to have sex with every other man attached to the chain gang. In response to repeated violations, Annie tells Pleasant that she "detached [her] nether parts from the rest of [her]" (207). The phrase "nether parts" not only implies a figurative partitioning of the body but that Annie's solution to her pain, in detaching parts of her body from itself, suggests that survival for her is not only to be found in dissociation from the forcible sex acts but also in the self-inflicted mutilation of her body and the rending of her own body parts/into parts.

Cliff's earliest short stories also abound in images of corporeality, rupture, and wounding. In "Screen Memory," for instance, one of the short stories from the third part of Cliff's collection, *Bodies of Water*, the narrator (an elderly Black woman who has adopted her white grandchild) compares the small white girl whom she has dressed in a pinafore with a "darker" tomboy on the playground, who, the reader is told, "could not pass the paper bag test" (1991a, 89), a reference to the crude discriminatory practice that compared the skin tone of dark-skinned Black people to the color of a brown paper bag, the results of which were used to make social judgments and determine the privileges an individual was granted. The narrator queries: "Where does she begin and the tomboy end?" Aside from the innate ambiguity in this question—it is not immediately obvious to the reader if the "she" here refers to the white girl in the pinafore or her Black grandmother, who is the focalizer of the story and whose ruminations on raising a white child comprises the remainder of the narrative—the question itself interposes the image of a bifurcated body, a body riven in two, and a body shared between the white child and the Black child whose physical margins are configured as indistinguishable from one another. Indeed, the corporeality of the scene is underlined somewhat paradoxically through the narrator's focus on the apparent translucence of the white child, whose veins, we are told, are visible through her pale skin but whose implied ghostliness carries spectral rather than somatic connotations. A bit later on in the story, when the grandmother muses on her most prized possession, a grand piano that the little white girl in the pinafore plays, the narrator describes in the following terms the expropriation from Africa of the ebony, ivory, and mahogany from which the piano is constructed, noting its provenance "[f]rom the forests of the Congo and the elephants of the Great Rift Valley, where fossils are there for the taking and you have but to pull a bone from the great stack to find the first woman or the first man" (91). The narrator's emphasis on the fractured bones of humankind here suggests a configurative alignment between the death (and desire of white culture for the retrieval) of originary Black cultures—a frequent theme in Cliff's work—and the somatic imagery of osseous matter. The narrator also alludes to the white child's birth mother (that is, the daughter of the grandmother character), who, we are told, has left very few remnants of herself behind for her child, save for a "heavy crazy quilt," which is described as "pieced like her mother's skin in the tent show where, as her grandmother said, 'she exhibits herself.' As a savage. A woman with wild hair. A freak" (98). That the child's mother is described as being in pieces ("pieced") puts the reader in mind, once again, of a literal dismemberment, the violent rendering of the Black body, torn asunder as it all too frequently is in Cliff's work.

Furthermore, this description must also surely put the reader in mind of the so-called "Girl from Martinique," the sideshow act and the part-narrator of "Burning Bush," another of Cliff's short stories from *Bodies of Water*. In this story, the Girl from Martinique is but one of a number of "freak" performers who are exhibited for the public as part of a touring commercial enterprise, described in the text as a "dark world of ... deformities" (75). Aside from the imagery of bifurcation conveyed in the appearance of the Girl from Martinique (she is described as "checkerboard" and "parti-colored" [76]), the segmentation of her body is also compounded by the "piece of cloth [which] wrapped her breasts and wound itself behind her, crossing her body beneath her navel." Here, the Girl's body is fractionated yet further by her costume, like the "heavy crazy quilt" she has left for her daughter (who, it is implied, is the white girl in the pinafore from the story "Screen Memory," discussed above); her body is presented as a patchwork of remnant parts. Within the "freak show" at large, though, deformed bodies seemingly abound, and the narrative is replete with images of interspecies cross-pollination—from the "Black Lobster Man" to the "White Penguin Boy" and the "Alligator Woman." In addition, the "[w]oman with a leg growing from her armpit" further connotes the body horror often associated with fractionated and conjoined appendages; she is described as an "[a]rmless, legless poet, a trunk of a girl," once again putting the reader in mind of the body as a segmentary form, a conjunction of pieces. Partway through this story, the narrative point of view changes from an omniscient heterodiegetic to the homodiegetic, first-person narration of the so-called Girl from Martinique herself. She reveals that she is not really parti-colored, but that she washes her skin using bottles of white shoe polish to achieve a mixed-race, biracial appearance (1991a, 78), while in "Columba," another story from the collection *Bodies of Water*, Charlotte's Cuban lover also purports to be white, a fact, as the narrator tells us, that "no amount of relaxers or wide-brimmed hats could mask" (15).

These images resurge in Cliff's later short stories, too. In "Stan's Speed Shop," a short story from Cliff's 1998 collection *The Store of a Million Items*, the eponymous Stan, a car repair shop owner with an intellectual disability who collects exotic curios and memorabilia, thrusts an Amazonian shrunken head at the unnamed narrator. Musing on the item, the narrator reflects that "[w]ithout a skull the head folded in on itself," concluding that it was "unbelievable" that the skull "once was attached to a human body" (1998, 61). Once again, Cliff underlines the (dis)connection between bodily forms in her writing, emphasizing the degree to which the dissociative trauma of colonialism and disembodiment or dislocation overlap. The same is true of her final novel, *Into the Interior*, which is comprised of a series of brief but interrelated vignettes. In one, titled "Night Nursery," the pederastic poet Richard is described by the narrator as having discovered on his travels a Burmese village "populated only by men and boys, missing limbs and fingers and toes and cocks and eyes," a so-called "island of mutilated Fridays" (2010, 62). Aside from the explicit cause of these atrocities (the narrator notes that the occupants of this village are "the casualties of a war unnoticed by the West," one cannot escape the uncomfortable implication of Richard's sexual imperialism—he is referred to as a "boy-fucker" (71) later on in the story—encapsulated in the allusion to Daniel Defoe's *Robinson Crusoe*, the ostensible urtext of British colonial practice. While there is no indication that Crusoe and Friday enjoyed a sexual relationship in Defoe's novel, that the narrator elects to utilize this particular frame of reference in the description of Richard effectively underlines the discomfiting association between subordination of the Black Carib Friday to Crusoe's white masculine power and Richard's pederasty, signaled by the mention of the boys' "cocks" and the title of the story itself, "Night Nursery," which suggests something of Richard's insidious paternalistic care for his younger subordinates. As a counterpoint to this scene, with its implication of stolen childhood innocence in the image of the boys' missing "cocks," another story in the same collection, "The Joy of Cooking," underlines the sexual imperialism of British colonial practice in a lighter, more parodic fashion. The narrator of "The Joy of Cooking," a young freelance journalist for an American magazine, is tasked with interviewing the British Museum staff member who is in charge of the so-called "penis room" (or "Member Restoration"), where the sculpted penises that have been resected from classical statues on the grounds of impropriety are reaffixed for preservation. The fact that every single penis that was removed from the statues is retained in storage not only underlines the hypocrisy of Victorian sexual standards ("bloody hypocrites" [2010, 89], as the London bureau chief of the magazine describes it), but it also reinforces the relationship, as Cliff sees it, between imperialism, somatic trauma, and disembodiment—as well as the rapacious sexuality that underpins the motivations of Richard the "boy-fucker" in the earlier story, itself facilitated by the conditions of economic imperialism. As Lauren Berlant argues, Cliff writes in "the language of embittering oedipalization, showing how still, long after the high imperial moment has passed, Jamaica and other postimperial sites must nonetheless continue to play the game of domination/castration beneath the caretaking skirt of the motherland" (148). Furthermore, she argues that "scenes of castration and sodomy are central to [Cliff's] exhaustion of patriarchal national politics as a source of emancipatory federation."

"Double Articulations": Reflection and Refraction

The successive images of fragmentation, splitting, and bifurcation that have come to characterize Cliff's formal literary approach—particularly in those images of wounded, rended, and dismembered Black bodies—result, then, in more than a diegetic split, more than a fragmentation in artistic form. Indeed, Cliff's work becomes multidiscursive or what Judith Raiskin refers to as articulations of a "double-voiced discourse" (1993, 58). These so-called "double articulations" (Ilmonen 2017, 58) are a consequence of the polyphony inherent in Cliff's seemingly dichotomous racial and cultural positions. As Caroline Rody notes, Cliff's "narrative strategy is strikingly, insistently *dual*" (153; my emphasis). Shirley Toland-Dix points out that a number of Cliff's characters—in particular, Clare Savage—exhibit a "*double* consciousness" and are the "embodiment of dualities" (40, my emphasis), while Angeletta K. M. Gourdine argues that Clare represents a "signifying duality" (57). In *The Land of Look Behind*, Cliff contends that "[n]o two people are the same" (1985, 88). However, unable to reconcile the duality inherent in her racial and cultural créolité, Cliff's writings actually end up replete with images of doubles and reflections. This is apparent from the beginning of Cliff's oeuvre, *Abeng*, the opening lines of which tell us that "[t]he island rose and sank. Twice" (1995, 3). Here, the Jamaica of Cliff's literary imagination is presented as a consequence of a double formation. The formation of the island's mythic genesis is predicated on duality: in rising and sinking twice, the island emerges from/as an act of double creation. Boy Savage's conception of the West Indies further emphasizes the dualism inherent in this creation myth: he notes that "the islands of the West Indies—particularly the Greater Antilles, which were said to once have been joined—were the remains of Atlantis," which had initially been part of a continent that had been riven by a "great and powerful earthquake" and which were "first joined in a chain and then [were] split apart into islands" (1995, 9). He also contends that the mythic Atlantis and the Mediterranean island of Crete "were one." Cliff replicates this doubling on the level of language, too: the narrative proper commences with the line "[i]t was a Sunday morning at the height of the height of the mango season," in which the repetition of the word "height" further serves to emphasize the quality of doubleness that underpins the irreconcilability of Cliff's—and some of her characters'—créolité. Doubles and doubling are an unassailable consequence of this créolité, a counterpoint to the bifurcatory mode employed by Cliff and her narratives' insistence on metaphors of (bodily) fragmentation.

This sense of doubling abounds in *Abeng*: from the mundane repetition of the figure "1" in the "ripe number eleven" (4) bananas both Clare and her sister Jennie carry with them to church, to the mythological originary narrative of *Abeng*'s Jamaica contained in the history of Nanny and Sekesu, two sisters who were there "[i]n the beginning" and from whom "[i]t was believed that all island children were descended" (18). Bifurcation and doubling are thus inherent to the cosmic foundational narrative of *Abeng*'s Jamaica. While Sekesu, we are told, remains enslaved, Nanny flees the shackles of her enslavement to become a revolutionary figure in Jamaica's Maroon history, one who embodies the myth of Jamaica's rebelliousness. The sisters' bifurcated histories, then, embody the dualism and doubling at the heart of Cliff's narrative, split as it is—as Clare Savage is; as Nanny was—between a maternal domesticity and a fierce rebelliousness. Indeed, Clare's "split personality," her fragmentary, doubled existence, is metaphorized yet further through the image of her grandmother's diamond-shaped cut glass pitcher that is "prismatic" and "*split* the light of the parlor" (13; my emphasis), "making a mirror in which Clare could detect her own reflection" (14). Here, Clare herself is doubled through her own reflection; her self-conception is literally fragmented between her embodied subjectivity and her diffuse, opaque "double" reflected in and refracted through the prism of the pitcher. The same is true for the narrator of "Down the Shore," one of the stories in Cliff's collection *The Store of a Million Items*, who sees the image(s) of herself both reflected and refracted in the mirrors of a funhouse and who notes the "elongation" of her body in "waves," "fluid" and "unsound" (1998, 40). The narrator's refracted self-image puts the reader in mind of Cliff's earlier (and more literal) body horror, as outlined above. That the narrator's body is something that might "melt away" through refraction suggests a rupturing and yet further fragmentation along the fault lines of the individual's subject position in which body and reflection are shown to come undone from one another. Of course, Clare Savage is also the semiautobiographical double or reflection of author Michelle Cliff—as is the character Annie Christmas from Cliff's third novel, *Free Enterprise*, argues Elena Sáez Machado, who says that the character is "symbolic of Cliff's ambivalence regarding her subject position as a Caribbean diasporic writer and whether she can teach her reader an ethical lesson about the history of Las Américas" (104).

Doubles, doubling, and images of reflection and refraction are to be found in some of Cliff's later writings, too. In *Into the Interior*, a number of the vignettes emphasize images of mirroring and duplication. In "Marooned," the narrator describes a passage in which she observes herself and her partner fighting. The scene is presented in such a way as to suggest that the narrator is undergoing a dissociative episode: disembodied, the narrator watches the scene from behind a "glass divider" in her "mind's eye" (2010, 38). Her repeated mention of being "stuck behind this glass" watching herself not only puts the reader in mind of the mirrors and mirroring in "Down the Shore," but it also underlines the duolocation of the narrator's fragmented subject position in this scene, doubled by and through the glass divider. The same is true of "Points of Departure," the first story from the same collection, in which a young girl is described as "bent double" (10). Precisely who this girl is remains ambiguous within the narration, as does the reason for her doubled condition. It may be that she is bent over in prayerful supplication (the preceding paragraphs make mention of a crucifix upon the wall of the room) or in the throes of a violent sexual act (the subsequent paragraph alludes to a neighboring landowner who impregnates his own daughter to secure his lineage). Regardless, the image of this body bent double connotes not only potentially further instances of racialized body horror but also suggests a literal doubling over/up of the characters' embodied subjectivity. The same can be said of the twin characters Elizabeth and Isabel in "The Joy of Cooking," yet another story from *Into the Interior*, who are described as "Orlando at each end of existence" (84). Not only does the allusion to Virginia Woolf's seemingly immortal transgender poet from her 1928 novel hint at the positional gender (and racial and cultural) binaries that Cliff seeks to explode in her novels in particular, but Elizabeth and Isabel's twinship is also a consequence of a monozygotic doubling, the literal splitting of a single fertilized egg into identical doubles: "two for the price of one" (98), as Isabel says.

2.

"The Third Division"

Michelle Cliff's Killing Ambivalence

So far, we have examined Cliff's imagistic use of fragmentation to articulate the multilocated racial and cultural subject positions inherent in her—and in some of her characters'—créolité. We have also seen the ways in which images of doubles, doubling, and reflections abound across Cliff's oeuvre, an obvious series of metaphors that she employs to express the bifurcatory nature of her split identities. Now I want to turn to the next iteration of Cliff's literary exploration of (her) identity that I have determined: the so-called "third division," through which she seeks to explode the duolocation of simple binary conceptions of identity formation. Having graduated from metaphors of splitting and fragmentation into images of doubling and replication, Cliff's imagistic motifs shift yet further to encompass this third space, the space of in-between-ness (as she sees it) that exists between two seemingly oppositional dyadic forces. The term "third division" is taken from the short story "My Grandmother's Eyes," the first in the 2009 collection *Everything Is Now*, about the secret love affair between the biracial female narrator and her closeted, same-sex lover, the unnamed J., a married, white American painter. J., we are told, "kept her life carefully divided" between the townhouse in which she resides with her husband and children and her studio "where she entertained her [female] lovers and led what she called her 'secret life'" (2009, 10). The "third division" in her life, the narrator tells us, is J.'s equally clandestine interest in the Harlem Renaissance and, specifically, in the art of Augusta Savage, the African American sculptor whom J. regards as her "equal in the arts" (11). J.'s "interesting take on race," the narrator notes, is such that it is J., with her cultivated interest in African American art and culture, who introduces the biracial narrator to the pleasures of Billie Holiday—and who also literally introduces the narrator to Savage. The narrator is, at first, concerned that Savage will "recognize" her—presumably, she means as multiracial, rather than in the sense of already knowing her—but this fear quickly subsides as she acknowledges to herself that she [the narrator] is "a race of one, unto myself." The narrator's perception of her own "oneness" here functions as a foil to her conception of J.'s all-encompassing wholeness: J.'s transgression of sexual and racial normative standards (in loving women; in loving Black culture) is such that her broad queerness as a subject may be read as representative of the burgeoning identity politics of the author Cliff herself, whose own autobiographical explorations of identity—as a biracial, bicultural, bisexual woman—is given expression and apotheosized through the figure of J.

The "third division," then, functions in Cliff's writing as a site of utopian potentiality; it is a conceptual space or imagined state of being in which traditional, duolocated binary oppositions (of race, of culture, of sexuality) are undone. This "third division" is neither one thing nor the other (neither Black nor white; neither hetero- nor homosexual, so to speak); it is the space or state of being that exists between and/or around those dyadic oppositions that is more than the sum of those oppositions. By way of illustration, the narrator of "My Grandmother's Eyes" offers a simple metaphor for this conceptual potentiality. In musing on her own eventual death, she hopes that the moment of her passing "resembles a thrilling orgasm like those [she] shared with J." (15). Rather than dualistic binary markers, this "third division" affords Cliff the opportunity to survey those spaces and states of identity that are neither one thing nor the other and that do not forcibly subscribe to traditional binary divisions. In the case of the above example, the pain of loss in death and the pleasure to be gained in sexual rapture are one and the same, a metonymic consolidation of Cliff's utopian vision of approximated wholeness.

Cliff attempts to conceive of this third space in *The Land of Look Behind*, in which she reflects on the "killing ambivalence" (1985, 103) of her créolité. It is as a consequence of her biracial, bicultural existence that Cliff imagines herself "speak[ing] from a remove of time and space," a space—as we saw in chapter 1—in which her metaphysical dissociation becomes topographized, firstly, and then literalized through various iterative metaphors of disembodiment and/or bodily dismemberment. Cliff notes that she is "*halfway between* Africa and England, patriot and expatriate, white and Black" (16; my emphasis), a figurative "white cockroach" (41), a hybrid being who is neither one thing nor the other, but a separate entity in which qualities of both are commingled—who, in Belinda Edmondson's words, is "simultaneously both and neither" (1993, 182). As Judith Raiskin reminds us, neither Cliff nor her most likely autobiographical counterpart, Clare Savage, identify as either white or Black; rather, their assumed créolité is actually a "shorthand expression covering a much more complex system of racial difference within the three-colour system (white, Creole, black)" (1996, 184). Indeed, as Raiskin also asserts, the central tension of Cliff's writings is the "shifting between sameness and difference in all relationships, a shifting that moves between defining and deconstructing identity" (185). The "third division" that Cliff seeks, then, is very much a corollary to this process of shifting between, as Raiskin describes it, and is very much part of the necessary step for Cliff in "seek[ing] a more coherent sense of self" (Strongman, 100) through an attempt to problematize and deconstruct "simple" binary oppositions. Indeed, much of Cliff's creative nonfiction in *The Land of Look Behind* captures her "process of finding a social space to inhabit that will not deny any of the complicated parts of her identity and history" (Kaplan, 195).

In much the same way as Edmondson identifies the hybrid nature of Cliff's créolité—the qualities of both-ness and neither-ness she ascribes to Cliff and her characters—so Caren Kaplan recognizes the manner by which Cliff elides yet further boundaries—"between homeless and origin, between exile and belonging"—in her search for the safety afforded by the spatio-conceptual "third division." The "third division," then, is a creative representation of Cliff's efforts to come to terms with the apparent void of her identity, an effort to reshape her racial and cultural "invisibility" (Cliff 1985, 71) and to reassert the indivisibility of her créolité. Of Cliff's duolocatedness and her rehabilitation of the concept of exile, Antonia MacDonald-Smythe notes that "[w]here the difficulty of being multiply located has occasioned a wide body of what I would call *distress literature*, a lamentation at the loss of voice and identity, Cliff has moved beyond this to proclaim the benefits of the choices wrought in exile" (87; emphasis in original). Thus, Cliff's assertion that "[w]e are triangular people, our feet on three islands" (1998, 22) is as much her thesis on identity as it is an expression of her own (and her peoples') move from a *duo*located conception of self to the *tri*partite space of multilocation. Caught in the interstices between "simple" binary configurations of race, culture, sexuality, class, etc., the triangular nature of identity which Cliff posits suggests that a true and proper recuperation of her créolité is to be found in this "third division," that spatio-temporal location that defies binary logic and represents neither one state of being nor the other but a *mélange* comprised of dualities and variances, yet indivisibly whole in and of itself. Thus, in this chapter, I explore the ways in which Cliff disrupts traditional conceptions of duolocated, split identities in her efforts to come to terms with her biracial, bicultural, and bisexual self. I argue that the triangular nature of identity that Cliff explores through her conceit of the "third division" represents a new conceptual location-space for locating créolité.

"Not Quite One Thing or the Other": Triangular People, Triangular Texts

If the "third division" of Cliff's créolité is to be (at least in part) characterized by the shared qualities of "both-ness" and "neither-ness," then it follows that an examination of this utopian spatio-temporal state is best carried out through an explication of those elements of Cliff's fiction that represent the condition of "not-quite-one-thing-or-the-other-ness." The phrase itself—"not quite one thing or the other"—appears verbatim (or almost verbatim) a number of times throughout Cliff's work. It is first mentioned in *Abeng* when an elderly Black woman approaches Clare Savage and her schoolmates at a bus stop and asks for the time. When Clare's peers "turned away from [the old woman] and told her to mind her own business," Clare responds almost instinctively, hissing at them: "[h]ow could you be so inhuman?" (1995, 77). In her reflections on the cruelty of her classmates and on her own use of the term "inhuman," Clare muses that "society had been built around an absolute definition of who was human and who was not. It really was that simple—except some people were *not quite one thing or the other*" (78; my emphasis). The concept or condition of "not-quite-one-thing-or-the-other-ness"—what Wendy Walters refers to as Cliff's "multilayered, both/and quality" (2005, 40)—underpins much of Cliff's writings; indeed, the very title of Cliff's first novel (*Abeng*) encompasses this quality particularly well. As Cliff herself explains in the front material, "*Abeng* is an African word meaning conch shell. The blowing of the conch shell called the slaves to the canefields in the West Indies. The *abeng* had another use: it was the instrument used by the Maroon armies to pass their messages and reach one another" (1995, iv). Thus, the novel's quality of "not-quite-one-thing-or-the-other-ness" is signaled in its title: as an object of both repression and resistance, the titular abeng refers to something that is both one thing and another; it is an intermediary item connoting in-between-ness. This is borne out in the many critical responses to the novel that emphasize the "both/and quality" of Cliff's narrative. For Walters, the abeng is "an instrument of both oppression and resistance [that] blurs the categories of oppressor and resister" (2005, 40). Similarly, Jeanine Luciana Lino Costa argues that the abeng is "both a sign of repression and rebellion, and so is the protagonist Clare herself, a mixture of these two" (117). Barbara Lalla recognizes that Cliff's employment of the abeng is "a call to break bonds and boundaries, to rupture epistemes ... to reject master codes, and to disorder and reorder existing imperatives" (5). The "both/and quality" of the novel's central image, then, suggests that the ambivalent nature of the abeng represents for Cliff the potential for continual revision and reconfiguration of boundaries and identity markers, a rupturing of the colonial status quo whereby the very tool of oppression also becomes a means for resistance. It is for this reason, perhaps, that Françoise Lionnet refers to the abeng of Cliff's novel as a "polysemic object, having both positive and negative connotations in the context of Caribbean slave societies," and which is "'double-voiced,' duplicitous, and susceptible to ambiguous reception and interpretation" (323).

The phrase "not quite one thing or the other" reappears in *No Telephone to Heaven* during an intimate exchange between Clare and her transgender friend Harry/Harriet. When Harry/Harriet asks Clare whether she finds them "strange," Clare answers, "[N]o stranger than I find myself. For we are *neither one thing nor the other*" (1996, 131; my emphasis). Melissa R. Stephens argues that, as friends, Clare and Harry/Harriet "share a general understanding of Jamaican class and race conflict as well as a unique understanding of society's intolerance towards same-sex desire and transgendered identities" (370). Harry/Harriet challenges Clare's presumption of their "shared sense of alienation regarding unitary identity"; however, when they tell her that "the time will come for both of us to choose. For we will have to make the choice. Cast our lot. Cyaan live split. Not in this world" (1996, 131). In Stephens's words, Harry/Harriet implies that "in times of crisis, one cannot necessarily afford to reside on the political border" (370). She elaborates: "Clare is encouraged by Harry/Harriet to choose between the political position embodied by her father, who has assimilated into a United States culture of whiteness, and that of her mother and grandmother, whose sources of political inspiration stem from Jamaican histories of Black female militancy." By telling Clare that they "cyaan live split," Harry/Harriet "signifies a predicament whereby certain historical contingencies necessitate forms of strategic identification that may compromise heterogeneity and reinforce singular notions of the political." Harry/Harriet urges Clare to "choose rather than to unquestionably inherit her political alliances" (371). Cliff never quite resolves the tension at the heart of Harry/Harriet's objection to Clare's "split" identification: Harry/Harriet believes one "cyaan live split," but, as Cliff makes clear, fragmentation and the burgeoning split to her own (and her other characters') consciousness becomes a necessary means to survival, a necessary means to assimilating her own créolité.[1]

The same might also be said for the names of certain characters in Cliff's oeuvre, whose denomination suggests a similar "both/and quality." This is certainly the case with Boy Savage, Clare's father in *Abeng* and *No Telephone to Heaven*, whose bifurcation is signaled through both his forename and surname. As *Abeng*'s narrator notes, "Mr. Savage was caught somewhere between the future and the past—both equal in his imagination. His first name was James, and his middle name, Arthur; in the family and among the friends he kept from school he was called 'Boy,' sometimes 'Boy-Boy'" (1995, 22). Here, Boy's identity is posited as triangular in nature, positioned as he is within the "third division" of neither-one-thing-nor-the-other-ness. Not only is he caught "between the future and the past"—and thus within the interstice of both—but his various designated appellations (James, Arthur, Boy) represent the tripartite division of his identity that is context- and place-specific, dependent on who it is that addresses him, and where. Thus, Boy's multilocated identity is, in this example, literally deltoid in nature. Moreover, there is yet a further iterative example of splitting and doubling to be found in Boy's nickname: the moniker "Boy-Boy" is, in effect, a double articulation, a consequence of yet further splitting and replication within Cliff's work. It is also worth noting, as Judith Raiskin has, that Boy's surname, "Savage," "betrays him by occupying the wrong side of the equation of colonial semantics" (1994, 164)—a betrayal which Cliff seeks to redress in her characterization of Boy's daughter, Clare. Indeed, Clare's full name offers an early indication to readers of the "third division" that she comes to occupy throughout the bildungsroman of her two-novel character arc: the quality of "both-ness" and "neither-ness" that she embodies semantically. Clare's surname—itself doubled in Cliff's later use of it (the real-life African American sculptor Augusta Savage appears in the story "My Grandmother's Eyes" from the collection *Everything Is Now*)—"evokes the wildness that has been bleached from her skin" (Lima, 40) and the "barbaric history of her father's supposed 'civilized' family of English planters" (Eldmair, 39). Here, Maria Helena Lima draws on Cliff's assessment of Clare from Cliff's own essay on "Caliban's Daughter: The Tempest and the Teapot" (1991), in which she states that her use of the word "wildness" is "ironic, mocking the master's meaning, evoking precolonial values, which are empowering and essential to survival, and wholeness, [Clare's] wholeness" (1991b, 44–45).[2] Of Clare's forename, a number of critics have commented on the significance of its paradoxical juxtaposition with the surname "Savage." Kaisa Ilmonen notes that the name "Clare" signifies "light-skinnedness" (2002, 117), while Barbara Eldmair argues that her name "calls our attention to her light skin, an obvious privilege in the world in which she grew up" (39). Silka Alaine Dagbovie concurs, arguing that Clare's name "connotes her color (*clair*, as in clear, pale, light-color)" (99). Nada Elia contends that Clare's forename carries another significance in that "it is the name of a college at Cambridge University, the matrix and dispenser of the British knowledge that the Savages claim as their cultural heritage" (2001, 45). Of Clare's forename, Cliff herself has stated that it "signifies light-skinned, which she is, and in the worlds she knows, light skin stands for privilege, civilization, erasure, and proximity to the colonizer" (1991b, 44).[3] Thus, between her forename and her surname, Clare Savage is caught in neither one space nor the other. The neither-one-thing-nor-the-other-ness of her créolité positions her, like her father, between her ancestors' past and her as-of-yet unexplored future but also between the interstices of racial and cultural identity: "her mother's version and the feminine history [and] her father's 'white' history of the schoolbooks" (Ilmonen 2002, 119).

It is for this reason that a number of critics have recognized the triangular nature of Clare as a character, a "paradoxical" (117) and "transitional" figure (Pollock, 208) who "belongs at least in two worlds" or cultural traditions (Lima, 40; see also Ilmonen 2002, 117). If Clare is split, then, it is not simply, as Silka Alaine Dagbovie states, "into two parts—white and not white" (95). Rather, her multilocatedness as a subject is conditioned by the triangularity of her créolité: a tripartite division. As Dagbovie herself says, "Cliff inscribes Clare's biracial identity as *not distinct from* (her) 'blackness'" (my emphasis). As such, Clare's biracialism (and the qualities of her bi-ness at large) suggest that she is at one and the same time both *a part of* and *apart from* those particular normative poles that mark her identity (race, culture, sexuality) while also occupying neither positional status of those paradigmatic binaries. In her triangularity, then, Clare is, according to Cliff, a "crossroads" character—the concept of which is evidently of such great importance to Cliff that she chooses to title her 1990 essay—a contribution to a volume of papers proceeding from the first conference on Caribbean Women Writers—simply "Clare Savage as a Crossroads Character." In this essay, Cliff describes Clare as a "crossroads character, with her feet (and head) in (at least) two worlds" (1990, 265).

The triangularity of Cliff's characterization extends beyond the Savage family, too. Indeed, a number of Cliff's other novels and short stories abound with characters who share the self-same qualities of "both-ness" and "neitherness" that Clare and her father Boy embody. In "Columba," for instance, the first story in the collection *Bodies of Water*, the eponymous Columba, a fourteen-year-old Black serving boy who is taken on by the white, landowning Charlotte, is also posited as semantically triangular. Columba, the narrator tells us, had been known by his mother as "Junior" prior to his baptism at age ten, "Collie" by some locals, and "Colin" by Charlotte, who anglicizes his name after purchasing him (1991a, 17–18). Thus, like Boy Savage from *Abeng* and *No Telephone to Heaven*, whose assorted designations represent the tripartite division of his identity, so too is Columba's identity figuratively deltoid in nature. Moreover, within this tripartite division, yet further segmentation occurs: "Collie soon turned Lassie and he was shamed" (18). Not only does this nominative slippage indicate the ease of semantic transformation that underpins much of Cliff's writing (and that I will discuss in more detail in chapter 4 in relation to *No Telephone to Heaven*'s transgendered character, Harry/Harriet), but it also underlines the casual social prejudices inherent in nonbinary identity markers within Cliff's Jamaica. That "Collie" (a male designation) should become "Lassie" (a female designation) represents not only the "simple" derogatory nature of casual sexism but is also suggestive of the fearful regard in which the "both/and quality" of not just racial but cultural and gendered créolité is commonly held.

The same is true for Peg-leg Joe, the one-legged sailor whose delivery of many enslaved Africans into freedom in the American South is enshrined in legend and whose mythic presence buttresses the focalizing character of "A Hanged Man," another story from *Bodies of Water*. The last paragraph of "A Hanged Man" reads:

> She got up, wiped her mouth with the corner of her apron, and walked on. She looked down at the muddy bank and recognized the trace of a track: human foot beside the circle of a peg leg. The mark of the journeyman. Spying this she walked forward. There was another track, then another, and after a hundred such tracks she was able to breathe deep, and take heart in this other human presence. (1991a, 52)

Not only is Peg-leg Joe's physical difference another iterative example of the violence of dismemberment and bodily segmentation that runs throughout much of Cliff's fiction and that I discussed in chapter 1, but the fact that the reader is told that "we do not know if Joe was black or white or Indian—or a combination thereof" (45) reinforces his mystique in the eyes of those who are equally "not quite one thing or the other." He is a veritable hero of créolité whose conceivably tripartite genealogical origin represents an aberration of traditional dyadic markers of identity. As a "black or white or Indian," Peg-leg Joe repudiates racial binaries in favor of triangularity.

Much like the titular abeng, a polysemic object connoting the "both/and quality" of Cliff's literary experimentation, so too does the title of Cliff's third novel, *Free Enterprise*, suggest a double-voiced in-between-ness. As Kaisa Ilmonen notes, the term "free enterprise" is a "poly-semantic signifier referring simultaneously to slavery and oppressive capitalism, as well as the actual possibility for oppressed people to gain prosperity" (2017, 77); it refers to both the business organized by Mary Ellen Pleasant, the capitalist philanthropist and first African American self-made millionaire, as well as the abolitionist enterprise in which she was an integral player.[4] Annie Christmas, the pseudonymous part-focalizer of *Free Enterprise*, is a Caribbean Creole who is described in partly similar terms to Clare Savage as a "migrant, displaced girl simultaneously privileged by her middle-class background and oppressed because of the ambivalent color of her skin" and who "does not accept her mother's values and dreams of passing as a privileged upper class white woman" (71). Between them, Mary Ellen Pleasant, Annie Christmas, and Clare Savage represent a triumvirate of characters who "connect the Caribbean diasporic experience to the American history of slavery and symbolize the counterhistory of the diasporic 'Black Atlantic,' the transatlantic cultural space." Moreover, the "third division," which characterizes Clare's créolité, is also to be found in the triangularity inherent in much of *Free Enterprise*'s linguistic economy. If Clare Savage's bi-ness marks her as a crossroads character, both a part of and apart from paradigmatic and normalizing identity poles, then so too in *Free Enterprise* does Cliff "[represent] the self as multiple," emphasizing the "constant shifting" of "multiple-provisional subjects" (Agosto, 11) between not-quite-one-thing-or-the-other-ness. Indeed, much of the novel's writing is indicative of the degree to which in-between-ness and triangularity typify Cliff's exploration of identity politics.

For instance, Annie Christmas is described as someone who, on account of her biculturalism and biracialism, could "come and go" (1993, 3) and whose "both/and quality" enables her to occupy the interstitial betwixt and between Jamaica's mulatto class and white America. Annie is described a number of times as existing "[o]n the very edge" and as someone who "lived her life on the edge, where most people who won't settle end up" (4). Annie's triangularity, her quality of "not-quite-one-thing-or-the-other-ness," is a consequence—or perhaps even a condition—of her borderwork; that is, her continual probing of the limitations of her own fragmented and pluralistic subjectivity on the edges and along the margins of normative identity markers. It is not a coincidence, then, that the title of the novel's first chapter in which Annie is introduced, is "*Gens Inconnu*," or "unknown people"—the "unknown" quality here being that of nonnormative or broadly queer racial, cultural, and sexual alterity. When asked by Mary Ellen Pleasant whether her family is comprised of enslaved or free people, Annie replies, "A bit of both" (24), and shortly after, when Mary Ellen Pleasant is recounting details of the real Annie Christmas, the preternaturally strong African American folk hero whose namesake Cliff's protagonist adopts, she notes that Annie Christmas "was very beautiful, drawing the stares of men as well as women" (26). Thus, the mythic Annie Christmas is positioned through the narrative along the edges of racial, cultural, and sexual borders. The quality of her bi-ness resulting, at first, from her racial and cultural créolité extends to her sexuality and to her sexual appeal to both men and women. As Cliff's Annie herself states, she is "a bit of both." Annie's indeterminacy as a subject, then, is reflected in the fact that she "[n]ever settled, never [felt] at home on the continent to the north, even after a lifetime in exile there" (19). Rather, of the quality of "placelessness" that she espouses, Annie notes that it "had always been hers," a syntactical arrangement that is suggestive of a certain possessiveness, but a possessiveness that is, of course, ironic, given her professed lack of attachment to any one space, place, or identity marker. Annie's placelessness, then, carries a metonymic quality: her bi-ness—that is, her cultural, racial, and sexual créolité—is not only out of place but can also be said to stand in for the placelessness she occupies at large. Annie has no place and there is no place for the "both/and quality" of her bi-ness within the normative racial, cultural, and sexual paradigms. Of Annie's triangularity, of the quality of not-quite-one-thing-or-the-other-ness, Bénédicte Ledent notes that, as a character, Annie "provides an even more complex and ambivalent version of Caribbean identity" and one that "transgresses a narrowly national or racial scope to encompass the black American experience but also that of oppressed peoples from all over the world" (78). Ledent argues that Annie's "plurality"—that is, the "third division" conditioned by her créolité—has "always been a part of her inner world" and that her translocation to the United States can be read as "an attempt to escape such institutionalized amnesia and reconnect with [that] plurality" (80).

Much like Annie Christmas, the character of Mary Ellen Pleasant is also configured as one who exists "on the very edge" of (1993, 3)—"stepping across, over, and through" (105)—a number of structural and conceptual interstices within the text. As an independently wealthy African American woman, the real Pleasant was known to pass herself off as a cook or housekeeper so that she could gain financial and political leverage: in Cliff's words, she "dressed as a dignified, unobtrusive houseservant" so that "she could move among [white people] easily, in and out of any station they required. Disguised" (1993, 105). In addition to the indeterminacy afforded her by her ability to pass as not-quite-one-thing-or-the-other as well as the implication that fragmentation of the Creole subject is presented to Pleasant as a necessary means to socialization, Pleasant is often framed within the narrative in terms of her characteristic qualities of "both-ness" and "neitherness"—those qualities that are characteristic more broadly of Cliff's writings. Indeed, Pleasant is almost literally framed by two other historical figures in the novel who may be said to be both present within and absent from the narrative: John

Brown, the abolitionist leader whose failed rebellion of enslaved peoples at Harpers Ferry was financed by Pleasant, and who never appears but is referenced numerously in Pleasant's letters to Annie; and Malcolm X, the African American human rights activist and Black empowerment leader who manifests variously in the form of a futuristic hologram. As Elena Machado Sáez notes, "Malcolm X makes several appearances as a hologram to Pleasant, as if he has become such a powerful symbolic figure (like Christmas and Nanny) that he can defy realist conventions. His time travel highlights the potential commonalities they could have conversed about: mixed-race identity, self-defense, and liberation" (100). Of John Brown, Pleasant notes in one of her letters that he is the "not-dead, not-alive man by [her] side" (142), while of the hologrammatical Malcolm X she shares that, in his (not)presence, she feels "alone, not alone" (153). Thus, her relation to these significant historical figures—as well her significance as a historical figure in her own right—is conveyed through the qualities of not-quite-one-thing-or-the-other-ness, the indeterminacy of both presence and absence, and the qualities of both-ness and neither-ness that abound throughout Cliff's oeuvre. Moreover, in much the same way as Annie's racial and cultural créolité extends to her sexuality (that is, the sexual appeal of the mythical Annie Christmas to both men and women), so too is it implied that Pleasant's "third division" is specifically gendered: "Didn't she have a penis?" (18) asks one of a number of disembodied voices stylistically employed by Cliff as a means of recounting the (many) largely unfounded but apparently reputed claims about Mary Ellen Pleasant. Not only does this particular query imply something of the "both/and quality" of intersexual nonbinarism, but the number of these successive claims position Pleasant at the divisory interstice of, among other things, optical heterochromia ("One blue eye and one brown eye?") and corporeal revenance ("Didn't she come back as a zombie?").

Indeed, we find throughout Cliff's later canon of writing various reiterative examples of divisory interstitiality that pervasive quality of both-ness and neither-ness. In Cliff's final novel, *Into the Interior*, the narrator of the third vignette, "Among the Christian Diabolists," evokes a number of collocations identical in conceit to *Free Enterprise*. Of Haiti, the adopted homeland of the narrator's mother, the narrator notes that it is the "[h]ome of the undead" (2010, 15). Not only does the image of corporeal revenance in the implied figure of the zombie ("the undead") put us in mind of *Free Enterprise* and some of the claims made about Mary Ellen Pleasant, but the juxtaposition of death and bodily reanimation suggests once again the significance of those qualities of not-quite-one-thing-or-the-other-ness. In describing his mother's death, the narrator notes that he "experienced [it] as a final absence;

she who had never been a presence" (16), calling to mind the indeterminacy of John Brown and Malcolm X's presence-absence in Mary Ellen Pleasant's life. The narrator's claim to be "a citizen of the world, belonging nowhere, with fealty to no one" (17) also puts us in mind not only of Annie Christmas's sense of placelessness as a Creole woman but of Anne Dillon, the focalizing character of "Bodies of Water," the title story of Cliff's first collection, who describes the house she lives in as "hers, not-hers" (1991a, 121), an admission that connotes a similar dissociative placelessness: the house is both hers and not-hers at the same time.[5]

Speaking more broadly, the quality of not-quite-one-thing-or-the-other-ness, that "both/and quality" that occurs repeatedly within Cliff's textual worlds, can also be said to characterize Cliff's literary style and her approach to textual practice at large. If a number of Cliff's characters might be described as "triangular" as embodying those both/and qualities that have come to define her exploration of Creole identities, then we might also think of Cliff's collected works as boundary-eliding entities in and of themselves. In other words, Cliff's writing "combines and rewrites a number of genres . . . from poems, folk songs, and texts that seem to be taken from a history book" (Schröder, 238); it "juxtapose[s] myths, superstitions, rituals, and songs signifying a forgotten past against the cultural embarrassments, oddities, and riddle of everyday life in the present" (Mohan, n.p.). As Ramchandran Sethuraman notes, "Cliff's hybrid narrative, in which several genres meet, jostle, and collide, defies all attempts at categorization; fiction, poetry, lyric, multiple references to both Western and non-Western contexts, canonical and noncanonical texts are all combined and recontextualized to serve the author's artistic purpose" (252). Renee Hausmann Shea also states that Cliff's work "mixes myth and story, fact and fiction, madness and sanity, [and] a range of time periods and even forms" (32). Finally, Kaisa Ilmonen asserts that Cliff's employment of paratextual elements—citations, poems, traditional hymn, proverbs—"foreground an assemblage of subaltern texts within which the (post)colonial subject is not spoken for" (2017, 115). The result is that Cliff's work takes on the quality of historiographic metafiction as she rewrites various real-world historical occurrences. That is to say, Cliff's writing "leaves the realm of the strictly 'fictional' since it engages in a critical discourse with historiography, rewriting dominant and authorized versions of the past" wherein "different literary discourses intersect and communicate with each other and hint at the numerous possibilities of reading and (re)writing" to be found within Cliff's literary imagination (Schröder, 239). Rajeswari Mohan argues that Cliff's literary invocations of past historical trauma are characterized, in her words, by "juxtapositions, contrasts, fortuitous coincidences, and the haunting presence of traces that we can only read as the return of the colonial repressed" (n.p.). This particular historiographic approach is borne out in Cliff's defence of the multilocatedness of the historical subject, caught as she/it is in the interstices of that spatio-temporal "third division" between recorded history and revisionist fiction. In her disdain for those strictly bifurcatory considerations of the novel (as one thing) and history (as the other), Cliff claims that she "can't stand the idea of the novel here, the history there, the biography there" (qtd. in Shea, 32) and that she "can't see why these things can't be mixed up," arguing that "[w]e have to bring our imagination to our history, because so much has been lost" (qtd. in Hudson, 111). In her essay titled "History as Fiction, Fiction as History," Cliff proclaims that "[i]t is through fiction that some of us rescue the American past" (1994b, 199).[6] It is for this reason, perhaps, that Cliff has been referred to as a literary archaeologist, concerned with "discovering if not 'what really happened,' then, at least, what might have happened" (Diedrich, n.p.). Cliff has also been called an "autoethnographer" precisely because her writings represent a new form of contemporary autobiographical text, the interest and focus of which are "not so much the retrieval of a repressed dimension of the private self, but the rewriting of . . . ethnic history, the re-creation of a collective identity through the performance of language" (Lionnet, 324). In Noraida Agosto's words, Cliff's writings "challenge standard forms that reflect the dominant tradition: though classified as novels, they read as autobiography and history and sometimes as poetry, thus eliding easy classification by genre. Her practices of intertextuality, word play, polyphony, and spatial and temporal fragmentation may be labeled postmodern; however, the revolutionary thrust of Cliff's texts distances them from that movement" (14). For Ramchandran Sethuraman, Cliff employs "multiple clashing genres" that both "inform and "cut across" the text (253). Furthermore, Cliff's works "evolve in their treatment of subjectivity, mapping the development of a subject that moves from the transcendental self—essential, individual, universal—to a being created in specific historical contexts and occupying multiple discursive positions at different moments" (Agosto, 103). Within the so-called "boundarylessness" (MacDonald-Smythe, 4) of Cliff's writing, then, which engages in "wilful border crossing between genres" and in which the "dramatic and the prosaic now exist within the same narrative frame," Cliff creates an "alter/native Caribbean aesthetic" (xiii).[7]

This boundary elision is evident from the earliest of Cliff's writings. As Belinda Edmondson notes,

> *Abeng*'s odd blend of narrative techniques is an attempt to show how these historical events created the cultural duality that is the legacy of the creole. The narrative reflects that duality: it moves in abrupt staccato from historical facsimile to historical fiction to autobiography ... and the choppy switching back and forth from genre to genre creates a restless tension in the narrative which is never resolved-or meant to be. (1993, 187)

Noraida Agosto continues, arguing that the relatively linear development of *Abeng* evolves into the "plurality" of *No Telephone to Heaven*, which is suggested by that narrative's particular "back and forth movement in place and time" (115). Lamiaa Hassan Ibrahim Abdulaal contends that *No Telephone to Heaven* actually "breaks down the linear conceptualization of time in order to challenge Western master narrative[s] and to represent the fragmented identities of those who are excluded from [these] master narrative[s]" (1,418).[8] For Irene Nicácio Lacerda, the postmodern underpinnings of *No Telephone to Heaven* are evident in Cliff's "patchwork" assemblage of narrative pieces that are "sewed together"; Lacerda contends that the structural relationality of the text's historico-fictional composition "represent[s] the site for the formation of new relations and new alliances" (12), not only for the construction of Clare Savage's identity but for the exploration of historical myth, too. In its "deliberately episodic and fragmented" form, "partially filtered through the sporadic 'rememoration' of Clare Savage," *No Telephone to Heaven* is thus a "creative rewriting of the past as opposed to a simple reminiscing" (Sethuraman, 252). Sethuraman argues that a "facile, ahistorical reading of the plot structure, character development, and stylistic nuances" of *No Telephone to Heaven* "can only yield a dominant version of the story" (254). Rather, he contends that "shimmering underneath the surface of the text lies another, more interesting tale that begs to be told."

The same can be said of *Free Enterprise*, both a work of fiction and a creative rewriting of history. As Mary Ellen Pleasant says to Annie Christmas, "For some, this is fantasy; for others, history" (1993, 29). While she is, in fact, discussing a number of reputed stories told about the mythic Maroon figure, Nanny, Pleasant's comment could equally be read as a metadescription of *Free Enterprise* itself. Elena Machado Sáez argues that *Free Enterprise*'s "ambivalence about storytelling [is] a means for disseminating a comparative approach to historiography" (99) and that the "alteration of voices is one way in which the novel's formal structure encourages the readers to see parallels between . . . different national and ethnic histories." Machado Sáez concludes, noting that "Cliff creates a temporal space for dialogue between historical figures that is possible only in the world of fiction." As Kaisa Ilmonen illustrates, the novel "offers a contrapuntal reading of the history of slavery, highlighting women's activity and the shared resistance of several people of minorities" (2017, 82).[9] Ilmonen argues that the narrative plurality of the Clare Savage novels is extended to the "multiple voices and perspectives" (2017, 82) to be found within *Free Enterprise*; "the boundary between fact and fiction is dissolved [as] written history proves to be only one possible narrative legitimized by the dominant knowledge-power episteme." Much like *No Telephone to Heaven*, then, the postmodernist ethic of *Free Enterprise* is signaled through the "nonlinear collection of memories, images, stories, old letters, and short narrated episodes, arranged without a single controlling narrative" (Pollock, 209).

Points of Departure: Hyphenation and Transition

Andrée-Anne Kekeh-Dika observes that the "crossroads pattern" that Cliff employs in *Free Enterprise* creates a narrative of "myth story, history, and memory" that "fus[es] past and present, combining fictional and 'real' characters" (267). For instance, Mary Ellen Pleasant and John Brown are not the only historical figures to feature in the novel; Cliff also includes the American photographer Clover Adams and her cousin Alice Hooper. Kekeh-Dika argues that "Cliff deliberately chooses to set her narrative at the intersection of history and fiction, of 'real' life and 'invented' life as if the *'truth' were to be found in the interstices* between those two narrative modes" (my emphasis). If, as Kekeh-Dika states, Cliff's narrative and/or historical "truth" is to be found in the "interstices" of her work, then it follows that yet further examination of these interstitial third spaces of in-between-ness proves necessary. In particular, the not-quite-one-thing-or-the-other-ness of Cliff's writing, that "both/and quality" that recurs throughout Cliff's textual worlds and that can be said to characterize her literary style and her approach to textual practice at large results in a certain "trans-ness." To be clear, by "trans-ness" I am not referring here to transgender identities or to the condition of being trans (although I will certainly return to this in my discussion of *No Telephone to Heaven*'s Harry/Harriet in chapter 4). Rather, by "trans-ness" I am alluding to the transitional quality of Cliff's writing resulting from the dialectical interchange that is conditioned by Cliff's and her characters' occupation of that space of not-quite-one-thing-or-the-other-ness. In other words, the transitional state between traditional epistemic polarities and/or binaried markers of identity—what I have referred to thus far as the "third division"—is signaled through the particular quality of motionality.

Kaisa Ilmonen argues that the Caribbean of Cliff's literary imagination "seems to be a *trans*locality constructed out of numerous movements and migrations, a site of diasporic journeys . . . a place with no stable origin" (2017, 2; my emphasis). Cliff's status as bicultural, biracial, and binational—a status which also befits a number of her literary protagonists—also signifies a transitionalist ethic, and it is this "hyphenated status" as a transnational, transcultural entity that "affords [Cliff] the freedom to occupy various discourse communities and to pick and choose from all traditions" (MacDonald-Smythe, 20). Indeed, Elizabeth Wilson also refers to Cliff's transitionalist ethic as her "hyphenated condition" (2), a term that indicates not only the divisory but the combinatory signification of meaning in Cliff's writings. Just as Cliff's "third division" is characterized by the shared qualities of "both-ness" and "neither-ness," so too does the hyphen simultaneously separate out and merge in one; it is, in itself, a linguistic symbol employed at once to both divide and compound. Moreover, Cliff's "hyphenated condition" is linked to the motionality inherent in her (and her characters') identity, itself represented by the forward-directional thrust of the hyphenation (e.g., bicultural, biracial, binational). It is for this reason, perhaps, that Nicole Branca suggests that "Cliff represents people in motion" (24);[10] while Antonia MacDonald-Smythe refers to Cliff as a "traveler through history" (144).[11] As a consequence of Cliff's transitional status (her occupation of the in-between; of the "third division") and as a result of her own positional ambivalence and the multipolarity of her subject-identity, "Cliff can ultimately not be securely placed anywhere" (Schröder, 201). It is, perhaps, for these reasons that Cliff's narrator notes with mocking wryness in the short story "Crocodilopolis," from the collection *Everything Is Now*, that "one of the only uses of Empire is ease of travel" (2009, 42).

Clare Savage is, of course, the most directly congruent embodiment of the hyphenated multipositionality of the "traveler." Jennifer Donahue argues that while Clare is "not a transitional citizen in the traditional context, as she does not physically leave Jamaica [in *Abeng*, at least]," she does, in fact, vacillate between the city and the countryside of Jamaica, "moving both spatially and between disparate cultures" in a manner that replicates "the very form of negotiation that transnationalism speaks of" (137). Indeed, as Wendy Walters has asserted, it is precisely Clare's nomadism,[12] her "shuttling between different national locations," that "forces her to confront the racial *métissage* of her own genealogy" (1998, 219). In Yolanda Martínez-San Miguel's words, Clare is a "bisexual or queer migrant" (186), and it is precisely through her "process of departure/return, this constant movement of migration" that

Clare "becomes the meeting place between different pasts, as well as between these pasts and the present of Jamaica" (Croisy, 143). In other words, it is in Clare's transitionality and motionality as a subject that she "becomes a figure of hope for the future, a positive vision of recovery from colonial lies, against cultural disavowal." The motionality of Clare's migrancy is yet further linked to her ability to racially "pass," that is, the ability of a biracial or multiracial person to be accepted and/or perceived as white, typically to escape the social and cultural ramifications of racial discrimination. The term "passing" also signifies movement, used to denote the passage of something (e.g., time) and/or transitionality (e.g., the passage from one state/space to another). In Noraida Agosto's words, "passing" is "a crossing over of ethnic religious, racial, class, and gender boundaries" suggestive of "movement and elusiveness" that "provokes anxiety because it demonstrates that categories defining subjectivity are constructed and, therefore, provisional and refashionable" (126). Isabel Hoving argues that Cliff's literary polyvalency is also rooted in the strategy of passing, which, in her words, "necessitates the adoption of the voices of others" (2001, 245), something which, as we have seen, Cliff's works are replete with. As Agosto sees it, passing is the primary means of Cliff's subversion and that which enables her (and her characters) to "underscore [their] cultural construction of identity" (10). Agosto argues that the collapse of racial, ethnic, and gender categories as a consequence of passing "promote[s] solidarity among oppressed groups by tearing down the barriers that isolate them," which leads to fundamental resistance. For Cliff herself, passing represents an act of camouflage, a manifestation of her desire to "blend in," to "become invisible," to "cultivate normalcy," to "stress sameness," and to live a "ghost life" (1985, 21, 23). Cliff has noted that "[m]any of the middle class who emigrated to Brooklyn or Staten Island or Manhattan were able to pass into the white American world—saving their blackness for other Jamaicans or for trips home; in some cases, forgetting it altogether. Those middle class [sic] Jamaicans who could not pass for white managed differently" (1985, 59–60). In *The Land of Look Behind*, Cliff's desire to pass is symbolized through the image of the ground lizards that she observes "rustle under a pile of leaves—some are deep-green, others shiny blue: all blend in" (19). Of this image, Joanne Chassot argues that Cliff's imagining is "an act of self-invisibilization" in which "passing is presented as a 'ghost-life'": Chassot asserts that "[f]or the passing subject, to be ghostlike means not only to look white, to make oneself inconspicuous in a white world, but also to make oneself un-raced" (2018, 165). Thus, Chassot contends that Cliff's efforts to lead a "ghost life" is an attempt "not only to escape and subvert the binarism of traditional racial categories by sliding through them and thereby making them inconsistent; it is also to fundamentally contest the essence of identity itself by making it utterly unstable" (171).[13]

Within Cliff's writings, the concept of passing is metaphorized not just in racial terms (e.g., Clare Savage) or gendered terms (e.g., Harry/Harriet from *No Telephone to Heaven* or Mary Ellen Pleasant and Annie Christmas from *Free Enterprise*) but also in terms of the transformational possibilities afforded to Creole identities. That is to say, passing—in the sense of the passage through, between, and within one particular sociocultural, racial, and/or temporal context to another—is metaphorized as a transformation, particularly of the body, from one state of being to another. As Nicole Schröder asserts, in *Abeng*, for instance, Clare's identity is "polysemic," "multidimensional, ever-changing, and layered" (207, 208), and we see this in the imagined body horror of the juvenile Clare, whose apprehensions concerning her own burgeoning (albeit already fluctuating) sense of identity are couched in terms of the fearful prospect of a very literal transformation. When, in their youth, Clare and her childhood friend Zoe are examining one of the British newspapers brought over to Jamaica by Clare's uncle, they are arrested by one story in particular: that of the report by an Edinburgh-based doctor who attests that "there was a rare disease which only girls could contract, in which they were gradually turned into men" (1995, 102). While Zoe is frightened by the possibility of simply *becoming* another gender ("Imagine, wunna could tun into one man, and wunna mama cannot do no-t'ing" [103]), Clare, it seems, is mostly horrified by the "irrevocable" (102) nature of this apparent transformation. In other words, she is struck less by the prospect of transformation *in and of itself* and more by the reputedly irreversible nature of the transition. There is a certain degree of logic to Clare's trepidation at large here, especially if we consider it in the context of her own "hyphenated" Creole status. Clare's identity, burgeoning though it is, is conditioned precisely by the transitional quality afforded her through her occupation of the space(s) and/or state(s) of not-quite-one-thing-or-the-other-ness. The transitionalist ethic of her nonbinary positionings—and that which has been borne out in our exploration, thus far, of the impossibility for Clare in having to choose between one racial/cultural/sexual subject position and another—further augments the notion that the "truth" or "wholeness" of Clare's identity is to be found in her capacity to transition between subject positions, whereby there is no originary or foundational identity marker but a series of identity markers (plural) between which she repeatedly vacillates.

It is also not insignificant, in this context, that Clare draws for the reader an implicit correlation between the ways in which she imagines her behavior will alter if she were to suddenly become a man ("[w]alking in a certain way.

Stroking their chins.... Spitting against the wind ... grow one of those things they called 'pepsis' [penises]" [103]) and the female menopause. Clare conceives of menopause as something to which "many strange things in women's lives were attached," including women's abilities to "develop paunches" and "grow beards" (159). In making analogous the physiological processes of female menopause and her own imagined prospect of becoming male (paunches, beards), Clare conveys to the reader her perception that, whether by catching this reputed disease or simply by growing into middle age, her transformation into some "other"—configured symbolically as male—is a totalizing rather than partial conversion. In other words, Clare is most fearful of being forcibly aligned with one subject position over another rather than being allowed to exist in the fluid interstices that her hyphenated state of in-between-ness already affords her. Thus, when Cliff argues in *The Land of Look Behind* that the purpose of her literary self-reflections is to "try and see when the background changed places with the foreground" and "[t]o try and locate the vanishing point: where the lines of perspective converge and disappear" (1985, 62), she is not simply talking about the harnessing of imperial powers by light-skinned, middle-class Jamaicans and the oppression of their Black counterparts. She is also acknowledging here that the "vanishing point" between one subject identity position and another is precisely where she exists: on the very edge. If the prospect of total transformation or conversion from one state or racial/cultural/sexual subject position to another is so fearful for Cliff, it is because she has always existed in a state of hyphenation: transitory and motional, and within the indeterminate in-between.

The transitionalist ethic of Cliff's writings can be found in her later novels and short story collections, too, which continue to underline the importance of motionality for Cliff in disrupting traditional epistemic polarities. In *Free Enterprise*, Cliff reimagines the ancestral lineage of her protagonist, Mary Ellen Pleasant, whose mother in the novel is presented to the reader as the folk heroine Quasheba, who is, herself, descended from Yemaya, the mythical mother of the seas. Aside from the implications of transoceanic movement embodied in the mythic Yemaya, "whose responsibility the churning waters were" (1993, 126), Mary Ellen Pleasant acknowledges that it had been her mother who "taught her daughter the need for movement" that she defines "in the sense of moving against, against, and toward, and away, and across." Mary Ellen Pleasant's reimagined ancestry, then, is one that explicitly foregrounds a certain transoceanic transitionality. Moreover, in her recitation of the foundational feminine mythology (which comprises most of the chapter on "Quasheba" in the novel) from which, it is implied, Pleasant is descended, Yemaya passes onto her daughter Quasheba the story of Shàngó, another mythic god who, we are told, "carried lightning bolts in her fists, his fists, and meteorites on his head, her head" (127). Thus, whereas Clare Savage struggles in a very mortal, temporal sense to position herself outside of those inherited binary paradigms of race, class, gender, and sexuality, in *Free Enterprise*, Cliff reconceptualizes the very cosmic foundations of her mythicized Caribbean by presenting one of its foremost deities as intergender, illustrating the nonnecessity of binaried gender subject positions altogether, as though nonadherence to gender markers were itself constitutive of a transcendent, celestial state.

Similarly, the titular story of *The Store of a Million Items* also contains a number of allusions to intergender identity that, I argue, metaphorizes Cliff's concerns with her own hyphenated, transitional status. Following the events of a devastating plane crash, after which disembodied torsos, arms, and legs appear to rain down from the sky, the townspeople find themselves unable to discern neither the gender nor the race of the various cadavers: "[Y]ou couldn't tell if they were a man or a woman, or colored neither" (1998, 51). The townspeople attempt to piece together the various assortment of body parts but are quailed by the sinful prospect of "bury[ing] people all mixed up." Thus, while the intergender quality of the mythic Shàngó in *Free Enterprise* is presented to the reader as achievable only in the transcendent realm, on the quotidian plane of "The Store of a Million Items" Cliff reinforces the notion that gender (and racial) nonbinary subject positions are framed in this instance as a by-product of an aberrant accident rather than as a consequence of a deliberate and sanctioned nonobservance of traditional markers of identity. Juxtaposed with this is the scene earlier in that story of the water fight on the school playground, before the plane crash, in which the "girls-against-the-boys" and the "boys-against-the-girls" face off against one another. Cliff refers to these team names as "ancient compound nouns, spoken in one rapid breath" (46). The compound names here represent something of a development within Cliff's literary canon. Whereas in both *The Land of Look Behind* (1985, 33) and *No Telephone to Heaven* (1996, 75), the oblique stroke was employed variously throughout to signify Cliff's earliest worldview of her own identity as something fragmented, split, and segmented, her use of the en dash in connecting "girls" and "boys" suggests that these two gender identity markers have perhaps become symmetric for Cliff. In other words, in conceiving of these supposedly gendered opposites not as "girls versus boys" but as "girls-against-the-boys" and "boys-against-the-girls," Cliff signals her maturing comprehension of gendered subjectivity as fluid and increasingly compound.

3.

"A Place for In-Betweens"

Michelle Cliff's Liminality

If chapter 1 was concerned with articulating Cliff's racial and cultural bifurcation through metaphors of fragmentation and doubling and chapter 2 elaborated on Cliff's exploration of the "third division" between supposedly duolocated markers of race, culture, and gender and sexuality, chapter 3 further examines her occupation of the bi-spatial in-between and the maturing assimilation of her own liminal ethnic, cultural, and gender identities. Here, we witness yet another shift from the simple multipolarity of the "third division," that space of not-quite-one-thing-or-the-other-ness, to a more considered and comprehensive melding or conflation of binary identity forms in which the space or state of the "third division" is reconciled within the individual entity and in which the erstwhile fragmented nature of Cliff's créolité is, arguably, reconstituted as indivisibly whole. It is in this "phase" of Cliff's writing, as Ramchandran Sethuraman notes, that "Cliff's ambivalent double articulation . . . explodes the fixed boundaries of identity and difference" as well as those "hackneyed binary oppositions" (251) by which her biculturalism and her biracialism, for instance, have hitherto been defined in relation to. Sethuraman further argues that the in-between spaces of the center/margin, the metropole/colony, the ruling class/subaltern—and, presumably, by extension, the Creole space between Black and white—give rise to new forms, posing questions as to the nature of transnational, transcultural identity.

The utopian potentiality of this interstice is further realized in Cliff's departure from a transitional conception of her own subjectivity; that is, her move away from and development beyond the simple "shifting [back and forth] between sameness and difference" (Raiskin 1996, 185) that previously constituted the conception of her own hybrid identity as a biracial, bicultural woman caught in the folds of multiple polar identity markers.

Here, Cliff is moving beyond ironclad deconstructions and (re)definitions of identity, beyond the need to define herself as "simultaneously both and neither" (Edmondson 1993, 182), and beyond that social and political space that would "deny any of the complicated parts of her identity and history" (Kaplan, 195) toward an in-between space which affords her the possibility to question even the value of the transitional contexts between which she previously situated herself. Sethuraman poses the question: "Is the process of hybridization always liberatory?" (251). For Cliff, it becomes apparent that the answer to this question is "no" and that the potential for recovering a totalizing wholeness of identity is one that is now not contingent upon earlier considerations of multipolarity—that is, of the strictly bifurcated conception of her transitional hybridity and her movement between multiple binaried polarities. Thus, in *No Telephone to Heaven*, when Mrs. Taylor (the school principal to whom Clare's father appeals on her behalf) informs Boy that her school is "[n]o place for in-betweens" (1996, 99), the implication is that Clare's biracial hybridity constitutes a despoliation of the white student populous. Here, Cliff acknowledges vis-à-vis Clare the liabilities and limitations of her own hybrid conception of self; the transitionality inherent in(-between) her occupation of multiple hybridized identity positions ("white cockroach"; "white chocolate") is presented not as empowering but as an impediment to her reconstitution of a social self. For Ginette Curry, this is most evident in Clare's declining relationship with her childhood friend, Zoe. Curry argues that "Zoe's comment about Clare being a worthless cuffy who tries to be white appears to have a double meaning. Zoe accuses her of being white on the outside and black on the inside. She points out her nebulous identity. She also derogates both Clare's black and white ancestry. Zoe implies she is not really black and that she feels superior because of the color of her skin" (235). Furthermore, Curry argues that, like Clare herself, Cliff is "caught between two contradicting sets of allegiances. . . . Cliff comments that the Jamaican whites want to enjoy white people's privileges but despise them at the same time" (237). If there is, indeed, no place for in-betweens in the context of Cliff's racialized Jamaica, then, Roberto Strongman's suggestion that Clare "seek a more coherent sense of self through identification with [Jamaica]" (100) is not quite satisfactory. Indeed, Strongman presents Clare's return to Jamaica after her various exploratory sojourns in London and the US as a matter of choice, as opposed to what Clare herself admits is the case: that she "returned to [Jamaica] because there was nowhere else" (1996, 193).[1] Thus, if there is nowhere else for in-betweens, either—that is, if Cliff cannot now conceive of her trans-itional hybridized identity in a topological sense (i.e., locating herself *in* a particular space or place)—then it follows that the way to do so perhaps lies less in positional or geospatial terms. Kaisa Ilmonen, for one, posits the notion that Cliff's identity, and the identity of the Creole subject at large, is constructed through the "political, historical, cultural, racial [and] even biological discourses, which all shape [their] reality" (2002, 114–15). She argues that it is precisely Cliff's disturbance and confusion of *language* (which we will see throughout this chapter) that affords Cliff the possibility of retrieving the "forgotten cultural matrix" of her identity (114).

Indeed, the importance of language and its constitutive role in Cliff's and her characters' identity (re)formation has been underlined a number of times in Cliff's fiction, particularly in *No Telephone to Heaven*. As I have previously mentioned, Cliff's use of the oblique stroke in her description of Boy Savage's multipolarity (1996, 75), as well as the declarative full stop in descriptions of Clare's pluralistic sense of self (91), underlines the symbiotic and relational nature, for Cliff, of language and identity. Moreover, this relationship is conditioned, to a certain degree, as a matter of choice. Take, for instance, the scene in *No Telephone to Heaven* in which Boy Savage checks his family into the motel in Georgia. In order to evade the suspicions of the racist white motelkeeper, Boy runs through a list of potential racial designations for himself: "What shall I say to this man? Boy wondered. . . . mulatto, offspring of African and white; sambo, offspring of African and mulatto; quadroon, offspring of mulatto and white; mestee, offspring of quadroon and white; mestefeena, offspring of mestee and white" (56). Though Boy elects to identify himself as white (without qualification) in order to endear himself to the motelkeeper, Cliff nevertheless underlines the point that it is a *choice* between a multiplicity of identity markers that is afforded him. Boy determines his own racial-linguistic designation in order to situate himself within various socioracial contexts. While Boy's preference seems to be to "counsel his daughter on invisibility and secrets," advocating for her "use of camouflage"—that is, using her white-presenting appearance to blend in and efface her hybrid racial identity (100)—it is the "ambivalent ethnic situation" (Gifford, 30) shared by both Boy and Clare that actually imbues them with a powerful liminal agency to redress the problems of racial and cultural bifurcation. Shirley Toland-Dix is adamant that the "eventual *choice* of racial identity that Clare will be required to make" (44; my emphasis) is irrefutable; and this choice certainly does form part of Clare's self-concern in her conversations with Harry/Harriet in the latter half of *No Telephone to Heaven*. However, what Toland-Dix seems to overlook is the transformative capacity of choice itself: it is Clare's capacity to *choose* that enables her to negotiate between subject positions. Such liminality, the ability to blend and mix between racial, cultural, and social strata, is not—or does not have to be—a consequence of otherization. Rather, it represents a subject position that is, in itself, indivisibly whole and in no further need of qualification. In other words, rather than attempting to reconcile a fluid, liminal subjectivity with one (or more) characterizing identity markers, Clare's racial, cultural, and sexual identity constitutes not a triangular but a blended or merged subjectivity.

Thus, in "Muleskin. Honeyskin," one of the stories from Cliff's final short story collection, *Everything Is Now*, when the narrator notes of the eponymous mulatta that she is "half-breed, possibly half-black, perhaps half-slave" (2009, 34), we are not only put in mind of Peg-leg Joe, the mythic figure in "A Hanged Man" (from the collection *Bodies of Water*) whose genealogical origins ("black or white or Indian" [1991a, 40]) also represent a racial mélange, but are reminded of Cliff's literary politics at large: that "we cannot be certain of anything" (2009, 34) pertaining to our identities, which Cliff suggests are fluid and unfixed, and which allow for the possibility of new forms to emerge and to reconstitute us. Indeed, in one of her later short story collections, *The Store of a Million Items*, Cliff signals her maturing comprehension of fluid subjectivities as increasingly compound and liminal. This is certainly borne out in the titular story and in the character of Gerald O'Brien, a young schoolboy who refers to himself as a "Gibson Girl" (the colloquial term for the personification of female attractiveness in the *fin-de-siècle* US) and who, we are told, "draped beads . . . around his waist and pretended he was a mermaid" (1998, 46). Gerald O'Brien's unselfconscious nonadherence to gendered socialization (he pretends he is a mer*maid*, and not a mer*man*) further signals to the reader Cliff's progressively more compound conception of fluid (in this case, gender) identity. When Gerald later inadvertently stumbles upon a man sexually assaulting a young woman among the "Mexican Rocks," a vacant lot of urban terrain located near the schoolyard, he scares the assailant off by smashing a Pepsi bottle on the back of the man's head. Gerald's father's reaction to his son's unlikely heroics—he "tries to reconcile his pansy of a son with the hero of the Mexican Rocks" (50)—might very well be said to be tantamount to Cliff's literary quest at large: that is, to reconcile seemingly irreconcilable constitutive parts of a whole identity and to underline the liminal forms of melded or blended identities. Thus, in this chapter, I will address the ways in which Cliff attempts to reconcile and amalgamate her multipolar bicultural, biracial, and bisexual subjectivities through conceptual liminality, arguing that Cliff expands on the bi-spatial in-between as a liminal space of identity (re)formation.

"A Space between Who You Are and Who You Will Become": The Language of Liminality

Liminality refers to the transitional or initial stage of boundary-crossing and/or the positional occupation of both sides of a boundary or threshold between two (or more) spaces or states of being.[2] The term has often been employed as a catch-all expression denoting "ambiguous, transitional, or interstitial spatio-temporal dimension[s]" (Downey et al., 3). Hitherto, I have referred to Cliff's burgeoning liminality as a state of "not-quite-one-thing-or-the-other-ness" or her conceptual "in-between-ness"—what Eric Prieto has termed the "entre-deux" (1). Prieto has argued that the "entre-deux" as a conceptual category has often been "misunderstood, maligned, or simply ignored." Liminality itself has been likened to a wide range of subject-positional categories: from "death, to being in the womb, to invisibility, to darkness, to bisexuality, to the wilderness, and to an eclipse of the sun or moon" (Turner, 81). However, as Downey et al. argue, the liminal entre-deux

> arises in-between two or more categorical definitions, but its spatial (physical and/or conceptual) position implies both integration of and resistance to whatever is either side of or outside of the in-between. In simple paradigmatic terms, one cannot occupy an in-between space or exist (in-)between two binary states without a resultant tension and/or mobility between both elements of the binary, which resist but also merge with the middle in-between. (6)

Furthermore, Bjørn Thomassen has asserted that it is in the liminal in-between that the "distinction between structure and agency cease to make sense" and that "structuration and meaning-formation take form" (1). In other words, thinking through liminality—what Thomassen advocates for as the understanding of "passages and passage experience" (13)—allows Cliff scholars to assimilate more closely Cliff's own de-structured approach to categorical structures in the age of increasingly fluid identity concepts.

According to Lilleth Trewick, it is precisely her liminal status that affords Cliff the possibility to "observe and participate in both the first world and third world as unconscious oppressor and oppressed, colonizer and colonized" (22). Trewick contends that, with her blended racial and cultural identity, Cliff is "imbued with the double vision necessary to depict the plight and resistance of the colonized" and that it is precisely through her liminal self-conception that Cliff (and her characters) "claim their multiple identities and achieve wholeness." From her earliest prose poetry in *The Land of Look Behind*, Cliff has always (albeit inadvertently, perhaps) expressed herself in terms of liminality; she describes her work as being "halfway between poetry and prose" and herself as "halfway between Africa and England, patriot and expatriate, white and Black" (1985, 16; see also Keulen, 200). Cliff acknowledges the necessary cost of her liminal borderwork: "I have tried to accept that reality and deal with its effect on me, as well as finding what has been lost in me from the darker side, and what may be hidden, to be dredged from memory and dream" (1985, 13). Here, Cliff is talking about the effects of internalized Anglocentrism on the "darker side" of her racial heritage, as well as the toll taken from herself by claiming an identity that is at once both hidden and revealed to her. It is also clear that Cliff considers (at least part of) her identity to be located in the nonquotidian dream world, the psychically liminal space of the unconscious that is both self and not-self.

The complexity of this liminal borderwork is made manifest in the characterization of Clare Savage. Shirley Toland-Dix contends that Clare's liminality, her capacity to choose her own identity, is radical in its potential to "undermine the whole fabricated system of racial classification" (46). Similarly, Trewick argues that Clare's radical liminality is also conditioned by choice: "[a]lthough she is bi-racial, [Clare] *chooses* to acknowledge, and identify with, only her Blackness" (42; my emphasis). Moreover, the complexity of Clare's liminality is, in Trewick's words, "compounded by her sexuality," split as she is "between the 'primordial polarities' of dating men while craving women." Trewick concludes that Clare's liminality is "heightened by her ability to move in and out of the primordial polarities of mainstream heterosexuality and homosexuality" and that she is "empowered . . . by her understanding of both [racial and sexual] realms." It is not insignificant, then, from Wendy Walters's perspective, that Clare's identity-quest ends not with "progress toward a stable whole at the end of the novel"—a notion that Cliff's earliest prose poetry seemed to explore with a certain hopefulness and that Walters refers to as a "defunct Enlightenment fantasy" (2005, 28)—but that her "fragmented and multiple" subjectivity, as well as her occupation of various liminal states of being "between childhood and adulthood, white and black, colonizer and colonized," illustrates the ways in which these subject categories are "discursive constructs." Such a position allows for a conception of identity as an "ongoing, adaptive process" and a form of "negotiation and transformation" (Donahue, 140) between multiple liminal states and positions. Indeed, Jennifer Donahue reads Clare's burgeoning bisexuality as a direct consequence of her creolization (140), which suggests that there is a conceptual relationship between Clare's biracialism/biculturalism and her hybrid sexual identity. To put this another way, then, Clare's identity is no longer to be conceived of in dualistic terms; she embodies not simply the "best of both sides" in a strictly binarial hierarchy—although some critics continue to conceive of Clare's identity in these dualistic terms: Irene Nicácio Lacerda, for one, argues that Clare is "the product of *two* different processes of dislocation" and the "result of *two* major geopolitical dislocations to the Caribbean area: the European migration to the West Indies and also the African migration as a result of the slave trade" (5, 13; my emphasis). However, the triunal state of her multihyphenated subjectivity—as biracial, bicultural, and bisexual—allows for a fluid blending and mixture of identity poles and a reconception of identity categories as deliberately bifurcated and unstable. Thus, when Clare's mother, Kitty, informs her daughter in *No Telephone to Heaven* that "[t]here is a space between who you are and who you will become," imploring her to "[f]ill it" (1996, 103), she is speaking of the liminal nexus of Clare's multihyphenation. If, as Irene Nicácio Lacerda notes, "the construction of one's identity is constantly incomplete" (35), then Clare's (lack of) sense of self is radically deconstructive of customary identity discourses, which has tended to posit individual subjectivity as indivisibly whole and as something one inadvertently "loses," rather than as a process of gradual, perhaps even lifelong, attainment.

The origins of Cliff's eventual transition from a both/neither dualism to a liminal-blended conception of her multihybrid identity can be traced back to her earliest prose-poetry reflections in *The Land of Look Behind*, in which she considers what she terms the "children of mixture / die Mischlingen / bambini de sangue misto / the crossover babies" (1985, 109). Cliff notes that these so-called "crossover babies," those racially hybrid offspring of parental miscegenation who we might also think of as culturally hybrid, more broadly, "number in the millions." Cliff's assertion that there are "millions of *us*" (my emphasis) is revisionist in that it presents racial and cultural créolité not as marginal but essential to the Caribbean mestizo experience. The pronoun "us" forcibly realigns the reader as the object and subject of the numerical preposition, thus underlining the diffusion of liminal identity beyond Cliff's own multihybrid conception and across the implied Caribbean Basin as a whole. Indeed, Cliff makes it clear that a liminal conception of her own (and others') identity is tantamount to the stripping away of boundaries and limitations; she refers to her liminal self-conception as a garden without walls: "Not a walled place—in fact, open on all sides. Not secret—but private. A private open space" (48). This "private open space," for one, is resonant of those contradictory syntactical juxtapositions in Cliff's writings we have discussed already but which are here, we might say, resolved in liminality.

Similarly, the epigraph to *Abeng*, Cliff's first novel, betrays Cliff's earliest aspirational longing for a freedom from limiting boundaried conceptions of identity:

> To know birth and to know death
> In one emotion,
> To look before and after with one eye . . .
> To know the World and be without a World:
> In this light that is no light,
> This time that is no time, to be
> And to be free . . . (1995, iii)

The epigraph is a quotation from Jamaican poet Basil McFarlane and, in some ways, can be seen to encapsulate the totality of Cliff's maturing literary vision, the hints of which are nevertheless perceptible in her earliest writings. It is apparent that the freedom Cliff seeks, the dangling prospect of which is presented (albeit unresolved) in the elliptical conclusion to the epigraph, is contingent upon the liminal fusion of multiple states of being in one. Thus, in wanting "[t]o know birth and to know death / In one emotion," Cliff is expressing her need to resolve the "not-quite-one-thing-or-the-other-ness" of her hybridity, that quality of both-ness and neither-ness that has largely defined her burgeoning conception of self. In order to "look before and after with one eye," in order to "know the World and be without a World," and in order to occupy a "time that is no time," Cliff must necessarily resolve her bifurcated self and embrace the radical potentialities of liminality.

Cliff's efforts to contend with the precepts of liminality are evident, firstly, in her metaphorization of the Middle Passage within a number of her novels. The Middle Passage, of course, refers to the trafficking across the Atlantic passage of enslaved peoples between the African, European, and American continents and the transportation of indentured African labor to the Americas. In *Abeng*, the young Clare Savage considers the African plague victims who contracted the disease while being transported to Jamaica and whose bodies are interred in a "monstrous packing case, made of lead and welded shut" that is then "dropped in the sea along the Middle Passage" (1995, 7). This oversized coffin is described as a "barracoon" or a "stockade" or "holding pen" (8). Here, the so-called "holding pen"—itself a liminal concept-term—literalizes the deathliness of the African enslaved people's liminality, caught as they are not in a radical but fatal in-between-ness. As Lin Knutson notes of the Middle Passage, enslaved Africans were "literally suspended—removed from the indigenous land and culture, in movement across the Atlantic, yet were nowhere at all"; she argues that in the liminal Middle Passage, "between their homeland and slavery, the chained slaves went through a psychological shift from freedom to colonization" (279). Knutson also argues that the middle three chapters of *No Telephone to Heaven* represent Clare Savage's Middle Passage: "These chapters reflect a major break with the narrative structure: rather than the omniscient third person narrative voice of the rest of the text, this narrative occurs in Clare's memory; here she re-makes her fragmented past into a present history" (286).

Similarly, in *Free Enterprise*, the central image of the novel (literally—the scene appears directly at the novel's midway point) is the unveiling by the wealthy white abolitionist, Alice Hooper, of J. M. W. Turner's painting "The Slave Ship" that depicts the forced drowning of a number of enslaved Africans who are thrown overboard from one of the ships crossing the Middle Passage. Thus, the Middle Passage is itself employed as a symbol of the erstwhile "killing ambivalence" with which Cliff has hitherto conceived of her own in-between-ness. However, Cliff's literary Middle Passage can also be read as the metaphoric fulcrum upon which her conception of liminality is reimagined. As Wendy Walters argues in relation to the Turner painting in particular, "Cliff makes the situatedness of the viewer central to the narrative of this painting's history as well as to the narrative the painting tells," providing in Mary Ellen Pleasant a "subject who views Turner's painting with an oppositional gaze" (2008, 517). Walters contends that "[b]y focusing on Turner's depiction of the violence of the slave trade, Cliff asks us to consider how a critical oppositional gaze is maintained in the face of images of terror."

The Middle Passage is also metaphorized throughout Cliff's oeuvre as a feature of language. Cliff's employment of neologistic portmanteaus—that is, words that blend the sounds and combine the meanings of two other words— replicates through language the interstitial liminality of her hyphenated state of being. Her figurative "middle passage," then, is configured in speech through the conflation of multiple word-states. Thus, terms such as "aristocoon" (2009, 1)—a portmanteau of the words "aristocrat" and "coon" (a derogatory designation for a Black person), or "politrickster" (2010, 8)—a running together of "politician" and "trickster," represent more than simple wordplay; they are political expressions of Cliff's (and her characters') multihyphenated liminality.[3] Equally, Cliff's juxtaposition of ostensibly divergent terms—such as "ripe sweet plague" (1995, 4) or "man-woman" (1998, 33) or even the compound nouns "girls-against-the-boys" and "boys-against-the-girls" (46)— metaphorize through language the conflation of liminal multihyphenation, the blended state in which Cliff has hitherto been unable to locate herself. In her own words, because Cliff is "halfway between Africa and England, patriot and expatriate, white and Black," she has often felt that "language and imagery had sometimes masked what [she] wanted to convey" (1985, 16). Her use of such portmanteaus and conflated word-images thus permits Cliff to express each hyphenated facet of her identity in a singular, totalizing utterance, or, to borrow a phrase from Lianne Vella, this "slipping between the two" compound words allow for the "lines between [both states to] become blurred" (37). Simon Gikandi has previously argued that "the struggle between language and speech in the Caribbean text is symptomatic of two radically opposed systems of representation—the oral discourses of the peasantry and the written texts promoted by the colonial school" and that Cliff and her characters (particularly Clare Savage) "[strive] to develop [their] identity between the two" (244–45). Gikandi further argues that a "third discourse" is "posited in the gap between the folk and official versions of history." But while he contends that this so-called "third discourse" is irreducible to language, I suggest that Cliff's compound juxtaposition of hyphenated portmanteaus is, in fact, part of her efforts to establish her burgeoning liminality in linguistic form. This so-called "linguistic creolization" illustrates the "integration of what were previously [Cliff's] rather disparate selves" (Donahue, 144) into a compound liminal whole. In her employment of ambivalent plural compounds and portmanteaus, Cliff dismantles "the supposition that there is an unambiguous position, or even only one position to speak from" (Hoving 2001, 243) in order that she might occupy an altogether more authentic pluralism reflective of her multihyphenated status. Isabel Hoving also argues that Cliff's strategy of ambivalent, plural pronouns is a tool that will eventually aid her in coming out as a queer woman (2001, 242). It is most likely for this reason that Cliff elects to construct her writings as heteroglossic in order to counter various hegemonic and monolithic cultural, racial, and national narrative scripts (see Barnes, 23). In her use of heteroglossic discourses, Cliff employs a "rebellious literary tradition" as well as "transliterations of vernacular language" in order that she might "transform the spoken subject"—that is, herself—"into a speaking subject" (Ilmonen 2017, 115).

Beyond her "linguistic creolization," Cliff's figurative "middle passage" is yet further conceived of in terms of the recurrent images of blending, melding, and conflation (of states of being) that represent her renewed efforts to articulate the multihyphenated pluralism of her identity. When, toward the end of *Abeng*, Clare professes that "there's all kinds of mixture in Jamaica. Everybody mixes it seems to me" (1995, 164), not only is Cliff reflecting on the so-called "crossover babies" she writes about in *The Land of Look Behind* who, she tells us, "number in the millions" (1985, 109), but Clare's admission of her biracialism, specifically, hints toward an acceptance of her own mixed, contradictory heritage (see Springer, 57) and an assimilation of the hitherto discomfiting "killing ambivalence" of racial and cultural ambiguity. Though she does not come to a place of acceptance until relatively later in her life, Cliff's burgeoning plurality is nevertheless signaled to the reader throughout even her earliest writings; her work is replete with images of melded and hybrid forms in such a manner as to indicate an early (though perhaps not fully realized) fixation on her own struggles with multihybridity. One of the earliest examples of this appears in the opening pages of *Abeng* and in the narrator's consideration of the mango crop, the largest crop of wild fruit grown in Jamaica. The narrative voice informs us that the local Jamaicans "did not cultivate the mango [for export]" but that they "made occasional efforts to change the course of its development" (1995, 4). These changes usually take the form of a grafting or transplantation of one shoot of the crop with the strain of another: "[a] branch was sliced from a common mango tree and replaced with a branch from a St. Julienne—the former could withstand all manner of disease or weather; the latter was fragile" (4–5). Here, the strain of one mango crop is compounded with that of another, grafted together in a process of literal hybridization. The mango crop—a prominent image throughout *Abeng*—is thus metonymically conceived of as a symbol of plurality, a metaphor for the hybridity that Clare cultivates and that "grows" within herself. In *Abeng*, in particular, Cliff underlines the pervasiveness of the mango plant across her literary Jamaica, often drawing attention to those various times throughout the narrative when "[t]he smell of the sea and the smell of the mangoes mixed with each other" or "the scent of ripe mangoes was present and heavy" (1995, 20, 22). Indeed, a number of critics have underlined the importance of the mango plant to Cliff's literary imagination. Marissa Petta argues that Cliff employs the symbol of the mango as a means of rewriting Jamaican history by "metaphorically representing the people of the island as mangoes to address the identity crisis among the large mixed-race population" (11). She elaborates:

> Cliff wants to put the Jamaican people back into their own history because they are misrepresented in the master narrative; the mango is the ideal symbol for the Jamaican people because it is so much a part of the island culture. While Cliff shows the natural and untouched fruit in its purest and wildest of states, she also shows the island fruit being manipulated for sale, becoming *mixed* like the people on the island. Cliff uses the island fruit to better show the complex mixed race identities that have been established due largely to colonization. (11–12; emphasis in original)

Thus, when Cliff notes toward the opening of *Abeng* that the people of Jamaica "did not cultivate the mango, but they made occasional efforts to change the course of its development" (4), Petta contends that "[t]he same could be said for Jamaican people who were products of biracial relationships, and were uninformed about their past. One race was often seen as weaker and fragile, while the other was more dominate and prevailing, which also shows the affects colonization had on the people of the island and their perception of race" (13). Furthermore, Françoise Lionnet argues that within Cliff's mythmaking, "the mango becomes a heterogeneous signifier that can readily be opposed, on the symbolic level, to the rigid classificatory practices of the colonial system," and that "[i]n order to create her own counterdiscourse to this disabling situation, Cliff establishes, on the first page of the text, the mango as emblem of the hybrid, mixed-race people of the island" (337). Finally, as Nicole Schröder asserts most succinctly, the mango is used as "a signifier of a diversity . . . in which the colors represent the island's cultural multiplicity" (209), which Cliff celebrates.

Clare Savage's genealogy, then, which is itself a form of cultivated hybridity, "parallels the varieties and mixings of mangoes" across the island of Jamaica (Walters 2005, 29) in a fashion not unlike the description Clare offers of the island's racialized social milieu. She refers to the "fabric" of Jamaican society as an "intricate weave" (1995, 28); that is, the process of entwining complex patterns from a number of interconnected components. This intermingling is further configured in *Abeng* through Clare's descriptions of blended bloodlines, often imagined throughout the narrative as a literal mixing of colors. The narrator tells us that Clare's maternal grandmother was "both Black and white" and that her father's racial origins were unknown; as a result of this, Clare's people are known colloquially as "red," the consequence of "a settling of blood as some light skins crossed over one or other of the darker ones" (54). Clare, we are told, has also "inherited her father's green eyes" (61); she is not just a liminal mélange but also a visual confusion of colors, the family's "crowning achievement" in a palette of black, white, red, and green, "combining the best of both sides." Indeed, at one point in the narrative, Clare seems to imaginatively transplant herself back in history to the eve of African freedom in Jamaica, the night her paternal (white) great-great-grandfather set fire to a stockade of enslaved Africans, burning them all alive. The narrator tells us that "Clare saw that afternoon behind the great house . . . remembering an event she would never know of" (1995, 40). Not only does Clare seemingly blend time and space in her figurative reconstitution of her ancestral past, but this sequence further demonstrates Clare's liminal positionality not just in space-time but also in terms of her political, social, and cultural alignment across both her father's ancestral landowning plantocracy and her mother's racially subjugated people. As Kathleen J. Renk notes, "Although the majority of the Savages take pride in their ancestor's cruel treatment of slaves and seemingly ignore their own slave ancestors, Clare Savage seems to see both worlds—the world of the slave and the world of the master—simultaneously touching her own life, and she sees the remnants of the slave culture buried within the landscape" (71).

The visual blending together of races/people continues in the opening segments of *No Telephone to Heaven*, in the description of the homogeneous attire of the revolutionaries riding through Cockpit County atop the open-backed truck. The narrator notes that this mix of men and women "were dressed in similar clothes [khaki], which became them as uniforms, signifying some agreement" (1996, 4). In their khaki getups, this admixture of people "seemed to blend together," their shared quality of "alikeness" emphasized over those otherwise disparate elements of their respective existences—"the shades of their skin, places traveled to and from, events experienced, things understood, food taken into their bodies, acts of violence committed, books read, music heard, languages recognized, ones they loved, living family"—which "varied widely" and which "came between them." Thus, when the narrator notes that Clare, as a "light-skinned woman, daughter of landowners, native-born, slaves, émigrés, carib, Ashanti, English" had "taken her place on this truck, alongside people who easily could have hated her" and that, together, this group of people were "making something new" (5), the narrative is signifying the transformative power of liminal plurality on both individual and collective identity formation. As Joanne Chassot argues, the identificatory "heterogeneity of the band, which is made up of people of diverse races, genders, nationalities, and backgrounds, is largely what makes its power, as each member brings something to the group— weapons, knowledge of the land and its ancestral language, experience of armed revolution, or, in Clare's case, an estate on which to grow sustenance, hide away, and prepare for the fight to come" (2018, 172). Cliff makes it clear to the reader, then, in these opening scenes, that the identificatory features of this particular hybrid group of people "are not fixed but dynamic" and that their liminality is conditioned as a result of "processes, action, [and] choices" as much as it is by their racial and cultural heritage, or their class and socioeconomic backgrounds.

When Clare elects to move to London to further her education, she notes that "[h]er place could be here" (1996, 109), underlining once again the liminal potentiality of choice; the conditional "could" here is suggestive of the not-yet-one-thing-or-the-other capacity of a decision in flux and of the "middle passage" of the liminal state itself. In the context of Clare's blended configuration of identity, then, London represents in *No Telephone to Heaven* "an intermediary moment in [Clare's] migration" (Stecher and Maxwell, 815). Luciá Stecher and Elsa Maxwell argue that, in *Into the Interior*, Cliff's final novel, London is alternatively positioned as "the diegetic sphere of narrative, although it also constitutes a counterpoint space of analeptic moments that recreate fragments of the protagonist's past in rural and isolated parts of Jamaica" (815). Clare is thus doubly liminal, caught as she is within both the intermediary space of London and the intermediary state of migration. As a liminal locale, London is the space in which Cliff "situates [her] protagonist within familial and social environments similar to those experienced by the author," thus "evoking sensations of isolation from both her family and Jamaican society" (818). It is telling, therefore, when Clare acknowledges to herself that "[no one in London] had called her white chocolate" (1996, 110), a term that is reminiscent of the pejorative portmanteaus—such as "white cockroach" or "white n----r"—often used in Cliff's textual world to designate light-skinned Jamaicans. Clare's recognition that such labels need not be applied to her in London denotes her figurative and literal move away from the irreconcilable both/and model of self-conceptualization and toward a more holistic reconciliation of the hybrid multiplicity she embraces in liminality. Indeed, the reader is told that, in her burgeoning and fluid liminal status, Clare is "able to hold two things in her head at the same time" (101), a comment that underlines the transformative development of her hybrid multiplicity and her capacity to reconcile her previous condition of "not-quite-one-thing-or-the-other-ness."

Cliff's reconciliation of hybrid identity forms is frequently metaphorized in her writings as a blending or melding together of heterogenous objects and/or states of being. For example, in "A Woman Who Plays Trumpet Is Deported," one of the short stories from the collection *Bodies of Water*, the narrative opens with a particular conflatory image: that of a Black trumpet player whose instrument, the reader is told, is "[n]ot made of flesh but of metal" (1991a, 55). Cliff's linguistic negation of this image (the "not") results in precisely its opposite: though the reader is told that the woman's trumpet is *not* made of flesh but of metal, we are immediately (if not unconsciously) put in mind of the image of a trumpet made of flesh. Cliff's double reminder of this fact—she emphasizes that the "instrument [is] not made of her [the focalizing character]"—reinforces the syntactical trickery at the heart of this image. On the one hand, Cliff is at pains to illustrate to us that the Black woman's "instrument" is not, in this case, her body (as it was in the days of slavery, the implication seems to be) but the trumpet. However,

Cliff also seems to deliberately undermine her efforts to disassociate the Black woman's instrument from the Black body by doubling down on her reinforcement of the syntagmatic alignment between the Black body and the trumpet-as-instrument. Both body and trumpet are repeatedly melded in one, a forcible blend of flesh and metal, subject and object in one. This melding is reinforced yet further through the focalizing character's musings on the instrument itself: as she "traces her hand along the ridges of silver," we are told that "[h]er finger catches the edge of a breast" (57), an image that only buttresses rather than dispels the notion that "body" and "instrument" are one. Most chillingly evidential of this conflation, perhaps, is that the woman appears to have come into possession of the trumpet only as a result of its previous owner (it is presumed to be her brother) having been burned alive in a tar fire. That is to say, her possession of the trumpet is a direct consequence of the transmogrification of the Black body from one form to another—and apparently from one gender to another as well, given the aforementioned image of the figurative breast that the woman's hands feel "along the ridges of silver."[4]

Similarly, in the first few pages of *Free Enterprise*, the image of the blended body-as-instrument becomes a synecdoche for the entire history of Jamaica's colonial servitude. Annie Christmas's imagined recollection of the subjugated enslaved body, which she visualizes "lying on [the plantation owner's] bed, having served the landowner well," conflates "[f]ather, uncle, cousin, family friend" (1993, 5) in one, in which the act of rape is multiplied as a contiguous act of sexual imperialism performed repeatedly upon the Black body-as-instrument. The image of the transmuted Black body-as-instrument also pervades the narrative of "Crocodilopolis" from Cliff's final short story collection, *Everything Is Now*. The narrative-focalizer of this story recalls in vivid detail the stories her grandmother recounted for her in her youth, of "[b]eings with umbrellas growing from their foreheads," "[w]omen with golden nipples," and "[v]olcanoes inhabited by fire-people who were in a constant state of burning" (2009, 44). While this final image, in particular, might very well put us in mind of the closing lines of "A Woman Who Plays Trumpet Is Deported," in which the narrator recalls her brother's death by fire (not to mention the often violent ends met by Black and biracial people across Cliff's oeuvre as a whole), the imbricated images of metamorphosed Black bodies as either "freakish" (e.g., "umbrellas growing from their foreheads") or fetishized (e.g., "women with golden nipples") transmutes the biracial subject into a hybrid subject-object form. Moreover, Cliff's frequent metaphorization of blended and/or melded states is also manifest in her metatextual habit of borrowing lines of text from one of her books in order to fashion titles for another. Thus, the title for her final collection, *Everything Is Now*, first appears in her third novel, *Free Enterprise*, during one of Mary Ellen Pleasant's late-night sojourns in her imagination, in which she muses that "everything seems like yesterday, tomorrow.... Everything is here, and now" (1993, 154). Of course, "Everything is now" is also a line from Toni Morrison's *Beloved*, which Cliff also quotes in the story "Lost Nation Road" in the collection titled *Everything Is Now*. Similarly, the title of Cliff's final novel, *Into the Interior*, appears earlier in her oeuvre, in the story "Transactions" from *The Store of a Million Items*. The focalizing character, a traveling salesman, is described as someone who "brings American things into the interior, into the clearing cut from ruinate" (1998, 4).

Contiguous Identities: Bodies of Water

Further to Cliff's use of portmanteaus as expressions of her "linguistic creolization" as well as the recurrent imagery of blended-melded states and/or objects, the liminalization of Cliff's pluralist identity is also metaphorized through her focus on contiguous bodies—that is, bodies that are presented as adjacent to one another and that, in their proximity (in time; in space; in narrative sequence) become for Cliff permeable and porous, through which the fluidity of her liminal state is made analogous. The fluid liminality inherent in the images of porous bodies throughout Cliff's oeuvre allows for the negotiation of the body-object as subject. In other words, it is through the interstitial forms of the body that Cliff and her characters reclaim a hybrid identity that is literalized as porously liminal. The term "contiguous" I borrow from Cliff's own work: from "Everything Is Now," the titular story of Cliff's final collection, in which the character Grace recalls with melancholy making love to her former partner at the foot of a gravestone. When asked whether she was nervous about disturbing the grave beneath her, Grace answers by saying that "[o]ur lives are contiguous": "[w]e touch [the dead]; they touch us" (2009, 22), in reference to the decaying corpses beneath her. Cliff's coalescence of sex and death here is perhaps the most hyperbolic her analogy becomes. Nevertheless, the contiguity of these liminal bodies, suspended as they are between the existential throes of *la petite mort* and *la grande mort*, is underlined by Grace's admission that "[a]fter a storm scraps of bone have been known to roam to the surface." The symbolic revivification of the dead in this scene (the animated scraps of bone) draws attention to the porous exchange between life and death that constitutes mortality. Indeed, the title of the story itself—"Everything Is Now"—further emphasizes the contiguously liminal nature of existence within the narrative: everything at once is here and now; both life and death, the present and the past, exist in one homogenous interstice. This is underlined once more by the fact that the woman Grace is speaking to, Cassandra, has the capacity to speak with the dead and is able to hear "a voice out of time, out of nowhere" (20) communicating with her.[5] Sex and death are conflated for Cassandra, too, who, upon leaving Grace, returns to her home and immediately initiates intercourse with her lover: "I need to make love" (22), she implores, as though sex itself were a necessary *memento mori*, a way of staving off the conscious realization of life and death's contiguities.

Porous and adjacent bodies pervade throughout the canon of Cliff's writings, from her earliest novels. As Kaisa Ilmonen argues, the principal focus of the Clare Savage novels is Clare's fluidity; that is, "her ability to pass as white, her dislocated self, [and] her crossing between categories of identity and geographical continents" (2017, 58). Ilmonen also contends that the fluidity of the content and subject matter of both *Abeng* and *No Telephone to Heaven* is also replicated in the fluidity of those novels' narrative structure, which "leaps from one scene to another, occasionally concentrating on minor characters." For instance, in *No Telephone to Heaven*, during Clare's short-lived sexual relationship with the wounded Vietnam War veteran Bobby, the narrative description of their lovemaking in the Adriatic Sea underlines the contiguous relationship between corporeality and liquidity. When Bobby has "entered [Clare]," we are told that he ejaculates into her "along with the salt sea" (1996, 155). In response, the narrator notes that "[Clare's] own liquid rushed out" and that she and Bobby "stood, bodies wrapped, one with the water." Of course, the porosity of the body is probably most evident here in the viscous exchanges of sexual intercourse (a literal trading of fluids). But this scene also underlines the transposition of bodily fluids with the oceanic fluid. Bobby's semen is blended with the salt water; Clare's sexual *jouissance* is, in this moment, as much conditioned by the fluidity of the ocean as it is by the physical act of lovemaking with Bobby. Clare's postcoital bliss is constructed in terms of her being "one with the water" and not necessarily being one with Bobby himself (though their bodies are wrapped together). At this stage of the narrative, Clare is obviously still in the process of negotiating her emerging fluidity as a multihyphenated subject, as is evident in her fearful regard for reproduction following Bobby's admission that his offspring may very well be deformed as a result of the chemical poison he ingested during his time in Vietnam. On the one hand, Clare's early experimental foray into a more fluidly liminal self-conception of her own biracial and bicultural subjectivity is bluntly metaphorized through her sexual embracement of Bobby, whose Blackness is pointedly relevant here. On the other hand, Bobby's Blackness—that which Clare, at least in part, covets for herself—is presented as metonymic to the imagined monstrosity of any of his potential offspring whom he conceives of in vivid detail: "a little Black baby with no eyes, no mouth, no nose, half a brain, harelip, missing privates, or a double set like some fucking hyena, missing limbs, or limbs twisted beyond anything you might recognize, organs where they are not meant to be, a dis-harmony of parts" (156). It is very clear for Clare, then, that the monstrously imagined offspring she and Bobby might produce, a literal product of miscegenation, is the potential price to be paid for a more fluid embracement of her own liminal hybridity embodied in the fluidizing jouissance of her union with Bobby. Thus, when Clare later undergoes a miscarriage—or a "heavy period for all she knew" (157); it is not clear which—the image of "[s]omething slid[ing] out of her suddenly" emphasizes once again the viscous and bloody porosity of the body-as-instrument. Moreover, the (imagined or literal) death of Clare and Bobby's unformed (potential) child symbolically prefigures the difficulties Clare is to face in reconciling her hyphenated status as a multihybrid subject.

The preeminence of corporeal porosity within Cliff's literary imagination is further spotlighted in Cliff's first short story collection—titled *Bodies of Water*, no less, the title of which alone centralizes Cliff's conceptual relationship between corporeality and liquidity. Indeed, fluid bodies—and bodies made of fluid—pervade this collection. In the very first story, "Columba," the narrator offers a description of her Aunt Charlotte, who is described as wearing such loose-fitting clothes that her "huge breasts slid outside, suddenly, sideways, pink falling on pink like ladylike camouflage" (1991a, 13). Here, Aunt Charlotte's rolling fleshiness suggests a viscosity, a certain liquid existence. Moreover, the narrator underlines the liquidly liminal nature of Aunt Charlotte's body when she notes that "[a]s [Aunt Charlotte] drank, so did she piss, ringing changes on the walls of chamber pots lined under the bed, all through the day and night." Aunt Charlotte's body, then, is presented as literally porous, a corporeal filter through whom liquid seems to pass unendingly. Moreover, her bedroom is constructed as a site of liquidity, a fluid admixture of "urine and bay rum and wet sugar" (13–14), an image that further suggests that Aunt Charlotte's body is housed by (and itself functions as a house for) liquids. It is also telling that the narrator frames her memories of Aunt Charlotte's Cuban love, Juan Antonio, in terms of Charlotte's bodily fluidity. The narrator's recollections of Juan Antonio are interrupted by the "sharp PING! of Charlotte's water [cutting] across . . . my imaginings," which dispels her memory: the narrator notes that a "sustained SPLASH! followed Charlotte's PING! and the young man slipped under the waves" (14). Here, it is not only the physical-corporeal that is syntagmatically aligned with water and liquidity but the metaphysical forms of memorization, too. Indeed, the narrator doubles down on this association in her admission that she has "never been able to forget [Juan Antonio], and capture him in a snap of that room, as though he floated through it, me" (14). Here, the narrator configures herself as a porously liminal subject through which she imagines her aunt's lover "floating." Aside from the latent psycho-sexual dimensions of this confession, the narrator imagines herself as part of the household's liquid triumvirate that is housed in an equally fluid space in which bodies seep and float through one another as the physical and noncorporeal are porously blended together.

Such liquid bodies recur throughout *Bodies of Water* and across a number of other stories. For instance, in "The Ferry," when the mother of the focalizing character, Vincent, appropriates one of Vincent's sports coats for Jimmy, the man she is currently dating, the narrator notes that Jimmy "swam in the sports coat" (26), an observation that is suggestive of the difference in stature between Jimmy and Vincent but that also implies that Jimmy's body is contained within the liquid form of the coat itself. A number of Cliff's other stories from the collection also conclude either in or beside bodies of water, such as "The Hanged Man" and "American Time, American Light," the former of which sees the focalizing character soaking her feet and praying to Oshun, the Yoruba river *orisha* (or goddess) most commonly associated with water, and the latter of which resolves with the discovery by a number of children in a river creek of a boy who has drowned himself. As the main character of the titular "Bodies of Water" is "drawn to lakes, yet afraid of water" (122), so too is Cliff preoccupied with water and its symbolic associations with porous corporeality and fluid identity formation. Within the canon of Cliff's writings, these associations are, for Cliff and her characters, initially ambivalent in nature. Rachel's assertion in *Free Enterprise* that "[t]he air was made of water. Unbreathable. Undrinkable" (1993, 187) suggests in its synesthetic central image that water is stifling and connotes a deathliness in keeping with the morbid conclusions to stories such as "American Time, American Light." However, toward the end of Cliff's oeuvre, these ambivalences are resolved in the totalizing encompassment of Cliff's later aqueous imagery. For instance, in "Crocodilopolis," one of the stories from Cliff's final collection, *Everything Is Now*, the homodiegetic narrator expresses her desire to "sink myself in the dark blue," in which she "would open my legs and the Nile would flood me" (2009, 43). Not only is this scene reminiscent of its earlier counterpart in *No Telephone to Heaven*, in which Clare Savage and her erstwhile boyfriend

Bobby are having sex in the ocean in a blend of seminal and oceanic fluids, but flooding and wateriness are presented here as a condition of sexual jouissance—as enlivening rather than deathly, as in the earlier image of the "[u]nbreathable," "[u]ndrinkable" water in Free Enterprise.

The resolve of Cliff's erstwhile ambivalence is also linked to her increasing comfort with her own liminal, hybrid subjectivity as a (sexually) fluid woman. Indeed, Cliff's sexuality is symbolically entwined with liquid fruit imagery throughout much of her earliest prose poetry and novels. As Wendy Walters notes, Jamaica's "island produce, the fruits of the landscape, are figured in terms of female sexuality, strengthening the female gendering of the Jamaican natural geography promoted by [Cliff's] narrative[s]" (1998, 222)—although Nada Elia contends that Cliff's use of fruit imagery is representative of "cross-cultural mixing" (2001, 53) more broadly and not just (or simply) her fluid sexuality. In her poem "Colonial Girl: And What Would It Be Like," Cliff conjoins the "sweet *liquidity*" of mangoes "*washed* down with coconut *water*," "ginep," and "*slippery* papaya" with female genitalia: the fruit imagery is immediately juxtaposed with the image of a "woman's thatch," a "bright, thick ginger womanly ... patch thatch" (2011, 251, 252; my emphasis), thus making analogous the wetness of the fruit and the female sex.[6] This analogy is made all the more explicit in the subsequent image of the "banana leaves wide as a girl's waist ... and as long as the girl's feathered legs" (252). This overlay of fruit and the female body suggests not simply an alignment between Jamaica's natural landscape and the sexual topography of the speaker's adolescent self-discoveries; rather, the syntactical arrangement of the subsequent sentence—"which exude the juice of the fruit without a taste of the fruit dependable as any aunt" (252)—makes it difficult to discern from whence the fluid of the juice comes: from the bananas and the banana leaves, or from (between?) the girl's "long" "feathered legs." Furthermore, the seemingly incongruous mention of the "dependable" fruit of the "aunt" connotes a certain matrilineal, inherited, or shared (if not potentially incestuous) liquidity. The repeated reference to the "aunt" figure throughout this poem would seem to suggest that it is under the aegis of more senior women that the young speaker apprehends her own burgeoning fluidity as a queer woman. It is in a river falls "once owned by an aunt" that the narrator speaks of an early experience of "taking our half-naked selves down the sweet into the salt water and women," an image that underlines within Cliff's imagination the porous interchange between the aqueous biota of the island's flora and a fluidizing Sapphic sexuality. Indeed, it is in the Jamaican bush, surrounded by luscious fruit, that Clare Savage realizes her burgeoning sexual fluidity in Abeng. The pleasure of "feast[ing] secretly on ... pears" (1995, 55) that Clare shares with her male playmate Joshua is transposed onto her desire for her childhood friend Zoe, with whom, the reader is told, Clare would normally have "feasted and played" (56).

The overlaying of fruit imagery and same-sex desire is also continued in the title story of the collection *Bodies of Water*, in which the narrator-focalizer reminisces about her lover, with whom she used to pick strawberries and peaches. The image of the girls' "[h]ands stained where the red tenderness gave way," the "thin cotton sticking to their upper legs," the "heavy fuzz of the fruit against their mouths," and the final jouissance of the girls' "two pink tongues [meeting]" (1991a, 128–29) aligns most explicitly the pleasures of eating and the fluid sensuality of same-sex desire. Finally, fruit is also associated in Cliff's work with the discovery of a shared matrilineal passion between mother and daughter. In *Abeng*, for instance, Clare's mother Kitty often takes her daughter into the bush to "hunt for mangoes out of season," an experience that, for Clare, constitutes a space of female abandon "away from her father and his theories and whiteness and her sister and her needs" (1995, 52, 80). The narrator also notes that Kitty, like her daughter, is quite light-skinned, "like the inside of a Bombay mango when the outside covering is cut away" (127)—a point that further underlines the association between matrilineal relations and fruit imagery.

4.

"Ways into Their Own Bodies"

Michelle Cliff's Queer Transactions

In this, the final chapter, I will extend the discussion begun in chapter 3 on the nature of transitional identities to incorporate a more focused discussion of transcorporeality and the trans-ness of Cliff's contiguous bodies. If, as I have already asserted, Cliff's liminal identity is metaphorized through her use of contiguous and porous bodies in a figurative sense, I now wish to turn my attention to the literal interpenetration of (and between) bodies, as well as to the intergendering of corporealized identities within the social, cultural, and gendered contexts of Cliff's Jamaica. This is constituted within Cliff's work by a move toward an embracement of interracial queer identities that have been belied by the fluid hybridizing of race, culture, and class throughout her oeuvre. Much like Kaisa Ilmonen, I take it as assumed that Cliff's use of "queer" is "always connected, along with her representations of Caribbean myths and oral histories, with those processes that question naturalized and monolithic categorizations rendering sexual identity positions intersectional" (2017, 199). As Ilmonen has further noted, "Cliff emphasizes the gendered and sexualized representations of de-colonized Caribbeanness [foregrounding] different kinds of Caribbean myths, rites and ceremonies, healing practices and many kinds of Afro-Caribbean tales, but she rewrites this tradition from the queer point of view, thus undermining the extremely homophobic Jamaican culture" (2005a, 182–83). Ilmonen elaborates: "Cliff claims an identity for the colonized Caribbean people by re-visioning decolonizing narratives, but her corollary aim is to revise Caribbean history in such a way that makes visible the existence of homosexuality" (184).[1] To this, I would add that Cliff is not only making visible the existence of homosexuality specifically but also the whole spectrum of queer sexualities. Ilmonen is correct in her assumption that there are "no functional heterosexual relationships in Cliff's fiction" (187), but Cliff's structural revision of colonial, patriarchal, and racial power structures, as well as compulsory heterosexuality, is not specifically centered on homosexual relationships. As we will see—particularly with the figure of Harry/Harriet in *No Telephone to Heaven*—it is much more pervasive than this, incorporating a number of nonnormative sexual identities that are linked to Cliff's overarching project of postcolonial resistance.

The most immediate of these means to resistance is, of course, the erotic intimacies between women that pervade Cliff's narratives, some of which I have already touched upon. Such intimacies are part-mythologized in Cliff's writing: for example, the relationship between Inez, one of Justice Savage's mistresses, and Mma Alli, the enslaved *obeah* woman (whose name is not an abbreviation but based on a Botswanian form of greeting), in Cliff's earliest novel, *Abeng*. When Inez falls pregnant with Justice's illegitimate child, Mma Alli performs a sexual rite upon her to rid her of the child: "Mma Alli began to gently stroke her with fingers dipped in coconut oil and pull on her nipples with her mouth," running "[h]er tongue all over Inez's body" until the "thick liquid which had been the mixed-up baby came forth easily and Inez felt little pain" (1995, 35). Here, Mma Alli's "magic of passion" is imbricated with her own sexual identity; the reader is told that she "had never lain with a man" and that "she loved only women in that way." Among the enslaved population on the island, it is reputed that "by being in bed with [Mma Alli], women learned . . . [h]ow to become wet again and again all through the night. How to soothe and excite at the same time. How to touch a woman in her deep-inside and make her womb move within her." Most significantly, we are told, Mma Alli teaches the enslaved women "[t]o keep their bodies as their own, even while they were made subject to the whimsical violence of the justice and his slavedrivers." Shared same-sex eroticism between women is thus presented as both a means to (self-)empowerment and a means of (cultural, social) resistance; the women's sexual pleasure discovered through the act of aborting Inez's unwanted fetus represents "a powerful subversion against the patriarchal systems because [Inez] reclaims her body by freeing it from the shackles of sexual violence" (Morguson, 37). Furthermore, Inez's seeking out of Mma Alli's "magic of passion" signifies the healing power of female interconnectedness and shared sexuality. As Kaisa Ilmonen notes, Cliff's "queered mythos subverts, or abrogates, the naturalizing power of white hetero-mythology," and characters such as Mma Alli become "carriers of the traditional, indigenous knowledge," "sources of strength for the most oppressed people" (2017, 148–49). Indeed, following her passionate sojourn with Mma Alli, the reader is told that Inez has discovered a "new-found power": "she remembered her mother and her people and knew she would return home" (1995, 35).

It is no coincidence, therefore, that immediately after this scene of shared female passion, the titular symbol of the abeng appears in the narrative for the first time: the narrator mentions almost as an aside that Mma Alli keeps an abeng "oiled with coconut and suspended from a piece of sisal and a fishhook" (36). Thus, Inez's capacity to remember her homeland constitutes a syntagmatic alignment between memory and resistance, between her free past and her indentured present. As I discussed much earlier in chapter 2, the abeng, of course, has been appropriated as a tool of Jamaica's historical rebellion of enslaved peoples, a means by which indentured laborers communicated and passed messages between one another, and a figurative symbol: a "call to break bonds and boundaries, to rupture epistemes . . . to reject master codes, and to disorder and reorder existing imperatives" (Lalla, 5). Thus, it is not just female sexuality but the practice of same-sex female sexuality that is presented as defiantly contrapuntal within the paradigms of patriarchal, colonial order. As Ilmonen argues, "Cliff creates localized queer practices, which highlight decolonized, or non-Western, Caribbean sexualities inseparable from the character's race, gender or social status" (2005a, 182).

In this final chapter, then, I engage with the issues of trans identities—both transcorporeal and transgender subjectivities—and the ways in which they are conceived of within the developing politics of Cliff's writing. I argue that, throughout her work, Cliff explores the logical endpoint of her "queering" of bifurcated, split identities along racial, cultural, and, in particular, sexual and gendered fault lines, and that this "queering" of race, sexuality, and gender is the means by which Cliff's characters reclaim their fragmented selves and, ultimately, find a "[way] into their own bodies" (1995, 120).

"A Girl Who Seemed to Think She Was a Boy": Intergender Frameworks

Of course, one of the most prominent examples within Cliff's writings of not just same-sex female sexuality but of hybridly fluidizing gender, racial, and cultural relations is that of the relationship between Clare Savage and her childhood playmate Zoe. While I touched briefly on this relationship earlier, I want to examine in greater detail the extent to which Clare "crosses lines of race, class, and sexuality in her love for the darker-skinned Zoe" (Bost, 682). I will also argue that Clare and Zoe's "boundary-crossing friendship" takes the form of a number of queer transgressions of corporeal limits: that is, the interpenetration of and between queer bodies. The earliest signs of these so-called transgressions, however, can simply be passed off as the habitual practice of pubescent schoolgirls: the narrator of *Abeng* notes that "[w]hen the wispy hairs began to grow between Clare's legs and under her arms . . . it was only Zoe she told, only Zoe she showed them to. And Zoe showed her own hairs" (1995, 81).[2] Here, Cliff situates both Clare and Zoe's burgeoning queerness within the continuum of a distinctly normative juvenile curiosity around one another's bodily development, a strategy that Cliff adopts, perhaps, as though she were attempting to offer some amelioration for those wider cultural and social concerns regarding the radicalization of queer female sexuality. Cliff emphasizes the extent to which the dawning relationship between both girls is directly corollary to a number of other ludic practices common to childhood. The narrator notes that "[t]he two girls walked the roads barefoot, and used the mud from the roadbed to make dishes and cups for their tea parties. But the creation of vessels from clay was the real aim of their activity, and the tea parties never came to an end" (93). The implication here is that the juvenile activities of youth are a socially sanctioned cover under which Clare and Zoe are permitted to engage with one another, especially in light of—or perhaps in spite of—their divergence in race and class. As the narrator notes, "This was a friendship . . . kept only on school vacations, and *because of their games and make-believe* might have seemed to some entirely removed from what was real in the girls' lives" (95; my emphasis). Of course, these ludic exchanges belie precisely "what was real in the girls' lives"; that is, Clare's burgeoning sexual interest in her friend and the imagined reciprocity she perceives in Zoe. Once again, it is under the cover of one kind of social, edificatory discourse (Zoe informs Clare about menstruation and how babies are made) that Clare imagines Zoe's physical self-exploration as part of her own exploratory sexual practices. Thus, when the narrator notes that "Clare never asked Zoe whether she stroked herself in her pussy or across her chest or squeezed her own nipples" and "Clare didn't mention to her friend the sweet and deep feeling when she did these things, nor the salty taste of her own moisture on her fingertips" (107), the narrative is, in effect, reifying Clare's desire for such intercourse, framed as it is here as an act of self-repressed longing (Clare "*never* asked"; she "*didn't* mention") for a shared discursive—and practiced—sexuality.

Clare's longing for Zoe's body is somewhat realized in their shared experience of bathing in the river. As the narrator notes, "This was the first time in her life that Clare had been naked with someone beside her sister. Another girl. Another female" (119–20). Focalized through Clare's longing gaze, the narrative lingers on the sight of Zoe's naked body, "lean and muscled," with narrow hips and long thighs, and the "patch of tight curly hair between her legs" (120). When the narrator notes that "the water cascaded between them, creating a shield which served their modesty," the reader is put in mind of Cliff's aforementioned viscously porous bodies and the syntagmatic alignment between fluidity and sexuality throughout her work. While Clare's postcoital bliss with her boyfriend Bobby in (the chronologically later) *No Telephone to Heaven* is framed in terms of her "oneness" with the water (when Bobby ejaculates into Clare, he does so "along with the salt sea," while at the same time "[Clare's] own liquid rushed out" [1996, 155]), in this earlier scene with Zoe, Clare has not yet become "one with the water"—and thus not yet one with her own sexual hybridity. The water acts as a "shield" to protect the girls' modesty rather than as a symbol of porous corporeality and fluid identity formation as it is to become.

This association between fluidity and female sexuality might also put the reader in mind of the same-sex affair in Cliff's short story "Crocodilopolis," from the collection *Everything Is Now*. Indeed, the "imagined" quality of Zoe's reciprocal desire for Clare also finds its counterpart in the narrator's description in that story of her closeted lover's passions:

> The passion between us, unlike anything I had known (had even imagined was possible, a young lady's imaginings should not venture there, into those dark, wet places), would not lie down, did not take what I imagined would be its natural (that word!) course but existed in spurts, followed by bouts of rage, terror. What possible future could we have? Two intelligent, beautiful women (my grandmother taught me to detest false modesty) going at each other hammer and tong, tongues, nipples, the glorious space between our legs. Madness. Complete. We had in our misbehaviour no center of gravity. (2009, 48)

The narrator even recalls a shared sexual dalliance beside a river, which further puts the reader in mind of the setting of Clare and Zoe's intimate encounter: "The body remembers what that mind thinks it has forgot. June. A rainy afternoon. Green outside the window. The commingled smell of earth, rain, green. A river behind the woods behind the cottage. Our nakedness in the rain, river. The body remembers, becomes wet" (49). Similarly, in Cliff's final novel, *Into the Interior*, the association between female sexuality, wateriness, and wetness continues. For instance, in the subsection titled "Below the Waterline," the narrator recounts her sexual encounter with another woman hidden in a lifeboat while traveling to London on an ocean liner: "We are suspended above the promenade deck, our motion matching the motion of the ship. I am lying at the bottom of the lifeboat in the darkness, her tongue is working me. I feel myself open as the flood rises. . . . Now we are face to face. I can taste myself on her tongue. Salt. Conch" (2010, 26). Also, in the section titled "Marooned"—which, like the title "Below the Waterline," also connotes a certain kind of watery, oceanic imagery—the narrator employs equivalent terminology when discussing her aborted sexual encounter with Jennifer: she describes her passion for visual art, which she says is "awash in nudes and ambiguities," and for the institute of advanced learning in visual arts where she is encouraged not to "look behind the canvas [and] stick our fingers in the wet fresco" (29–30).

Clare's Sapphic imaginings in *Abeng*, then, are more closely realized shortly after her watery encounter with Zoe, when the two girls are lying on the shore, sunning themselves dry. The narrator notes that their bodies "stretched against each other" and they "touched hands" (1995, 120). More explicitly, the sexual overtones of the girls' interchange are underlined by the narrator's following aside: "Pussy and rass—these were the two words they knew for the space-within-flesh . . . the ways into their own bodies." However, the subjunctive form in which the girls' sexual exchange is syntactically constructed—"Their fingers *could* slide through the hair and deep into the pink and purple flesh and touch a corridor through which their babies *would* emerge and into which men *would* put their thing. Right now it *could* belong to them" (my emphasis)—suggests that the girls' sexual jouissance is not literally realized but, rather, is a product of Clare's wistful imagination, a projection of her own burgeoning desires for same-sex fulfillment with her friend. Nevertheless, in characteristic fashion, Cliff's narrative retains its ambivalence, forever withholding from the reader any clear-cut or decisive interpretation of events. Thus, when the narrator notes shortly after this scene that Clare "could not now analyze or explain to her friend what she felt about their given identities in this society, where they met and where they diverged" (121), we are not simply talking about the conflatory racial, social, and class-based contexts of both girls' respective upbringings: Clare as light-skinned biracial descendant of the English plantocracy; Zoe as dark-skinned, working-class servant girl. Rather, this admission also implies that Clare is unable to discern not only between her and Zoe's divergent markers of identity (childhood playmates as they are) but also between what she *imagines* of Zoe's reciprocal desire for her and her own projected sexual longing for her childhood friend. On these divergent markers, H. Adlai Murdoch asserts that, between Clare and Zoe, there are "stark differences, in race, class, social standing, and education [that] inalterably joined when they meet during vacations. Zoe, who is visibly black, lives in a one-room shack in the country and attends a one-room country school, all of which locate her in opposition to Clare, who is upper middle class, light-skinned, lives in an expensive suburb and attends an exclusive school . . . their friendship is maintained despite these multiple patterns of division" (34). As Laura Sarnelli also notes, "Issues of gender and sexuality are strictly intersected with those of race and class in the novel; indeed, the pleasurable encounter between the girls is marked by the discovery of the multiple differences written on their bodies: the gold of Clare's light skin contrasting with Zoe's dark skin makes Clare reflect upon her privileged social position as the daughter of a descendant of English slave-owners in Caribbean plantations opposed to Zoe's disadvantaged status as working class and black" (103). Finally, Noraida Agosto argues that the girls' intimacy "allows for the intense clash between their provided subject positions. Although Zoe's color and class are supposed to make her Clare's social inferior, her grasp of 'who she is' and 'where she comes from' gives her an advantage over Clare" (110–11). That the only sexual jouissance between these girls is an imagined one and one that resides within Clare's fantasies suggests that the real and imaginary realms are also conflated, wherein Clare's sexual longing is conditioned by that quality of not-quite-one-thing-or-the-other-ness of Cliff's writing: it is not quite imagined and not yet wholly realized. Nevertheless, the shared intimacy between the two girls serves to release them from the "mechanisms of colonial and patriarchal power, which separates them": that is to say, "[t]he power of the black, feminist and lesbian erotic challenges compulsory heterosexuality" (Ilmonen 2005a, 188) and "contradict[s] existing sexist and homophobic narratives of the Caribbean experience that often silence or render invisible women's resistance and . . . homosexual relationships" (Springer, 45). In spite of the potentially revolutionary politics of her desires, however, Clare necessarily qualifies the feelings she possesses for Zoe as "safe," "secluded," and as "something she had wanted all along" (1995, 124).

Clare's description of her feelings for Zoe might also be read as connoting a desire for maternality. Indeed, Clare admits as much to herself: the narrator informs us that "[i]n her love for Zoe, Clare knew that there was something of her need for her mother" (1995, 131). Moreover, during that moment in which Clare "had wanted to lean across Zoe's breasts and kiss her" (124) in the sunlight, the reader may very well be put in mind of an earlier scene in the novel which underscores the psycho-sexual and explicitly maternal nature of Clare's sexual interest in Zoe: "At twelve Clare wanted to suck her mother's breasts again—to close her eyes in the sunlight and have Kitty close her eyes also and together they would enter some dream Clare imagined mothers and children share" (54). This dream state that Clare describes may also be a fitting appellation for the desirous fantasy she imagines for herself and Zoe. Belinda Edmondson has argued that "Clare's love for Zoe is a manifestation of her more deeply rooted yearning for her mother's love and approval; her mother prefers [Clare's sister Jennie] because she is darker and therefore closer to Kitty's black heritage, while Clare is considered to be her father's child" (1993, 188), while Christine Cloud asserts that "Clare looks elsewhere for the Space of the Mother. She looks to the country, to her grandmother, and to her friend Zoe. While bathing in refreshing water and sitting on a rock far away from the 'civilized' world, she thinks she has finally rediscovered this part of herself" (12).

Notwithstanding the imagined nature of their mutual sexual attraction, Clare's projected desire is transmuted into near-action when she admits to herself that "*she had wanted* to lean across Zoe's breasts and kiss her" (my emphasis), thereby exchanging the subjunctive tense ("could," "would") for the past perfect tense ("she had wanted"). In this exchange, Clare's desire for Zoe is transformed from the conditional into something of the past, as something that, in the narrative's linguistic syntax, is rendered obsolete, passing as it does in this moment from the potential kinesis of the girls' sexual tension imagined by Clare to a synergy between the girls that is expired by the arrival of an anonymous male cane-cutter on the other side of the river, whose slight smile at the sight of the girls' nakedness dispels the privacy (and potential) of their sexual interchange.

Clare's sexual longing for Zoe is further associated with fruit imagery. During Clare's imagined sexual assignation with Zoe by the riverbank, the narrator points out that "if [the girls] *would* open their eyes, they could see orange and mango trees [and] dwarf coconuts" (1995, 120–21; my emphasis), an admission that seemingly undermines the subjunctive condition of Clare's sexual overture (or, at the very least, that complicates the reader's interpretation of its unreality), given the recitation by the omniscient narrator of those surrounding flora and fauna which are, presumably, not products of Clare's imagination. Fruit is also mentioned at other points throughout the narrative, during which Clare and Zoe's relationship is focalized. For example, when the girls are making dishes and cups out of mud, the reader is told that "they were interrupted by a desire to climb a star apple or custard apple tree" and that "[t]hey crushed blossoms from bushes and mixed them with water, and with the dye drew patterns on the branches where they sat together and dripped from the juices of the apples" (93–94). Fruit imagery also abounds in *The Land of Look Behind*, particularly in those scenes in which Cliff recounts her own real-life friendship with her actual childhood playmate Zoe. Cliff observes the "fruit of the ackee" (1985, 63) on the riverbank where she and Zoe play and describes the childhood freedom she enjoyed with Zoe as a "fruitful place" (75). That said, as Lindsay Pentolfe Aegerter notes, "Cliff's own voicing of her sexuality, and her love for Zoe, remains quite muted even in this essay ['The Land of Look Behind'] that illuminates so many other conflicting aspects of her subjectivity. She states her sexuality largely in parenthesis [sic]; it is still secret from certain people, still caught in the interstices of identity. She names it as part of the matrix of her identity that gets played out in the fragments that constitute the 'whole,' but she is not yet ready to burn people with it as she is with race, class, gender, culture" (912).

It is no coincidence, then, that shortly after their interruption by the male cane cutter, Clare and Zoe's friendship falls apart, their desire thwarted by Clare's "recollection of her obligations under compulsory heterosexuality and the consequent homophobia that surrounds her" (Gourdine, 91). Concurrent with this scene, Clare recalls (seemingly at random) the fate of her "uncle Robert" (who is not really her uncle but a distant cousin on her father's side), who, it is heavily implied, is a queer man. It is also no coincidence, as Joanne Chassot contends, that Clare's recollection of Robert "significantly surfaces in the narrative, and in Clare's consciousness, in the midst of her confused feelings and reflections regarding her friend Zoe" (2018, 180). Clare remembers that Robert had "caused some disturbance when he brought a dark man home from Montego Bay and introduced him to his mother as 'my dearest friend'" (125). Robert is described as "funny" and "a little off" and as a "battyman," the colloquial Jamaican term for a homosexual. To the juvenile Clare, whose lack of compassion spawns from ignorance—both of Robert's situational context and of her own as-of-yet burgeoning queer desire for Zoe—Robert is a source of fearful embarrassment, a progenitor of a certain kind of "illness for which the victim was liable" (126) and whose later drowning is attributed by the family to the "uncommonly strong riptide that afternoon" and pointedly not to the tragedy of Robert's self-directed suicide.

Robert is not the only tragic queer character in *Abeng*; a similar fate befalls Clinton, a man who also drowns himself while onlookers chant the word "battyman" at him. It is also rumored that Clinton's "duppy" (or ghost) wanders the pastures of his erstwhile home. As Joanne Chassot notes, "Not only did Clinton die, but because the men his mother paid to take care of the proper burial rites ignored her instructions, his duppy rose from the grave to restlessly roam the land. The people's indifference to Clinton's life and to his death, denying him the right to either because of his deviant sexuality, literally condemns him to the limbo of living death, in effect defining his identity as unliveable" (2018, 180). Like the potential revolutionary politics of the young Clare's same-sex, queer desires, Clinton's duppy "signifies the troubling return of the queer presence that will not let itself be erased completely" (190); it is a "bastardly trace of social transgression, in how

[Clinton] is 'queer' in many ways: black, non-human, fatherless, sexually deviant, outcast... [an] abomination to the heteropatriarchal order and an assault on black Jamaican masculinity" (Gairola, 29).

As Noraida Agosto argues, "Clare is led to believe that homosexuals become undesirables whose stigma the family and community are relieved to remove" (109). But the unfortunate Robert and Clinton also become foils for Clare, who must now herself attempt to reconcile "those swift and strong feelings—largely unspoken feelings—she had for Zoe [with] the category of 'funny' or 'off' or 'queer'" (126) she has previously designated to Robert. Timothy S. Chin argues that the tragedy of Robert's repressed life, in particular, functions "as an implicit warning to Clare against the dangers of transgressing the boundaries of what is culturally sanctioned as acceptable or 'normal' sexual behaviour" (137; see also Sarnelli 103); and that "[b]y loving, like Robert, someone who is not only of the same sex but also darker than herself, Clare would act in double contradiction to her father's exhortation to lighten up the family" (Chassot 2018, 180). Clare's transgression of boundaries, then, imbricates both her sexual and political development: her queer sexuality (in her desire for Zoe) and her contrapuntal politics (her same-sex, queer desire, in and of itself) become one. The apex of Clare's early political awakening follows swiftly on the heels of her first menstrual cycle, which she experiences just after her initial frisson of sexual desire for Zoe (Schwartz 1996, 292). In spite of her inability to label her desire for what it is, she certainly has a sense of its political importance; she sees it as a "force that transgresses not only class and race barriers but gender barriers as well" and as a means to "erode the barrier[s] between her and otherness" (Agosto, 112).

I have previously mentioned Clare's misapprehensions over her fear of suddenly becoming another gender—that is, becoming other to herself (see chapter 2). As such, in her growing desire for Zoe, Clare is both fearful and yet expectant of the prospect of the otherizing queerness she harbors within herself. The ambivalence Clare feels in regards to her own gender and sexual identity is evident from the narrator's tender admission that Clare is "[a] young girl of twelve [who] was feeling her way into something" (1995, 149), an acknowledgment that suggests something of Clare's gentle yet persistent probing of her own sexual and gendered subjectivity, burgeoning though her own understanding of her desire for Zoe may yet be. In response to her mother's insistence on sending Clare away to stay with one Mrs. Phillips to "learn once and for all just who are in this world" (150), Clare acknowledges to herself that she "[does not] want to be a lady," an expression that may be read not only as a rejection of the processes by which formal gender roles are encoded within young women, but a rejection of her own socialized, gendered status. Indeed, Clare's denial of her own supposedly innate "femaleness" or femininity can be seen a number of times throughout *Abeng*. Toward the beginning of the novel, we are told that "Clare's relationship with her father took the form of what she imagined a son would have" (8). As previously mentioned, Clare feels an affiliation with Pip, the character from Dickens's *Great Expectations*, which she reads and who "reminded her of herself in some ways" (36). She rejects traditionally gendered behaviors, too: "She hated to cry and she hated now that she couldn't control her tears—she was acting like a girl" (58), and she accidentally shoots her grandmother's prized bull: "She was a girl, she had taken a gun and ammunition; perhaps that was forbidden act enough" (115).[3] Finally, Clare makes it very clear in her interactions with Zoe that "she [Zoe] should be a princess and that Clare would be the prince" (101). To all intents and purposes, then, Clare very much represents "a girl who seemed to think she was a boy" (134). While I take issue with Michael Carosone's unnuanced assertion that "Clare is [simply] a lesbian" (1; see the introduction and the section on Harry/Harriet below), I think that Carosone's contention—that "if [Clare] is not allowed to be a lesbian, then she wants to be a boy"—certainly captures something of the struggle Clare faces in (re)locating herself between her various gender and sexual subject positions. It is for this reason, perhaps, that Kaisa Ilmonen refers to *No Telephone to Heaven*, *Abeng*'s sequel, as "a story of passings, becomings, and transformations" wherein the "binary structures of gender and sexuality are . . . contested" (2017, 58). Indeed, as M. Keith Booker and Dubravka Juraga argue, Clare and Zoe's experimentation "certainly does not reach the level of demonstrating unequivocally that either . . . is a lesbian" (120). The difficulty in locating her gender and sexual identity is literalized by the "sharp pain" Clare feels in her vagina the night she dreams of her and Zoe fist-fighting by the river (a stereotypically adolescent male pursuit). Though this pain represents the onset of Clare's first menstrual cycle, the figurative transmogrification of her genitals ("It felt as if the lips were being pulled back and forth from within. Her pussy throbbed and hurt" [165]) is suggestive of a violently transformative realignment, as though her genitals themselves were being manipulated to reflect Clare's growing resistance to nonbinary gender and sexual subject positions.

Such imagery is further literalized in *No Telephone to Heaven* and specifically in the violently anatomical transmutation of Paul's parents' genitals by the vengeful Christopher. Christopher—an impoverished, Black Jamaican subaltern who works as a yard boy for his childhood friend Paul's wealthy white family—requests of his employers a small plot of land in which to bury his grandmother. When he is refused with scorn, Christopher murders

Paul's parents in a sweeping act of brutality: he cuts off Paul's father's penis "so that it hung from his crotch as if on a thin string, dangling into the place between his open legs" (1996, 26); and he inserts a glass bottle into Paul's mother's vagina. Later, when Paul discovers his mother, the reader is told that "[t]he base of a rum bottle was caught between her legs" and that when Paul removes the bottle, he "saw that the neck was broken. Jagged." Thus, the young Clare's figurative denial of gender roles and her own supposedly innate gender identity at the onset of menstruation in *Abeng* is transposed in *No Telephone to Heaven* onto the violent transmogrification of Paul's parents' sexual organs, which undergo a forcible intergendering. Paul's father is literally and symbolically castrated, while Christopher grafts for Paul's mother a makeshift phallus. This is not simply an inversion of Paul's parents' sexual organs but a conflation. Much like the young Clare at the onset of menstruation, Paul's mother's makeshift penis also bleeds; the reader is told that "[b]lood poured from between her legs, catching in her fine curled hair." Christopher and his act of violence have been read variously by critics; he is at once a "symbol of a divided Jamaica" (Branca, 32) and a "fundamentalist," a "terrorist whose experiences and actions are radically and incomprehensibly intolerable to Western sensibilities" (Addante, 149). As such, if we are to read Christopher's actions as a "revolutionary gesture" (Lima, 42) and as "defin[ing] the limits of subaltern revolt" (Moynagh, 119), then Cliff seems to be suggesting that we interpret Christopher's revolutionary politics—and the revolutionary politics of Jamaican political culture at large—in terms of a distinctly intergendering framework.

"Claiming Their Fragmented Selves": Genderqueer Revolution

Nancy Backes has argued that, in *Abeng*, Cliff insists on gender categories;[4] however, in *No Telephone to Heaven*, Cliff elects to collapse them altogether. The transitionalist framework around which *No Telephone to Heaven* is constructed is one that deconstructs reductionist visions of sexuality, gender, and race alike. As Noraida Agosto argues, "passing cross-dressing, and transsexuality [serve] as metaphors but also subversive actions that underscore the cultural construction of identity" within *No Telephone to Heaven*, in which the "collapse of racial, ethnic, and gender categories promote solidarity among oppressed groups by tearing down the barriers that isolate them" and that, in turn, leads to solidarity (10; see also Edmondson 1993, 190). It is the collapsing into fragments of such racial, ethnic, and gender barriers that dissolves the broader sociopolitical structures upon which these barriers are based (Moynagh, 117). Nowhere is this more apparent in Cliff's oeuvre than with Harry/Harriet, Clare's close friend and sometime lover, who is as "ambiguously gendered as Clare is ambiguously raced" (Richards, 30; see also Martínez-San Miguel, 188),[5] and whose gender and sexual identity throughout *No Telephone to Heaven* becomes a foil for Clare's own unresolved, fragmented sense of self. As such, Harry/Harriet and Clare are, in Judith Raiskin's words, "racial and sexual 'doubles' for one another" (1996, 190).

Within the narrative's chronological progression, Harry/Harriet is first introduced to the reader simply as "Harriet"; she is one of the revolutionaries traveling in the open-backed truck through Cockpit Country. Though the reader is not meant to know it yet (given the achronological, nonlinear presentation of the narrative), Harriet has, by the time she finds herself in the back of the truck, reached the culmination of a lifetime's work of gender and sexual identity exploration: she has decided to embrace her life as an openly transgender woman. For most of the narrative, which takes place prior to the scene in the truck, Harriet is known to others as "Harry/Harriet." Much like Cliff's use of the oblique stroke to denote Boy Savage's racial multipolarity ("mestee/sambo/octoroon/quadroon/creole" [1996, 75]), so is the visual construction of Harry/Harriet's nominal identity on the page representative of their portmanteaued and bifurcated subjectivity. Again, the reader might not realize the implications of what they are reading at first, but Harry/Harriet's eventual choice to live as Harriet is signaled from the beginning of the narrative: she is listed as "Harriet" and not "Harry/Harriet," the moniker by which they are commonly known throughout the rest of the narrative. Perhaps even more tellingly, Cliff also signals to the reader in this scene the performative nature of gender identity in and of itself through Harriet and the group's androgynizing attire. The reader is told that the revolutionaries have obtained camouflage khaki jackets with the names of their former owners—male soldiers—taped to the breast pockets. As such, the line "in the jacket, [Harriet] became Thorpe" (7) takes on far greater significance once the reader comes to understand that, in this scene, Harriet is not simply dressing up as a man (the anonymous Thorpe) but is a transgender woman whose performativity as "Thorpe" belies the cultural and social misgendering of her identity at large throughout the narrative. Rosamond King has argued that the khaki uniform is "meant to override . . . differences" in gender, and that even while the revolutionaries "attempt to reject race, class, and other differences . . . [they] remain committed to binary gender" (2009, 597). She argues that "Harriet challenges the system with her presence as a trans person, but reinforces it by largely conforming to her society's notion of womanhood."[6]

The rhetoric employed by the narrator to describe the revolutionaries who are masquerading as soldiers—"but that *is* what they were, what they *felt* they were, what they *were* in fact" (emphasis in original)—might also readily be interpreted in the context of Harry/Harriet's trans identity: Harry/Harriet has always *felt* like a woman because that is what in fact she *is*: Harriet—a woman. Thus, if we are encouraged to read Christopher's violent actions against Paul's parents in terms of a distinctly intergender framework, it follows, then, that Harry/Harriet, Cliff's genderqueer revolutionary is, in fact, the text's "true soldier" (1996) within the gender war Cliff wages throughout her novel, challenging as they do "oppositional sexual identities and [blurring] conventional dualisms" (Ilmonen 2017, 217; see also Agosto, 114). Indeed, Cliff herself refers to Harry/Harriet as the "real revolutionary in the book" (qtd. in Schwartz 1993, 602).

This becomes apparent during Harry/Harriet's first appearance within the chronology of Clare's narrative history. For instance, though the oblique stroke remains throughout to denote their "subjective multiplicity" (Agosto, 114), the first description of Harry/Harriet—"boy-girl, Buster's brother-sister, half-brother-sister actually" (1996, 21)—signals to the reader the fluid intergendering that will come to define this character's radicalism. The use of the short en dash between those paradigmatic social and gender poles ("boy-girl"; "brother-sister") connotes the interstitiality within which Harry/Harriet finds themselves for most of the novel. That the en dash is also normally used to mark ranges and could easily be replaced with the preposition "to" within the syntactical and grammatical structures of language further suggests that Harry/Harriet's position is inherently transitional; they are neither one thing nor the other but are moving from one (space/position) to another—a point that is doubly emphasized by the qualification that they are Buster's "half-brother-sister." Thus, not only is Harry/Harriet half-siblings with Buster, but they are, quite literally, half-brother and half-sister. The use of hyphenation here, as Pin-chia Feng notes, "materializes Harry/Harriet's multiple gender identities and highlights Cliff's refusal to follow the rules of gender naming," embodying as it does the "slippage and indeterminacy of queer identity" (27). Harry/Harriet, then, occupies an unusually powerful position with Jamaica's otherwise queerphobic social and cultural strata: the reader is told that, in spite of the fact that Harry/Harriet was "always strange, since childhood," "everyone tolerates him, as if measuring their normalness against his strangeness" (1996, 21). Cliff's switch from the third-person plural pronoun to the third-person singular ("him," "his") is demonstrative of the apparent position Harry/Harriet holds within Jamaica's social sphere: they are thought of as a man dressed in woman's clothing, and nothing more. In this sense,

Harry/Harriet performs a particular function within their social network; for the people around them, they act as a gauge for others to "measur[e] their normalness against"; Harry/Harriet's fragmentary bifurcation serves to "[remind] [those around him] of their wholeness." Harry/Harriet is seen as incomplete, as in some way deficient. While there are certainly instances throughout the novel in which Harry/Harriet can be said to perform the problematic role of the magical Negro whose function seems to be enabling the white-presenting Clare to attain her own sense of racial, cultural, and gendered wholeness,[7] for the most part, Harry/Harriet seems perfectly aware of their own revolutionary potential, dressing as they do in gender nonconforming apparel ("bra stretched across his hairy delicately mounded chest, panties cradling his cock and balls") and adorning their face in flamboyant makeup ("spangled eyelids glistening red, gold, green in the candlelight" [121]).

That said, those moments in which Harry/Harriet's nonconformist gender and sexual politics are shown to be at their most radical coincide with their incitement to gender and sexual revolution in Clare herself. Aside from their gentle mocking of Clare for whose sake they are wearing a proper (male) dinner jacket for an evening out together ("I draped myself in this drab garb, without so much as an earring to recommend me, for your sake, you might be more appreciative" [122]), Harry/Harriet deliberately goads Clare to reflection when they ask her whether she has ever been tempted by "[p]ussy . . . loving your own kind." With no mention of her longing for her childhood friend Zoe, Clare offers one dissimulatory comment after another, wanting to evade the question[8]—although she does, she admits, concede to the temptation of self-pleasure and to the exploration of her own "pussy." As a woman who is yet to fully realize her own Sapphic passions, Clare is enamored of Harry/Harriet's daringly probing nature; "[H]ow were you able to question, to know to question, so early?" she asks them with both naiveté and longing. Thus commences a sequence in which Clare and Harry/Harriet engage in heavy sexual petting with one another: "[t]ouching gently, kissing, tongues entwined, coming to, laughing" (130). William Tell Gifford contends that neither Clare nor Harry/Harriet ever sexually arouse one another (60), but from Cliff's description, this is clearly not the case; theirs is certainly more than a traditional friendship. Here, Cliff explodes assumptions around the gender and sexual identities of both characters—and of these identity categories, more generally. Clare, an erstwhile heterosexual-performing woman with an ever-burgeoning sexual interest in women, finds pleasure with Harry/Harriet, a self-professed transgender "battyman." Their sexual dalliance becomes not only a matter of political urgency but also connotes for Clare feelings of homeliness ("I feel drawn to you. At home with you" [1996, 131]).

Such feelings of homeliness put the reader in mind of the psycho-sexual relationship between Clare's childhood attraction to her friend Zoe and her desire for maternality; as Joanne Chassot argues, Clare and Harry/Harriet's "trips through the country and the moments of intimacy they share by the sea and the river are reminiscent of the times Clare shared with Zoe as a girl" (2018, 189). Myriam J. A. Chancy also argues that Clare and Harry/Harriet's relationship is "rendered parallel to that Clare begins with Zoe" (161). Moreover, Clare and Harry/Harriet's shared sexual interchange is framed in terms of fruit imagery in much the same way that Clare's sexual longing in *Abeng* is. Just before their sexual assignation, Harry/Harriet "sliced two [coconuts] open with his cutlass and they poured rum into the sweet water, the mixture dribbling over them." The narrator notes that "[s]oon they would be covered with mango juice, salt water, and the spicy oil of the meat" (1996, 130). Furthermore, Jenny Odintz contends that "[l]ike her experience with Zoe, this closeness with Harry/Harriet is a realization of the dream of female community. This time, no man appears to disrupt what she and Harry/Harriet create together. There is also none of the fragility that appeared with Zoe—Clare's belief then that they could only have the 'right now,' before their bodies were inevitably possessed by men and pregnancy" (173)—and by the seemingly inevitable onslaught of socialized expectations around traditional gender and sexual roles. In their flagrant overthrowing of considered gender and sex roles, Clare and Harry/Harriet's personal liaison becomes—and *is*—a matter of sociopolitical revolution, a disruption of the entire fabric of Jamaica's gender-sexual topography.

As a precursor to their sexual performance, Clare and Harry/Harriet also "perform" the roles of "Princess Cunnilinga" and "Prince Badnigga" for the benefit of gullible white tourists. On a night out together, when they are approached by one of the tourists, they pretend that they are the crown prince of Benin from Africa and his first wife, who are themselves visiting Jamaica for the "International Festival of Practitioners of Obeah" (1996, 125). The man's evident fear and fascination is a source of much amusement for Harry/Harriet in particular. As Irene Nicácio Lacerda argues, "Harriet is totally conscious that she is playing a role, aware that she is performing as if she were on a stage. In this scene, Harriet is a man/woman who constructs, consciously, her gender identity. . . . Harriet mixes both masculine and feminine looks and by doing so, she does not necessarily add another category of classification. Here, she mixes the physical traits of both men and women" (65). In their guise as an African resistance warrior, Harry/Harriet's "war paintings are turned into makeup foregrounding transsexuality, and thus undermining biological gender binaries" (Ilmonen 2005b, 101). Also in this scene, "the narrative voice does not employ the usual 'he/she' to refer to Harriet; it uses 'his' instead. Here, although Harriet has an ambiguous gender identity, the narrative voice decides to highlight her masculine traits in order to make her fit into her performance of a prince from a faraway place in Africa" (Lacerda, 66; see also Zabus 2014).

As Noraida Agosto argues, "If Clare as a heterosexual can be eroticized by a male who sees himself as a female, then gender identity is dangerously unstable" (121). Clare and Harry/Harriet's realization of their own liminality is, as Lilleth Trewick attests, the "defining moment of truth that pushes them to claim their fragmented selves" (50). Their sexual experimentation definitively underlines Cliff's political ethos, encapsulated within a familiar refrain that runs throughout Cliff's oeuvre: Clare reasons out their sexual assignation, claiming that "we are neither one thing nor the other" (1996, 131). The implications of this refrain are fully realized in this scene: for Clare is not simply a straight woman nor Harry/Harriet simply a "man" no more than Harry/Harriet is not (yet) simply a "woman" nor Clare simply a lesbian. Lianne Vella does note, however, that, in *No Telephone to Heaven*, there are "more than explicit hints that later in life Clare might have had an affair with her friend Liz while in London" and that "Clare and Harriet might have followed on into a relationship or Clare might have openly acknowledged her lesbianism had circumstances been different" (181). Cliff herself has gone on record saying that "[i]f Clare had had an affair in Britain with Liz, which is suggested very strongly in the novel, it wouldn't have led her back to herself. It would have made her more foreign to the place she came from. But her love for Harry/Harriet is a step towards herself. And if she wasn't killed she probably would have gone the whole way. Harry/Harriet is the novel's lesbian in a sense" (qtd. in Schwartz 1993, 601). For Clare, her "journey towards multiplicity also entails recognizing homosexuality as a subject position" (Agosto, 119), while Harry/Harriet is "both man and woman, black and white, gay and straight" (Ilmonen 2017, 64). The sexual/gender mélange of these characters emblemizes the text's true revolutionary potential, while it is Harry/Harriet, in particular, who becomes a "metonymy of the wide range of deconstructions and hybridities envisioned in the novel, a figure in whom many sides of Jamaican créolité unite." While Clare maintains that she is "neither one thing nor the other," it is Harry/Harriet's belief that "the time will come for both of us to choose" (1996, 131)—meaning that, at some point, Clare will have to choose her sexual identity in much the same way that Harry/Harriet will have to choose their gender identity.

Harry/Harriet's assertion that "[c]yann live split. Not in this world" as well as their eventual choice to live as "Harriet" and not "Harry/Harriet" would seem to complicate Cliff's revolutionary gender politics in one sense. Harry/Harriet's belief that duality is a "temporary stage to be overcome" as well as Clare's obsession with her own need to choose between one racial/sexual subject position and another would seem to undercut the text's politics of racial, sexual, and gender pluralism (Agosto, 119). Moreover, it would also seem to undermine and contrast with Harry/Harriet's own assertion that they were "born this way" (128), which suggests not binary gender essentialism but the radical capacity for *non*binary depolarization, for Harry/Harriet's "subversive body" could be said to "[twist] or [queer] the gendered imperatives of the heteronormative gender binary" altogether (Ilmonen 2017, 220). Ironically, though, it is Clare—by far the less outwardly queer of the pair—who problematizes Harry/Harriet's contention that one "cyann live split," enduring as they do over the course of the narrative the irresolvable discomfort of an in-between-ness that becomes, in and of it itself, an interstice of radical potentiality. Judith Raiskin is only partially correct in her assertion, then, that there is "nothing utopian in Cliff's vision of in-between racial or sexual positions" (1996, 192), for Cliff is not striving for utopianism. In Clare and Harry/Harriet's relationship and in their own embodied identity politics, Cliff is striving for a language not of perfection but of potentiality, of possibility. Raiskin claims that the "choices Clare and Harriet make are not freely chosen, nor do they guarantee freedom," but it can hardly be said that the alternative—repressive sociopolitical structures of hegemonic racial, sexual, and gender interpellation—guarantees any more freedom.[9] Harry/Harriet *elects* to live as Harriet; it is a *choice* conditioned neither by race, science, nor sexology or by the fact that she retains biological male sex organs. Unlike Clare, who, in *Abeng*, conceives of her own multipolar racial, cultural, and sexual subjectivity as/in fragments, Harriet represents a "reconciliation with the various elements that make up their identity, a spiritual healing that gels these elements in viable wholeness rather than fragmentation" (Elia 2001, 61). That is to say, Harriet embodies and "envision[s] a womanhood beyond biology" (Ilmonen 2017, 221). As Ramchandran Sethuraman argues, "Besides militating against the authority of biological determinism, Harry/Harriet reaffirms, to use the terms of Judith Butler's argument, that gender is not fundamentally an interior state but a performative act" (274). Rather than being fragmented, Harriet represents "the most whole and clear-sighted character in the book" (Raiskin 1996, 190).

Like Harriet, it is Clare's *choice* of relationships with people who "accept her as a multicultural, ethnically mixed individual" (Gifford, 49) that defines her, and it is through their respective choices that each has "challenged the boundaries of racial and sexual classifications and stepped beyond the biological [and socioracial and sexual] determinism of [their] positions" (Raiskin 1996, 191).[10] In Raiskin's own words, they "*choose* roles that permit them to perform the political actions they believe in" (192; my emphasis). That is to say, both characters "blur the boundaries that have been considered absolute and natural . . . namely those of race, gender, and sexuality" (Ilmonen 2017, 214). In spite of the obvious dangers, Harriet "chooses to step out of [the role of Harry/Harriet] and claim subjectivity" (Agosto, 121). This ambivalence[11]—which might be said, perhaps, to call into question the extent to which one "cyann live split"[12]—renders the binary model of identity obsolete, even though Harry/Harriet's choice to live as Harriet might seem to reinforce certain conditions of gender hegemony. However, Noraida Agosto is quick to remind us that "Cliff's constructions are not traditional or final" and that she "privileges the undervalued female identity [which] does not entail a sex change" (122). By the end of *No Telephone to Heaven*, Harriet is "capable of refusing the Harry part of herself, and chooses to be Harriet, in Harry's body," abandoning all biological or genetic categories precisely through her underlining of their "performative constructedness" (Ilmonen 2005a, 188), thus "locating [her] political and social identity through performance rather than in essential physical manifestation" (Stitt, 67). In biological, essentialist terms, Harriet retains the sex organs she was born with ("castration ain't de main t'ing" [1996, 168; see also Agosto, 122]). In sociological, gendered terms, the text honors her transitional, transgender identity and interpellates her femaleness within the narrative consciousness: immediately following Harriet's revelation of her assumed identity, the narrative switches from the use of third-person plural pronoun ("their") to third-person singular ("her").

In spite of this fundamentally quite comprehensible shift, it is surprising to find in critical discourses around Cliff a disparity in the ways in which Harry/Harriet—and, in turn, Harriet—is described. They are referred to variously as "transexual" (Agosto, 11; Potocki, 69), "transgender" (Smith 2009, 151), or "trans" (Martínez-San Miguel, 188); as a "transvestite" (Emery, 272),[13] a "transgendered transvestite" (Sarnelli, 104), a "non-operative transgendered transvestite" (Elia 2000, 352), a "non-operative, transgendered biologically male queer" (Lacerda, 61), or as a "bit of a cross-dresser" (François, 122); as a "hermaphrodite" (MacDonald-Smythe, 101); as a "homosexual" (Agosto, 114); a "gay, mixed-race hermaphrodite" (Raiskin 1996, 190), a "homosexual who can 'pass' as man or woman" (Cartelli, 93), or a "gay man who himself shifts between gender identifications by cross-dressing" (Edmondson 1998, 224); as a "man who sees himself as a female" (Agosto, 121), a "man who wants to be woman" (Lacerda, 53), someone who "chooses to live as a woman" (Stitt,

67), or as someone "who claims that he/she was born as a female within a male body" (Agosto, 119). Equally, critics are unsure as to which pronouns are best suited to describe the character, who is referred to as "he/she" (Agosto, 11; MacDonald-Smythe, 101), "him/her" (MacDonald-Smythe, 101; Sarnelli, 104), "his/her" (Agosto, 114; Sarnelli, 104), "s/he" (Addante, 156; Sarnelli, 104), and as "him/herself," "their," "his," "he," and "she" (Addante, 156). Kaisa Ilmonen opts for the gender-neutral pronoun "ze" (2017, 64). In a sense, the disparity within the critical nomenclature around Harry/Harriet's identity is largely reflective of Cliff's position that language is an inadequate servant of gender and sexual politics. Harry/Harriet's (later Harriet's) particular gender and sexual identity are, perhaps, not yet reconcilable in/through language. That is to say, there is a disjunction between the actualities of Cliff's characters' identities and the critical lexicon through which we may conceive of them linguistically. For instance, Angeletta K. M. Gourdine argues that Harry/Harriet does not embody homosexual attraction specifically; rather, they represent the "hybridization of . . . a biological male's heterosexual desire conflated with female gender identification" (92).

This disjunction extends, in part, to Clare Savage as well; however, while it is the case that language may not (yet) simply be able to conceive of Harry/Harriet's (later Harriet's) gender and sexual identity, the failure of most critics to accurately label or name Clare for what *she* is is not so much an issue of nomenclature as it is one of suppression. Clare is not simply a lesbian, and her lovemaking with Harry/Harriet does not simply connote homosexual desire. Like Harry/Harriet, Clare is both "sexually and racially indeterminate" (Raiskin 1996, 191); she is not *just* a lesbian—as both Raiskin (1996, 191) and Ilmonen (2017, 217) suggest—but, in M. M. Adjarian's words, an equally indeterminate "lesbian/bisexual woman" (72). There is an unpleasant irony to the fact that Adjarian is one of the only critics to label Clare as "bisexual" (see also Paravisini-Gebert, 39): in much the same way that Michelle Cliff's bisexuality is often invisibilized in critical discourse around her work (see Chassot 2018, 161), so too is Clare Savage's sexual identity often erased from considerations of her biracialism and biculturalism. Similarly, Nada Elia is one of the only critics to refer to Harry/Harriet (later Harriet) in terms of their "bisexuality"; indeed, she explicitly does so in the context of a discussion around the interrelated concepts of biracialism and biculturalism (2002, 61), illustrating the complex nexus of race, culture, and sexuality that is to be found in Cliff's work. Elia suggests that it is through an embracement of multiple (sexual, racial, cultural) subject positions that both Clare and Harry/Harriet (later Harriet) become "empowered" and "politically aware" (63). Doubling down on Elia's assertion, Kaisa Ilmonen advocates for a "genderless or bigender" (2017,

216) reading of Harry/Harriet, a point that is not often borne out in critical responses to Cliff's text but which opens up new conceptual avenues not just of Cliff's novel, specifically, but of the ways in which we think about the limits of language to delineate multiple performative gender and sexual constructs in general. Cliff herself attests that Harry/Harriet (later Harriet) is a "man who wants to be a woman and he loves women" (qtd. in Elia 2000, 352). As such, in Amy Woodbury Tease's words, "Cliff's [and her characters'] refusal to rest comfortably in a single category ... collapses the binary *either/or* and articulates the possibility of a *both/and*, tearing through normative categories and making them bleed into one another" (96).

Thus, it is not for nothing, then, that Cliff juxtaposes Harry/Harriet (later Harriet) with the mythical figure of Mawu-Lisa (1996, 171), the creator goddess of Dahomey mythology (in what is now present-day Benin). Mawu-Lisa embodies "both the sun and the moon, or power and wisdom combined to represent a synthesis of many dualities common to Western culture" as one who "resists the essential nature of biologically defined gender" (Ilmonen 2005b, 95–96). Like Mawu-Lisa, Harry/Harriet (later Harriet) is the "sun and moon trickster," an "anomalous being, in-between genders" who "fails to neatly categorize himself as either male or female" (Renk, 137). Kaisa Ilmonen points to the scene in which Harry/Harriet (later Harriet) performs the role of "Prince Badnigga" (1996, 125) as evidence for her claim that the character represents a trickster figure within the novel—that is, a figure who symbolizes the "transitivity between oppositional dualities" and signifies the "collision of culturally constructed binaries" (2005b, 85). Ilmonen contends that "in Cliff's novels the functions of the trickster characters and trickster-rhetoric are associated with a critique and problematization of normative systems of signification" and that the trickster enables Cliff to "undermine the stability of stereotypes related to a colonized Caribbean culture" as well as question and challenges "socially oppressive practices, such as patriarchal traditions and colonialism" (86). Harry/Harriet is a queer trickster who "creates positions for non-normative sexualities in the largely homophobic Jamaican culture" (87). As a queer trickster, Harry/Harriet "not only undermines the binary thinking of gender categories and stereotypical representations of black macho masculinity, but the limits of heteronormative sexuality" (98). Harry/Harriet (later Harriet), then, "intentionally and optimally functions in the liminal spaces, playing all the cards at hand"; their "passing" is "not an act of capitulation but a strategic ruse that admits [them] into ever wider circles" and allows them to "live [their] life in the most fulfilling and productive way possible" (Elia 2000, 354, 358). Harry/Harriet (later Harriet)'s bi positionality suggests they are the ultimate embodiment of Cliff's bifurcatory politics, whose "crucial power" is that of "self-definition": "physically a male, socially a woman" (363). Their choice allows them to "engage more deeply in a continuous unfolding of their stories which will lead them to a continuous discovery of possibilities of actions" (Lacerda, 72). Harry/Harriet (later Harriet) "bears the Shaman's threshold status as standing between worlds," a figure of ambiguity, of the margins, and one who "makes porous the boundaries between dichotomies and presents possibilities of a fluid subjectivity" (Knutson, 292). As Lilleth Trewick puts it most succinctly: "In the end, [Harry/Harriet's] ultimate act of resistance is [their] decision to be both Harry and Harriet, to not privilege one state over the other. As Harriet, she wears her penis under her skirt, a move perhaps to suggest that identity and sexuality are constantly being negotiated. Within her liminal space, Harry/Harriet eludes the politics of polarity" (50). Thus, it is Harry/Harriet (later Harriet)—rather than Clare Savage—who is Cliff's true alter ego, transgressing boundaries, exploding gender essentialisms, and redefining identity politics.

"Like the Bisexuality I Clung To"

Some Concluding Thoughts

I began this book with a discussion of the opening scene of *No Telephone to Heaven*, in which Clare, Harriet, and their fellow guerrilla revolutionaries are traveling through Cockpit Country in an open-back truck. This scene also happens to be the chronological closure of that novel, arranged in such a way that the teleological endpoint of the narrative is its opening scene: its opening moments, in fact, chronicle Clare's and the narrative's end. Because the telos of the narrative is its very origin, as Roberto Strongman notes, *No Telephone to Heaven* not only "performs a critique of time as a continuously unfolding stream progressing towards some as-yet-unattained goal" but also "presents the possibility of thinking of past, present, and future as simultaneous occurrences" (100). Rather than a simple condition of narrative time, I have argued that simultaneity is fundamental to the bi-politics of Cliff's writing at large; indeed, her *bi*racial, *bi*cultural, *bi*sexual, and *bi*gender characters can be read as totalizing embodiments of simultaneity itself. That is to say, Clare Savage's multipolar subjectivities, for one, are exactly coincident; her whiteness and her Blackness, or her sexual attraction to men and to women, or her cultural affiliation with Jamaica, with the US, and with London exist within her or occur simultaneously. Equally, Harriet's bigenderism and bisexuality also coexist and occur at the same time. As I have illustrated, Cliff's writings have thus not only "cleared a discursive space for the articulation of an 'indigenous' gay/lesbian subjectivity" (Chin, 136) but have also paved the way for a series of multiple positionalities that are unconditioned by binary modes of thought. With both Clare and Harriet, boundaries that are supposedly separate—"male from female, upper from lower classes, insider from outsider, self from 'other,' 'natural' from 'unnatural' sexuality"—are continuously transgressed, making way for an "interstitial space designated by the conjunction 'both/and' rather than 'either/or'" (138). In other words, my investigation has shown that Cliff offers her readers a potentially new vocabulary for conceiving of and shaping into existence the possibilities of bifurcatory, simultaneous subjectivities. Harriet's plurality, in particular, defies categorization, and it is the language of decategorization that, I have argued, Cliff embeds within her writing. In Myriam J. A. Chancy's words, Harriet is "made up of diverse parts, each of which [she] acknowledges and embraces . . . dark and light, Black and white, male and female" (160), and it is Clare's relationship with Harriet that enables her—and the reader—to recognize their own potential in-between-ness and ambivalent positionality (see also O'Callaghan 1998, 311).

Of course, Clare and Harriet's nonnormative bipolitics pave the way for a raft of other ambivalently positioned characters within Cliff's oeuvre who also trouble categorization and who attempt to navigate their own pluralistic contexts. In Noraida Agosto's words, "Cliff not only eschews proposing a grand goal that unifies the different subject-positions but expands the notion of multiplicity by adding more identities and insists on the unfixedness of subject-positions" (124). *Free Enterprise*'s Annie Christmas, for one, "continues with the themes of non-normative sexualities connected to political resistance and compulsory heterosexuality" (Ilmonen 2005, 189). Like Harry/Harriet, Annie cross-dresses ("[s]he looked as close as could be to a man" [1993, 24]), while Mary Ellen Pleasant describes how she "turned [herself] back into a woman in New York City" (140) as she transitions from one guise to another, transgressing boundaries of race, gender, and class simultaneously. Like Annie, Mary Ellen Pleasant "traverses multiple boundaries and becomes a protean subject" (Agosto, 129); it is precisely the liminality conditioned by her multipolar positionality that allows her to narrate herself into being. Other cross-dressing characters in Cliff's canon include the protagonist of "Transactions," the first short story in *The Store of a Million Items*, whose gender is doubly concealed: "She dressed in a boy's shirt . . . which serves her as a dress" (1998, 3). Such gender and racial ambiguity can also be seen in "My Grandmother's Eyes" from the collection *Everything Is Now*, in which the narrator dons darker stage makeup to play the part of a West Indian "Negress." Also in that story, the narrator encounters Patrice, a Haitian chanteuse who had once gone to see a witch doctor in the hopes of turning himself into a little girl. This encounter takes place in a nightclub called "Ambiguities," no less. Indeed, I argue that Cliff is a writer of ambiguities at large, a crafter of ambivalences—not just in herself (as a biracial, bicultural, bisexual subject) but also in terms of the teleological design of her characters' circumstances and of her texts at large. Cliff's writings "unsettle identity categories and imagine new ones" while articulating the ways in which different axes of identity (sexuality, class, ethnicity, gender) must be articulated through one another (Ilmonen 2017, 200). Each of these identity categories is deconstructed as performative and contingent and are repeatedly interrogated, historicized, and localized (2005, 192). As such, Cliff's writings make it clear that there is "something for everyone" (2010, 76), to quote the narrator of *Into the Interior*, Cliff's final novel. Like that narrator, who, we are told, "clings" to their bisexuality, so do Cliff's writings on the whole bear testimony to the "pluralities of postcolonial existence," enabling the reader to "become multicultural subjects as well" (Lionnet, 341). Cliff's lexicon of pluralities proves that, unlike Clare Savage, Cliff does not need to choose between the multiple polarities of her subjectivity because, ultimately, for Cliff, the need to choose between one determining category and another "means the death of possibilities" (MacDonald-Smythe, 88).

On the Very Edge: Bidentities in Michelle Cliff's Fiction has shown that Michelle Cliff's literary canon is focused almost entirely on the redefinition of conceptual boundaries and the binaried fault lines of race, nationality, and gender/sexuality. I have argued that Cliff's emphasis on categorical indeterminacy, her antagonism of traditional identity markers and categorical conventions, is not simply an aesthetic choice but also a form of resistance that is fundamental to her literary politics, which presages the redemptive powers of liminal subjectivity. The leitmotif of split subjectivities that runs throughout Cliff's canon represents the conceptual fulcrum upon which her burgeoning self-determination as a hybrid biracial, bicultural, and bisexual woman/writer pivots. Her writings, I have contended, open up the possibility of a world in which traditional polar identity markers are challenged and reconceptualized, while her liminal occupation of the (racial, cultural, sexual) space in between, that site of not-one-thing-or-the-other-ness, is reflective of Cliff's embodied "bi-ness," the aesthetic, political, and formal occupation of multiple bifurcated, fragmentary subject positions. It is in this intersection of race, nationality, and sexuality, I contend, that Cliff (and many of her characters) seek to (re)locate themselves. Uniquely, my research extends the most recent scholarship in Cliff Studies in its direct response to Kaisa Ilmonen and Joanne Chassot's cri de cœur for future Cliff scholars to examine Cliff's treatment of race, gender, and sexuality from an intersectional perspective (see Ilmonen 2017; Chassot 2018, 153). In *On the Very Edge: Bidentities in Michelle Cliff's Fiction*, I have explored the complete range and scope of Cliff's literary canon—from the "Clare Savage" duology to Cliff's later novels and from her short story collections to her prose poetry writings—and I have done so precisely through the intersectional lens of Cliff's "bi-ness," which, I have argued, not only takes "bi-ness" as a categorical imperative within Cliff's writings, but which enables us to think through new and emerging paradigms of identity within Cliff's writing and, perhaps, beyond.

Notes

"The Bifurcated Female": An Introduction in Fragments

1. For an overview of pre-twentieth-century Caribbean literature, see Evelyn O'Callaghan and Tim Watson, eds., *Caribbean Literature in Transition 1800–1920* (Cambridge: Cambridge University Press, 2021); A. James Arnold, ed., *A History of Literature in the Caribbean—Volume 2: English and Dutch-Speaking Regions* (Amsterdam: John Benjamins Publishing, 2001); A. James Arnold, J. Michael Dash, and Julio Rodriguez-Luis, eds., *A History of Literature in the Caribbean—Volume 3: Cross-Cultural Studies* (Amsterdam: John Benjamin Publishing, 1997); Thomas W. Krise, ed., *Caribbeana: An Anthology of English Literature of the West Indies, 1657–1777* (Chicago: University of Chicago Press, 1999); and A. James Arnold, J. Michael Dash, and Julio Rodriguez-Luis, eds., *A History of Literature in the Caribbean—Volume 1: Hispanic and Francophone Regions* (Amsterdam: John Benjamins Publishing, 1994).

2. Chassot writes very eloquently about the "ghosting" of sexuality within Cliff's fiction, too. In her reading of "Bodies of Water," the title story from Cliff's 1990 collection of the same name, Chassot illustrates the effects of collective queer cultural trauma as a result of society's repeated repression, denial, and "punishment" of nonnormative sexualities. See *Ghosts of the African Diaspora: Re-Visioning History, Memory, and Identity* (New Hampshire: Dartmouth College Press, 2018: 182–83). Cliff herself has spoken at length about this particular story and its overlap with her own experience of repressed sexuality: "The title story of *Bodies of Water* is about a boy who is gay, and he writes in his diary that he is gay. Now, when I wrote that story I did not connect it consciously to my own diary incident at all. But then when I went and looked back, I said, 'Gee, this is interesting, because you're transferring yourself into a gay boy.' Flashbacks are very strange events. I had remembered the incident of the reading of the diary. What had happened was I went back to school and I had a breakdown, and my parents had to take me out of school. And now, after having conversations with friends, I've remembered what was in the diary, which was that I was in love with another girl. She was taken out of school and sent to a boarding school, and we were never allowed to see each other" (qtd. in Schwartz 1993, 603–4). Chassot further notes that "Ecce Homo," one of the stories from Cliff's final collection,

Everything Is Now, also "offers a particularly dramatic account of both the symbolic erasure of queer sexuality and the literal elimination of the queer subject" (179).

3. For a broad overview of gender and sexuality studies within the Caribbean context, see Keja Valens, *Desire Between Women in Caribbean Literature* (New York, NY: Palgrave Macmillan, 2013); Omise'eke Natasha Tinsley, *Thiefing Sugar. Eroticism Between Women in Caribbean Literature* (Durham: Duke University Press, 2010); Thomas Glave, ed., *Our Caribbean: A Gathering of Lesbian and Gay Writing from the Antilles* (Durham, NC and London: Duke University Press, 2008); Gloria Wekker, *The Politics of Passion: Women's Sexual Culture in the Afro-Surinamese Diaspora* (New York: Columbia University Press, 2006); Alison Donnell, *Twentieth-Century Caribbean Literature: Critical Moments in Anglophone Literary History* (Abingdon: Routledge, 2006); M. Jacqui Alexander, *Pedagogies of Crossing: Meditations on Feminism, Sexual Politics, Memory and the Sacred* (Durham: Duke University Press, 2005); Rosamond King, "Sex and Sexuality in the English Caribbean Novels: A Survey from 1950," *Journal of West Indian Literature* 11, no. 1, 2002: 24–38; M. Jacqui Alexander, "Erotic Autonomy as a Politics of Decolonization: An Anatomy of Feminist and State Practice in the Bahamas Tourist Economy," in *Feminist Genealogies, Colonial Legacies, Democratic Futures*, eds. M. Jacqui Alexander and Chandra Talpade Mohanty (New York: Routledge, 1997), 63–100; Makeda Silvera, "Man Royals and Sodomites: Some Thoughts on the Invisibility of Afro-Caribbean Lesbians," in *Piece of My Heart: A Lesbian of Colour Anthology* (Toronto: Sister Vision Press, 1992), 14–26; and M. Jacqui Alexander, "Redrafting Morality: The Postcolonial State and the Sexual Offences Bill of Trinidad and Tobago," in *Third World Women and the Politics of Feminism*, eds. Chandra Talpade Mohanty, Ann Russo, and Lourdes Torres (Bloomington and Indianapolis: Indiana University Press, 1991), 133–52.

1. "Split into Two Parts": Michelle Cliff's Double Consciousness

1. In recalling her adolescent life in New York City, Cliff emphasizes those strategies adopted by her family in order to survive white America: "First of all, we never assimilated into America at all. Most of the time my mother was employed by the British government, and my father by various businesses, but they only socialized with Jamaicans. And whenever they had to socialize with Americans there was huge tension in the house. They never fit in, and I think one of the reasons they were very uncomfortable was because of racism.... [T]hey were never comfortable with that kind of thing at all, and they always felt that white Americans were very sick. So you went back [to Jamaica] to get recharged, then came to this cold place [New York], then returned [to Jamaica] to get recharged again. It was two completely different lives" (1994a, 274–75).

2. Maryam J. A. Chancy notices the similarities between Clare and her maternal grandmother, Miss Mattie, and, like Smith, she too recognizes the "autobiographical silence" of Clare's maternal line: "Born of a Black father and white mother, Clare's grandmother also occupies a position of 'in-betweenness,' but she has chosen her identity long ago.... With a foot in both the 'Black' and 'white' worlds, Miss Mattie has chosen to be

faithful to the 'darkness' in herself, but her existence between these two identities—canecutter yet landowner—also results in her silence" (148).

3. As Cliff writes in *Abeng*, "[Clare] thought about Pip now because the great house [of her ancestors] reminded her of Miss Havisham's room. Dingy and mindful of the past. *Both the source of her and not the source of her.* The house carried over to her a sense of great disappointment—maybe of great sadness. It was a dry and dusty place—not a place of her dreams. She felt a sense of loss and betrayal . . . she wished that the fire in the canefields would spread to the house and that it would burn down to the ground" (37; my italics). Note the ambivalence with which Clare conceives of the edificial monument to her white ancestry.

4. A number of critics have commented on Cliff's intertextual usage of Bertha Mason and Jean Rhys's novel *Wide Sargasso Sea* (a famous rewriting of Brontë's *Jane Eyre*) in the context of Clare's quest for fulfillment and wholeness. Belinda Edmondson notes that "Clare's final destination [in *No Telephone to Heaven*] is not England and a descent into madness [á la Bertha], but Jamaica and a conscious resistance, though she, like Bertha, dies in the act of resisting" (1993, 185). Edmondson elaborates: "Unlike Rhys, whose novels reveal simultaneous attraction to and fear of Afro-Caribbean society. . . . Cliff understands that an understanding of black consciousness is crucial to resolving the complexities of being a white colonized subject, and more importantly is empowering not only to black people in the Caribbean, but to white people as well; her novels attempt to reclaim her African identity, which was 'bred out' of her during her child- hood in Jamaica" (186). Sidonie Smith argues that "Clare's identification with Jane signals the mis/recognition of herself as universal 'white' woman. Her shift in identification to Bertha exposes the cultural construction of whiteness as universal norm" (54). While Lisa Walker suggests that "[b]y drawing on the narrative structure of [*Jane Eyre* and *Wide Sargasso Sea*] to write a lesbian Bildungsroman, *Abeng* invites a rereading of the first two novels that delineates a connection between the desire for identification across boundaries of visible differences and the emergence of the 'lesbian novel'" (141).

5. Writing in his obituary to Cliff in the *New York Times*, William Grimes refers to the aforecited essay "Notes on Speechlessness" as the "keynote for her subsequent work, which navigated the complexities of her life situation" (n.p.).

6. Of the conceptual relationship between landscape and the female body, Jennifer J. Smith contends that "[i]n colonial discourse, the land was compared to a feminine body, an analogy that rendered both ripe for conquest. The actual invasion and occupation of land was reinforced through its subjugation in language; women, fetishized as markers, also fell under the purview of narrative conquest. Despite their very different aims, Cliff's novels distinctly feminize the Jamaican landscape. The island, particularly the rural landscape, is lush, fertile, and pregnant with meaning" (144). Smith further argues that "marginalized maternal identity [is] coterminous with the trademarks of most national self-definition" and that this formulation "aligns Africa, mother, culture, and nation, causing slippage between these terms and the privileging of African history in the Caribbean" (145). Na'Imah Hanan Ford goes one step further in aligning "land" with "woman" and suggests that, in Cliff's writings, "the island of Jamaica [is] a metaphoric mother for Clare's development" (16). Ford does add the caveat that "reading [Jamaica] as feminine is problematic because it denotes negative connections of feminine landscapes

deriving from colonialism," although she does, nevertheless, insist on reading Cliff's Jamaica as a metaphoric womb. Furthermore, Smith argues that Cliff's novels actually "invert the meaning of this land/body alliance." She elaborates, "Instead of being mutually vulnerable to conquest, the land and women can potentially protect each other, and the land as female becomes a symbol of power rather than one of subjugation. In a very real way, women gain power through the land" (144). Izabella Penier takes up Smith's work, commenting that Smith's essay theorizes two colonial myths: the imbrication of colonial space with the native female body and postcolonial conflation of the female/mother with the newly born nation state (165). As Penier argues, the Clare Savage novels "subvert both myths . . . because Cliff wanted to show the reader that identification of the colonized land with the female body and treating maternity as a site of resistance and empowerment for Black women is no longer a viable strategy." Penier concludes that "all the readings of Cliff that uncritically espouse the notion that building matrilineal lineages can be the best hope for resisting oppression impoverish the concept of these texts."

2. "The Third Division": Michelle Cliff's Killing Ambivalence

1. For an expanded treatment of the relationship between Clare Savage and Harry/Harriet, see chapter 4.

2. Cliff elaborates, noting that the past has been "bleached from [Clare's] mind, just as the rapes of her grandmothers bleached her skin. And this bleached skin is the source of her privilege and power, too, she thinks, for she is a colonized child. She is a light-skinned female who has been removed from her homeland in a variety of ways and whose life, and narrative, is a movement back—ragged, interrupted, uncertain—to that place. She is fragmented, damaged, incomplete" (1991b, 45).

3. Cliff further notes that "[l]ight skin—in the world in which Clare originates, the island of Jamaica in the period of British hegemony, and to which she is transported, the United States in the 1960s; and to which she transports herself, Britain in the 1970s—is meant to ordain [Clare's] behavior. She is not meant to curse or rave or be a critic of imperialism; were she to do so, she would be considered at least deviant, possessed perhaps by a rogue gene. She is meant to speak softly and to keep to her place. And to keep others to their places; that is, of course, key" (1991b, 44).

4. Ilmonen elaborates: "The name ['free enterprise'] clarifies that capitalism, profitseeking, and entrepreneurship are more complicated issues than simply imperialist imports. For Mary Ellen, capitalism is a reality that might offer a way to rescue enslaved people from poverty or noble savagery. In this sense *Free Enterprise* is not ready to reject the ideal of American liberalism" (2017, 77).

5. Ramchandran Sethuraman also argues that this "both/and quality" is also to be found in *No Telephone to Heaven*: "One can partially and only imperfectly say at the outset that *No Telephone to Heaven* is about [the] "not-there" place of the dispossessed within both the geopolitical context of Jamaica and a transnational framework" (252).

6. Cliff further contends that it is the job of the artist to imagine the unimaginable in history: "[t]he history of the slave ship, for example. The rush to suicide of the cargo,

for example. But also: the resisters, female and male. Those who organized and armed themselves and fought back" (1994b, 199). She also contends that "[t]he history of armed and organized African-American resistance has been made unimaginable by the official histories of this country. One or two incidents are allowed in these sanctioned pages, but these more often than not end with the hanging of the hero. The extraordinary extent of ordinary people involved in a centuries' long struggle goes unacknowledged."

7. Carmen Birkle elaborates: "For Cliff, literature is an important vehicle for the expression of history because it can take up seemingly minor events of the past and turn them into lively and meaningful stories of the present, thus connecting past and present of a given civilization and opening up more space for both the historical and fictional narratives. Using this postmodern technique, she thereby transgresses the strict genre boundaries between fact and fiction, and shows that history (or, more precisely, historiography), and literature are not two separate fields but two essential concepts of representation that influence each other. Through fluid and permeable boundaries between fact and fiction Cliff questions the existence of fact" (62–63). As Andrée-Anne Kekeh-Dika observes, Cliff "reworks official literary, historical or mythical versions of 'America' to reconstruct a New World" and to "make a textual crossroads" (267).

8. Abdulaal elaborates: "History must be retold and rewritten by the persons excluded from the written records of western history [in order] to gain access to their knowledge of their past" (1,420–21). She further contends that "Cliff marginalizes western narrative[s] of Caribbean history and demonstrates how many voices, stories, mythologies and oral traditions are excluded. Moreover, the rewriting of history and the use of memories are Cliff's primary tools for creative resistance and political self-recovery. She creates narratives that challenge official versions of history. She situates herself inside the fight against the suffering of humanity because of slavery and racism. Furthermore, Cliff manipulates the suppressed fragments of history to create a vision of resistance that challenges official historical versions."

9. Of her stated intent to reposition women's roles in American historical metanarratives, Cliff says the following: "Part of my purpose in [*Free Enterprise*] is to show the problems of different lives of women in the nineteenth century, not just black women. Clover Adams is someone who intrigued me way back in the 1970s, when I was an art history student. My interest in her and Mary Ellen came together in this book. What I wanted to show was how the privilege of a woman of the upper class in this country, Brahmin Boston, pales beside the privilege of Mary Ellen as an activist. Clover Adams was more encumbered by her place in society than Mary Ellen was. Mary Ellen was able to transcend what was seen as her place by resisting. Unable to do that, Clover Adams committed suicide. I wanted her to stand for those women in the nineteenth century who were artists and who were passionate but were unable to practice their art or fuel their passion except in a very limited way, because of gender, class, and race" (qtd. in Shea, 32).

10. Branca elaborates: "Cliff creates characters that are changing and can be viewed as if they were characters in a movie. Cliff's characters question what it means to be Jamaican. They do not accept the status quo but are rather constantly grappling with different identities for themselves and where they fit in the wide spectrum of what it means to be Jamaican" (24).

11. MacDonald-Smythe argues that Cliff "travel[s] through history" as a consequence of the fragmentation and hybridity of her gender identity, the politics of her queer

location, and her biracial heritage, which "issue out of her various locations and the reality of early exile to foreign lands" (121).

12. The focalizing character of "Ecce Homo" (from the collection *Everything Is Now*), a queer American soldier who is sectioned in a mental institution and who is visited by the ghost of his same-sex lover, is also described as "nomadic," as one "always in search of a better place" (2009, 66).

13. Chassot notes that "the [trope of the] ghost enables Cliff to re-vision traditional narratives and discourses. More specifically, it serves to address, question, and destabilize fixed definitions of identity. It appears as the repressed that haunts racist, heterosexist discourse and society. In relation to race, it conveys the condition, experience, and paradox of passing, which is simultaneously presented as a protection and the promise of a privileged life through invisibility and suffered as the painful absence of connections to community and culture. In relation to sexuality, the trope conveys the abjection and invisibilization of the queer subject by patriarchal, heteronormative society. Yet because the repressed is also that which keeps returning, the ghost not only signifies what, or who, has been effaced and silenced but also exposes the workings of this effacement and silencing. A deconstructive trope that breaks down the hierarchizing and normalizing binaries that underpin the dominant discourses on race and sexuality, the ghost allows Cliff to contest these dominant discourses by debunking their essentialism and denouncing their inherent paradoxes" (153).

3. "A Place for In-Betweens": Michelle Cliff's Liminality

1. Cliff herself has noted in *The Land of Look Behind* that "although I have lived in the United States and in England I travel as a Jamaican. It is Jamaica that forms my writing for the most part, and which has formed to the most part, myself. Even though I often feel what Derek Walcott expresses in his poem 'The Schooner Flight': 'I have no nation now but the imagination'" (1985, 12).

2. From the Latin word "*limen*" ("*lmn*"), liminality as a critical concept derives originally from Arnold van Gennep's discussion of scared rites of passage. Van Gennep argues that social-symbolic events (e.g., marriage, birth, puberty, death) presuppose the subject's symbolic passage "from one defined position to another which is equally well defined" vis-à-vis an intermediate transitional stage known as the "liminal" or "threshold" stage (3). Van Gennep further argues that this liminal threshold space is specifically bound up in "magico-religious" rites that accompany the liminal subject's passage from one symbolic state to the next (18). Victor Turner later reformulated van Gennep's original conception of liminality, noting that the liminal figure "passes through a cultural realm that has few or none of the attributes of the past or coming state," before they are reaggregated within a "relatively stable state once more" with the "rights and obligations vis-à-vis others of a clearly defined and 'structured' type" (80). Turner identifies "liminal entities" as those marginal figures who are "betwixt and between the position assigned and arrayed by law, custom, convention, and [ceremony]" (81).

3. Beata Potocki offers an expansive reading of the portmanteau "Apocalypso," which appears at the end of Cliff's final novel, *Into the Interior* (2010, 122): "Conflating the millenarian

notion of apocalypse and the Caribbean music 'calypso,' *apocalypso* constitutes a joint venture of universal and local. The first term comprising 'apocalypso'—apocalypse, from the Greek *apocálypsis* ('un-covering')—refers to a disclosure of knowledge, as in a lifting of the veil or revelation of something hidden. In the millenarian Christian tradition, the Revelation of St. John also connotes the end of an age to clear space for the future recreation of the world. . . . The other part of this neologism—calypso—is a specifically Caribbean referent, even though the musical style itself is a transcontinental hybrid. The Afro-Caribbean music drew on French and West African music and was popularized in Trinidad and Tobago. At its inception in the Caribbean islands, calypso was used as a means of communication between slaves and as a voice of mockery and resistance to the masters. This specifically Caribbean style of music, with roots in West Africa . . . is tinged with strong political implications, as it shows how an aesthetic form was repurposed in a struggle for independence, becoming a vehicle for expressing the sentiment of solidarity between the oppressed as well as a medium for articulating their opposition to the dominant powers" (81).

4. As Clare Savage acknowledges to herself in *No Telephone to Heaven* that "[no one in London] had called her white chocolate" (1996, 110), so too does the focalizing character of "A Woman Who Plays Trumpet Is Deported" note of her time in Europe that "no one calls her n----r. Or asks her to leave. Or asks her to sit away from the window [of the restaurant] at a darker table in the back by the kitchen" (1991a, 58).

5. In her review of *Everything Is Now*, Claudia Buonaiuto notes that the titular story is "a macabre ghost story in which Cassandra, a woman with the gift of speaking to the dead, gets into contact with 'a shadow of a former self'" (22). The ghost is reporting about a lover who died during the War, "the great adventure where as usual the USA saved the world" (19). "War" is capitalized in the text as a way to refer to the warfare system that has characterized American history in the last fifty years. The issue here is the silenced voice of the 'twenty-three thousand fallen' (21) in an unspecified war that haunts the living" (129).

6. See also "Obsolete Geography" from Cliff's *The Land of Look Behind*: "On a hillside I search for mangoes. As I shake the tree the fruit drops: its sweetness splits at my feet. I suck the remaining flesh from the hairy seed. The sap from the stem stains my lips—to fester later. I am warned I may be scarred" (1985, 24).

4. "Ways into Their Own Bodies": Michelle Cliff's Queer Transactions

1. Ilmonen expounds further: "Queered identities in Cliff's novels are not constituted in the margins of the communal cultural tradition. In her writings, feminist mythologies and queered identities become a crucial part of the collective postcolonial Caribbean identity process. . . . Cliff's counterdiscourse becomes a strategy for revisionist mythmaking in its aims to queer the Caribbean past rather than to create separate lesbian histories" (2017, 148).

2. Of course, Clare's friendship with Zoe is drawn from Cliff's own real-life childhood friendship with a Jamaican girl, also called Zoe. In *The Land of Look Behind*, Cliff recounts the historical occasion upon which the scene of Clare and Zoe's mutual examination of each other's bodies in *Abeng* is based: "We were standing under the waterfall at the top of Orange River. Our chests were just beginning to mound—slight hills on either side. In the

center of each were our nipples, which were losing their sideways look and rounding into perceptible buttons of dark flesh. Too fast it seemed. We touched each other, then, quickly and almost simultaneously, raised our arms to examine the hairs growing underneath. Another sign. Mine was wispy and light-brown. My friend Zoe had dark hair curled up tight. In each little patch the riverwater caught the sun so we glistened" (1985, 57).

3. Jennifer Donahue argues that "[b]y going against the gendered nature of the [Maroon] ritual [of hunting wild pig], and sneaking out in the wee hours of the morning to perform this imitation of ritual, Clare indeed negotiates tradition. Her use of the gun as opposed to a machete suggests that she is not yet able to fully claim the ritual, and therefore must operate under a mediated experience, unlike Zoe, who as a child of the bush, wields a machete with ease. Clare's revision of the ritual's weaponry, the substitution of gun for machete, parallels her own hybridity. With this ritual and throughout the text, Cliff develops the possibility of a hybridized, or creolized identity for Clare, rather than an either/or situation" (140).

4. A debatable point. See the previous section for a reading of the ways in which the young Clare rejects traditional gender roles and her own apparently innate "femaleness" in *Abeng*.

5. Harry/Harriet has also been likened to the androgynous nymph Ariel from Shakespeare's *The Tempest*. Both characters are, for instance, "forced to cross-dress during the narration in order to serve the master's purposes," and both share "experiences of violence, oppression, and abuse" (Ilmonen 2017, 13) at the hands of those masters (in Ariel's case, Prospero, while in Harry/Harriet's case, the more diffuse cultural prejudices of Jamaican society at large). Cliff herself draws on the comparison in her essay "Caliban's Daughter: The Tempest and the Teapot," wherein her direct quote from Roberto Fernandez-Retamar's own essay on Caliban gives the reader a further indication as to how we might interpret Harry/Harriet: "There is no real Ariel-Caliban polarity; both are slaves in the hands of Prospero, the foreign magician. But Caliban is the rude and unconquerable master of the island, while Ariel, a creature of air, although a child, is the intellectual" (qtd. in 1991b, 39).

6. Further to this, Yolanda Martínez-San Miguel elaborates on what she sees as the reductive gender and racial politics of *No Telephone to Heaven*. She argues that "[i]t seems that in order to be able to identify with Jamaica as a national project, Clare first needs to identify with the marginalized and almost outcast location of Harry/Harriet within the Jamaican collective imaginary. The ambiguously race *mulata* woman must identity with the ambiguously male to female transgender . . . in order to produce another master-narrative beyond the *madre patria*, or the colonial/imperial logic" (189).

7. For instance, Clare notices that her "[Jamaican] twang was coming back, rapidly, in Harry/Harriet's presence, voice breaking the taboo of speaking bad. Discouraged among her people" (1996, 121). Here, Harry/Harriet performs the function of cultural, racial, and linguistic interlocutor, enabling Clare to reconnect to her Jamaican homeland in a manner that is framed distinctly in terms of their efficacy to Clare's narrative journey toward self-wholeness. It is Harry/Harriet who convinces Clare to "[c]ome home. . . . Come back to us" (127), encouraging Clare in her cultural, racial, and social connections to Jamaica. Indeed, toward the end of the narrative, the narrator notes that "[i]t was with Harriet and at her suggestion that Clare went to St. Elizabeth for the first time in twenty years, to find her grandmother's place, now left to her, and visit the river and forest of her girlhood"

(171). As Kaisa Ilmonen notes, "[i]t is Harry/Harriet who understand Clare's sense of emotional fragmentation and helps her to overcome her inner conflicts"; they "[heal] Clare's emotional scars and [unite] the fragments of her subjectivity," thereby enabling her to "reconnect herself to Jamaica and her childhood" (2017, 214, 215). Laura Sarnelli argues that "Harry/Harriet plays a central role in the novel insofar as s/he helps Clare to recover her past, her cultural roots, and a deeper sense of self which enables her to identify with her blackness and queerness" (104). Yolanda Martínez-San Miguel asserts that "Harry/Harriet provides Clare with an alternative space to explore and deconstruct metropolitan stereotypes about Afro-Caribbean identities, as well as a safe space to explore her problematic detachment from her bodily sexual pleasures"; they are her "only consistent interlocutor" (187, 188). Kaisa Ilmonen notes that "Harry/Harriet introduces [Clare] to the guerrilla fighters and makes her realize the importance of resistance" (2005a, 188). Jennifer J. Smith suggests that Harry/Harriet "offers Clare an alternative to the other available maternal models: by being both mother and friend, s/he straddles the responsibilities of mentor and peer" and "provides a model of a maternal figure who is non-reproductive" (151). Smith elaborates: "Harriet represents a nearly ideal maternal figure in the novel: she encourages Clare to challenge herself, she cares for Clare when she is sick, and she exposes Clare to things she did not know about her history, culture, and self" (152).

8. Quincey Michelle Hyatt notes that "Clare grows irritated with Harry/Harriet's insinuations regarding her sexuality. When he asks whether or not she is gay, Clare suddenly drops her patois and begins speaking Standard English and French, hoping to make him feel as uncomfortable as he has made her. . . . A true "borderland" character, Harry/Harriet easily alternates and negotiates patois, English, and French, suggesting that language, like race and gender, is an unstable category of social classification. For Harry/Harriet, one's language is a political choice, and by mocking Clare's use of Standard English and French, he underscores the fact that she still identifies with the white and light-skinned elite" (33).

9. Nada Elia notes that "queer theory, and the naming of oneself as 'queer,' came as a response to the binarism implicit in homosexuality, which defines its sexual practices as non-heterosexual, while excluding other possibilities. The shift from 'gay and lesbian' to 'queer' is more than a semantic evolution and was meant to include bisexuals and transgenders, but the latter two continue to be excluded from discussions of non-monosexual, non-heterosexual identities. Thus the transgender community, which includes, but is not restricted to, pre-, post-, and non-operative transexuals, drag queens, transvestites, and hermaphrodites, remains excluded from lesbian and gay activism" (2000, 357).

10. Joanne Chassot does argue, though, that by "[t]urning her protagonist into an actual ghost, rather than allowing her to live as a metaphorical one, Cliff ultimately seems to confirm that this world . . . has 'no place for in-betweens.'" That is to say, by "[r]efusing to naïvely celebrate ambiguity, instability, and elusiveness as essentially productive and empowering for personal and political affirmation, Cliff recognizes the cost and the anxieties that an unconventional positioning outside master categories entails. Despite its subversive and liberating potential, for Cliff's protagonists, to live a ghost-life is confusing at the least, more often painful, and sometimes simply no life at all" (2018, 173).

11. Harry/Harriet can also be said to embody the ambivalence of Cliff's Jamaica as a whole; "on the one hand, as a place of fear and violence, but on the other, as a home and a site of life" (Ilmonen 2005a, 188).

12. Jocelyn Fenton Stitt argues that Harry/Harriet's contention that one "[c]yann live split" "does not refer to a biological essentialism, but instead to the choice to participate in political action rather than accepting the status quo" (68).

13. Of the character Harry/Harriet, Cliff herself notes that she was "consciously determined because I come from such a homophobic society to make the most whole and sane character in *No Telephone to Heaven* somebody who was homosexual, which is what Harry is. People may want to think of him as a transvestite or something, but he's not. I think to live in this world as somebody like Harry, you have to be courageous, and he is, and he knows who he is" (qtd. in Raiskin 1993, 69).

Bibliography

Abdulaal, Lamiaa Hassan Ibrahim. 2016. "Writing History Against the Grain: Counter-memory as a Site of Reconstructing Postcolonial Identity in Michelle Cliff's *No Telephone to Heaven*." *JARTF*, no. 29: 1553–87.

Addante, Martha. 2009. "Mapping the Global Landscape in Women's Diasporic Writing." Unpublished dissertation. Western Michigan University.

Adjarian, M. M. 2000. "Michelle Cliff's Fictions of Self and Fantasies of Return in *Abeng* and *No Telephone to Heaven*." *West Virginia University Philological Papers* 46: 70–76.

Aegerter, Lindsay Pentolfe. 1997. "Michelle Cliff and the Paradox of Privilege." *College English* 59, no. 8: 898–915.

Agbor, Sarah Anyang. 2009. "The History and Growth of Caribbean Literature." *Lagos Papers in English Studies* 4: 147–63.

Agosto, Noraida. 1999. *Michelle Cliff's Novels: Piecing the Tapestry of Memory and History*. New York: Peter Lang Publishing.

Aguiar, Marian. 2001. "Decolonizing the Tongue: Reading, Speech, and Aphasia in the Work of Michelle Cliff." *Literature and Psychology* 47, nos. 1–2: 94–108.

Alcocer, Rudyard. 2004. *Narrative Mutations: Discourses of Heredity and Caribbean Literature*. London and New York: Taylor & Francis.

Alexander, M. Jacqui. 1991. "Redrafting Morality: The Postcolonial State and the Sexual Offences Bill of Trinidad and Tobago." In *Third World Women and the Politics of Feminism*, eds. C. T. Mohanty, A. Russo, and L. Torres. Bloomington and Indianapolis: Indiana University Press, 133–52.

Alexander, M. Jacqui. 1994. "Not Just (Any) Body Can Be a Citizen: The Politics of Law, Sexuality and Postcoloniality in Trinidad and Tobago and the Bahamas." *Feminist Review* 48: 5–23.

Alexander, M. Jacqui. 1997. "Erotic Autonomy as a Politics of Decolonization: An Anatomy of Feminist and State Practice in the Bahamas Tourist Economy." In *Feminist Genealogies, Colonial Legacies, Democratic Futures*, eds. M. J. Alexander and C. T. Mohanty. New York: Routledge, 63–100.

Alexander, M. Jacqui. 2005. *Pedagogies of Crossing: Meditations on Feminism, Sexual Politics, Memory and the Sacred*. Durham: Duke University Press.

Anim-Addo, Joan, ed. 1996. *Framing the Word: Gender and Genre in Caribbean Women's Writing*. London: Whiting and Birch Ltd.

Arnold, A. James, ed. 2001. *A History of Literature in the Caribbean, Volume 2: English and Dutch-Speaking Regions*. Amsterdam: John Benjamins Publishing.

Arnold, A. James, J. Michael Dash, and Julio Rodriguez-Luis, eds. 1994. *A History of Literature in the Caribbean, Volume 1: Hispanic and Francophone Regions*. Amsterdam: John Benjamins Publishing.

Arnold, A. James, J. Michael Dash, and Julio Rodriguez-Luis, eds. 1997. *A History of Literature in the Caribbean, Volume 3: Cross-Cultural Studies*. Amsterdam: John Benjamins Publishing.

Babín, María Teresa. 1980. "Trends in Caribbean English Fiction." *Caribbean Studies* 20, no. 1: 69–74.

Backes, Nancy. 2001. "Growing Up Desperately: The Adolescent 'Other' in the Novels of Paule Marshall, Toni Morrison, and Michelle Cliff." In *Women of Color: Defining Issues, Hearing Voices*, eds. D. L. Hoeveler and J. K. Boles. Westport, CT: Greenwood Press, 147–57.

Balderston, Daniel and Mike Gonzalez. 2004. *Encyclopedia of Latin American and Caribbean Literature, 1900–2003*. London and New York: Routledge.

Barnes, Erin Marie, Lily L. Miles, and Lauren Curtright. 2004. "Michelle Cliff." *VG: Voices from the Gaps: Women Artists and Writers of Color*. Website. University of Minnesota.

Barnes, Fiona R. 1992. "Resisting Cultural Cannibalism: Oppositional Narratives in Michelle Cliff's *No Telephone to Heaven*." *Journal of the Midwest Modern Language Association* 25, no. 1: 23–31.

Baytop, Adrianne. 1976. "The Emergence of Caribbean English Literature." *Latin American Literary Review* 4, no. 9: 29–38.

Benítez-Rojo, Antonio. 1996. *The Repeating Island: The Caribbean and the Postmodern Perspective*. Durham and London: Duke University Press.

Beriault, Janie. 2017. "'I Guess That's Another Place They've Ruined for Us': A Spatial Struggle Against the Development of Commercial Tourism in Jamaica Kincaid's *A Small Place* and Michelle Cliff's *No Telephone to Heaven*." *Journal of Postcolonial Writing* 53, no. 6: 659–72.

Berlant, Lauren. 1994. "68 or Something." *Critical Inquiry* 21, no. 1: 124–55.

Bhabha, Homi K. 1994. *The Location of Culture*. London and New York: Routledge.

Birkle, Carmen. 1998. "Colonial Mother and Postcolonial Daughter: Pocahontas and Clare Savage in Michelle Cliff's *No Telephone to Heaven*." In *Postcolonialism and Autobiography*, eds. A. Hornung and E. Ruhe. Amsterdam-Atlanta, GA: Brill, 61–75.

Blázquez, Eva María Méndez. 2016. "Unstable Identities: Michelle Cliff and Olive Senior 'Shortstorytelling' Jamaica." Unpublished thesis. Universidad Autonoma de Madrid.

Boehmer, Elleke. 1991. "Stories of Women and Mothers: Gender and Nationalism in the Early Fiction of Flora Nwapa." In *Motherlands: Black Women's Writing from Africa, the Caribbean and South Asia*, ed. S. Nasta. London: The Women's Press, 3–23.

Booker, M. Keith and Dubravka Juraga. 2001. *The Caribbean Novel in English: An Introduction*. Oxford: James Currey.

Bost, Suzanne. 1998. "Fluidity without Postmodernism: Michelle Cliff and the 'Tragic Mulatta' Tradition." *African American Review* 32, no. 4: 673–89.

Boyce Davies, Carole and Elaine Savory Fido, eds. 1990. *Out of the Kumbla: Caribbean Women and Literature*. Trenton, NJ: Africa World Press.

Brah, Avtar and Annie E. Coombes, eds. 2000. *Hybridity and Its Discontents: Politics, Science, Culture*. London and New York: Routledge.

Branca, Nicole. 2007. "Language, Gender and Identity in the Works of Louise Bennett and Michelle Cliff." Unpublished thesis. Rhode Island College.
Buonaiuto, Claudia. 2010. Review of "Michelle Cliff, *Everything Is Now* (Minneapolis and London: University of Minnesota Press, 2009)." *Anglistica* 14, no. 1: 127–30.
Carosone, Michael. "Another Side of Clare Savage's Identity Crisis: A Queer Theoretical Analysis of Michelle Cliff's *Abeng*." Unpublished paper.
Cartelli, Thomas. 1995. "After the Tempest: Shakespeare, Postcoloniality, and Michelle Cliff's New, New World Miranda." *Contemporary Literature* 36, no. 1: 82–102.
Carvalheiro, José. 2010. "Is the Discourse of Hybridity a Celebration of Mixing, or a Reformulation of Racial Division?: A Multimodal Analysis of the Portuguese Magazine *Afro*." *Forum: Qualitative Social Research* 11, no. 2: 1–29.
Chancy, Myriam J. A. 1997. *Searching for Safe Spaces: Afro-Caribbean Women Writers in Exile*. Philadelphia: Temple University Press.
Chassot, Joanne. 2009. "Fragmentation as Condition and Strategy: History, Narrative and Resistance in the Works of Michelle Cliff." *The Society for Caribbean Studies Annual Conference Papers* 10, no. 1: 1–8.
Chassot, Joanne. 2018. *Ghosts of the African Diaspora: Re-Visioning History, Memory, and Identity*. New Hampshire: Dartmouth College Press.
Chin, Timothy S. 1999. "'Bullers' and 'Battymen': Contesting Homophobia in Black Popular Culture and Contemporary Caribbean Literature." *Small Axe* 5: 14–33.
Cliff, Michelle. 1978. "Notes on Speechlessness." *Sinister Wisdom* 5: 5–9.
Cliff, Michelle. 1980. *Claiming an Identity They Taught Me to Despise*. Watertown, MA: Persephone Press.
Cliff, Michelle. 1985. *The Land of Look Behind*. New York: Firebrand.
Cliff, Michelle. 1990. "Clare Savage as a Crossroads Character." In *Caribbean Women Writers: Essays from the First International Conference*, ed. S. R. Cudjoe. Massachusetts: Calaloux Publications, 263–68.
Cliff, Michelle. 1991a. *Bodies of Water*. London: Minerva.
Cliff, Michelle. 1991b. "Caliban's Daughter: The Tempest and the Teapot." *Frontiers: A Journal of Women's Studies* 12, no. 2: 36–51.
Cliff, Michelle. 1993. *Free Enterprise*. London: Penguin.
Cliff, Michelle. 1994a. "Journey into Speech: A Writer Between Two Worlds: An Interview with Opal Palmer Adisa." *African American Review* 28, no. 2: 273–81.
Cliff, Michelle. 1994b. "History as Fiction, Fiction as History." *Ploughshares* 20, nos. 2–3: 196–202.
Cliff, Michelle. 1995. *Abeng*. London: Plume/Penguin.
Cliff, Michelle. 1996. *No Telephone to Heaven*. London: Plume/Penguin.
Cliff, Michelle. 1998. *The Store of a Million Items*. New York: Houghton Mifflin.
Cliff, Michelle. 2009. *Everything Is Now*. London: University of Minnesota Press.
Cliff, Michelle. 2010. *Into the Interior*. London: University of Minnesota Press.
Cliff, Michelle. 2011. "Colonial Girl: And What Would It Be Like." In *Sex and the Citizen: Interrogating the Caribbean*, ed. F. Smith. Virginia: University of Virginia Press, 251–55.
Cloud, Christine. 2009: "Rediscovering the Repressed: The Search for the M/Other in Michelle Cliff's *Abeng*." *An Online Feminist Journal* 2, no. 4: 9–13.

Cohen, Robin. 2007. "Creolization and Cultural Globalization: The Soft Sounds of Fugitive Power." *Globalizations* 4, no. 3: 369–84.
Costa, Jeanine Luciana Lino. 2006. "Remember Me: Identity Formation in Clarice Lispector, Isabel Allende, and Michelle Cliff." Unpublished dissertation. University of North Carolina at Chapel Hill.
Croisy, Sophie. 2008. "Michelle Cliff's Non-Western Figures of Trauma: The Creolization of Trauma Studies." *The AnaChronisT* 13: 131–56.
Cudjoe, Selwyn, ed. 1990. *Caribbean Women Writers: Essays from the First International Conference*. Wellesley, MA: Calaloux.
Cummings, Ronald. 2012. "Queer Marronage and Caribbean Writing." Unpublished thesis. University of Leeds.
Cummings, Ronald and Alison Donnell, eds. 2021. *Caribbean Literature in Transition, 1970–2020*. Cambridge: Cambridge University Press.
Curry, Ginette. 2007. *"Toubab La!": Literary Representations of Mixed-Race Characters in the African Diaspora*. Newcastle: Cambridge Scholars Publishing.
Dabydeen, David and Nana Wilson-Tagoe. 1987. "Selected Themes in West Indian Literature: An Annotated Bibliography." *Third World Quarterly* 9, no. 3: 921–60.
Dabydeen, David and Nana Wilson-Tagoe. 1997. *A Reader's Guide to West Indian and Black British Literature*. London: Hansib.
Dagbovie, Silka Alaine. 2006. "Fading to White, Fading Away: Biracial Bodies in Michelle Cliff's *Abeng* and Danzy Senna's *Caucasia*." *African American Review* 40, no. 1: 93–109.
Dalleo, Raphael. 2017. *Caribbean Literature and the Public Sphere: From the Plantation to the Postcolonial*. Charlottesville: University of Virginia Press.
Dash, J. Michael. 1998. *The Other America: Caribbean Literature in a New World Context*. Charlottesville: University Press of Virginia.
Derrick, Arthur. 1969. "An Introduction to Caribbean Literature." *Caribbean Quarterly* 15, nos. 2–3: 65–78.
Diedrich, Lisa. 1996. "Michelle Cliff." Postcolonial Studies. Emory University Blog. Accessed March 28, 2022.
Donahue, Jennifer. 2014. "Taking Flight: Caribbean Women Writing from Abroad." Unpublished thesis. Florida State University.
Donnell, Alison. 2006. *Twentieth-Century Caribbean Literature: Critical Moments in Anglophone Literary History*. London and New York: Routledge.
Donnell, Alison and Sarah Lawson Welsh, eds. 1996. *The Routledge Reader in Caribbean Literature*. London and New York: Routledge.
Downey, Dara, Ian Kinane, and Elizabeth Parker, eds. 2016. *Landscapes of Liminality: Between Space and Place*. London: Rowman and Littlefield International.
Edmondson, Belinda. 1993. "Race, Privilege, and the Politics of (Re)Writing History: An Analysis of the Novels of Michelle Cliff." *Callaloo* 16, no. 1: 180–91.
Edmondson, Belinda. 1998. "The Black Mother and Michelle Cliff's Project of Racial Recovery." In *Postcolonialism and Autobiography*, eds. A. Hornung and E. Ruhe. Amsterdam-Atlanta: Rodopi Brill, 77–86.
Eldmair, Barbara. 1999. *Rewriting History: Alternative Versions of the Caribbean Past in Michelle Cliff, Rosario Ferré, Jamaica Kincaid and Daniel Maximin*. Wien: Braumüller.

Elia, Nada. 2000. "'A Man Who Wants to Be a Woman': Queerness as/and Healing Practices in Michelle Cliff's *No Telephone to Heaven*." *Callaloo* 23, no. 1: 352–65.

Elia, Nada. 2001. *Trances, Dances, and Vociferations: Agency and Resistance in Africana Women's Narratives*. New York and London: Garland.

Emery, Mary Lou. 1997. "Refiguring Postcolonial Imagination: Tropes of Visuality in Writing by Rhys, Kincaid, and Cliff." *Tulsa Studies in Women's Literature* 16, no. 2: 259–80.

Enszer, Julie R. 2019. "'Creating Alchemy': On the Work of Michelle Cliff." *Sinister Wisdom* (Spring): 102–12.

Fanon, Frantz. 2008. *Black Skin, White Masks*. London: Pluto Press.

Feng, Pin-chia. 2013. "Narratives of Passing: Racial and Gender Politics in Michelle Cliff's *Abeng* and *No Telephone to Heaven*." *Feminist Studies in English Literature* 21, no. 1: 5–37.

Flores, Juan. 2009. *The Diaspora Strikes Back: Caribeño Tales of Learning and Turning*. New York: Routledge.

Ford, Na'Imah Hanan. 2004. "Toward a Theory of Yere Wolo: Michelle Cliff's *Abeng* and Paule Marshall's *Brown Girl Brownstones* as Coming of Age Narratives." Unpublished thesis. Florida State University.

François, Irline. 2010. "Unchaining the Unconscious: An Interview with Patricia Powell." *Anglistica* 14, no. 1: 121–25.

Gairola, Rahul K. 2017. "Bastardly Duppies and Dastardly Dykes: Queer Sexuality and the Supernatural in Michelle Cliff's *Abeng* and Shani Mootoo's *Cereus Blooms at Night*." *Wagadu: A Journal of Transnational Women's and Gender Studies* 18: 15–54.

Gifford, William Tell. 2003. *Narrative and the Nature of Worldview in the Clare Savage Novels of Michelle Cliff*. Oxford: Peter Lang.

Gikandi, Simon. 1992. *Writing in Limbo: Modernism and Caribbean Literature*. Ithaca: Cornell University Press.

Gilroy, Paul. 1993. *The Black Atlantic: Modernity and Double Consciousness*. Cambridge, MA: Harvard University Press.

Glave, Thomas, ed. 2008. *Our Caribbean: A Gathering of Lesbian and Gay Writing from the Antilles*. Durham and London: Duke University Press.

Glissant, Édouard. 1989. *Caribbean Discourse: Selected Essays*. Charlottesville: University Press of Virginia.

Gourdine, Angeletta K.M. 2002. *The Difference Place Makes: Gender, Sexuality, and Diaspora Identity*. Columbus: Ohio State University Press.

"The Grand Mixture of Trinidad's Culture." 1971. *Carib* (St. Thomas, Virgin Islands), October 28: 8–9.

Greene, Sue N. 1990. "Report on the Second International Conference of Caribbean Women Writers." *Callaloo* 13, no. 3 (Summer): 532–38.

Grimes, William. 2016. "Michelle Cliff, Who Wrote of Colonialism and Racism, Dies at 69." *New York Times*, June 18, https://www.nytimes.com/2016/06/19/books/michele-cliff-who-wrote-of-colonialism-and-racism-dies-at-69.html.

Hashimoto, Tomohiro. 2020. "Ruinate Landscape and Anti-Anthropomorphism in Michelle Cliff's *No Telephone to Heaven*." *Language Society* 14: 84–98.

Hoving, Isabel. 2001. *In Praise of New Travelers: Reading Caribbean Migrant Women Writers*. Stanford, CA: Stanford University Press.

Hoving, Isabel. 2011. "Michelle Cliff: The Unheard Music." In *The Routledge Companion to Anglophone Caribbean Literature*, eds. M. A. Bucknor and A. Donnell. Oxon: Routledge, 27–33.

Hudson, Lynn M. 2003. *The Making of "Mammy Pleasant": A Black Entrepreneur in Nineteenth-Century San Francisco*. Urbana and Chicago: University of Illinois Press.

Hyatt, Quincey Michelle. 2002. "In Praise of Michelle Cliff's Créolité." Unpublished dissertation. North Carolina State University.

Ilmonen, Kaisa. 2002. "Rethinking the Past, Rewriting the History: Counter-Narratives in Michelle Cliff's *Abeng*." *Atlantic Literary Review* 3, no. 2: 110–29.

Ilmonen, Kaisa. 2005a. "Creolizing the Queer: Close Encounters of Race and Sexuality in the Novels of Michelle Cliff." In *Close Encounters of an Other Kind: New Perspectives on Race, Ethnicity and American Studies*, eds. R. Goldblatt, J. Nyman, and J. A. Stotesbury. Joensuu: University of Joensuu, Studies in Literature and Culture 13, 180–95.

Ilmonen, Kaisa. 2005b. "From Borders to Bridges: Trickster Aesthetics in the Novels of Michelle Cliff." *American Studies in Scandinavia* 37, no. 2: 85–104.

Ilmonen, Kaisa. 2017. *Queer Rebellion in the Novels of Michelle Cliff: Intersectionality and Sexual Modernity*. Newcastle upon Tyne: Cambridge Scholars Publishing.

James, C. L. R. 1967. Introduction to *Tradition, the Writer and Society*, by W. Harris. London and Port of Spain: New Beacon.

James, C. L. R. 1969. "Discovering Literature in Trinidad." *Journal of Commonwealth Literature* 7: 73–80.

James, Louis. 1999. *Caribbean Literature in English*. London and New York: Longman Ltd.

Johannmeyer, Anke. 2005. "Claiming the Wholeness She Had Always Been Denied: Place and Identity in Michelle Cliff's Novels *Abeng* and *No Telephone to Heaven*." Unpublished dissertation. Uppsala University.

Johnson, Erica L. 2012. "Inventorying Silence in Michelle Cliff's *The Store of a Million Items*." *Contemporary Women's Writing* 6, no. 3: 267–83.

Johnson, Lemuel A. 1990 "A-beng: (Re)Calling the Body in(to) Question." In *Out of the Kumbla: Caribbean Women and Literature*, eds. C. Boyce Davies and E. Savory Fido. Trenton, NJ: Africa World Press, 111–42.

Kaplan, Caren. 1987. "Deterritorialization: The Rewriting of Home and Exile in Western Feminist Discourse." *Cultural Critique* 6: 187–98.

Kekeh-Dika, Andrée-Anne. 2003. "Michelle Cliff's *Free Enterprise*: Writing the Americas as Crossroads." In *Cross Perspectives on African Americans: Celebrating Michel Faber*, ed. C. Julien. Tours: Presses Universitaires François-Rabelais, 267–75.

Kempadoo, Kamala. 2009. "Caribbean Sexuality: Mapping the Field." *Caribbean Review of Gender Studies* 3: 1–24.

Keulen, Margarete. 1993. "From Silence to the Fragmented Self: Michelle Cliff and Edward Kamau Brathwaite's Subject Constitution in Literature and Non-Fictional Prose." In *Bridges Across Chasms: Towards a Transcultural Future in Caribbean Literature*, ed. Bénédicte Ledent. Liège: Liège Language and Literature, 199–210.

Kilinski, April Conley. 2006. "Embodying History: Women, Representation, and Resistance in Twentieth-Century Southern African and Caribbean Literature." Unpublished dissertation. University of Tennessee.

King, Bruce, ed. 1979. *West Indian Literature*. London and Basingstoke: The MacMillan Press Ltd.
King, Rosamond. 2002. "Sex and Sexuality in the English Caribbean Novels: A Survey from 1950." *Journal of West Indian Literature* 11, no. 1: 24–38.
King, Rosamond. 2008. "Re/Presenting Self and Other: Trans Deliverance in Caribbean Texts." *Callaloo* 31, no. 2: 581–99.
King, Rosamond. 2014. *Island Bodies: Transgressive Sexualities in the Caribbean Imagination*. Gainesville, FL: University Press of Florida.
Knutson, Lin. 1996. "Michelle Cliff and the Feminization of Space: *No Telephone to Heaven* as Female Limbo Gateway into History." *Journal of Caribbean Studies* 11, no. 3: 276–300.
Krise, Thomas W., ed. 1999. *Caribbeana: An Anthology of English Literature of the West Indies, 1657–1777*. Chicago: University of Chicago Press.
Lacerda, Irene Nicácio. 2009. "Home and Abroad: Identifications and Identities in Michelle Cliff's *No Telephone to Heaven*." Unpublished thesis. Universidade de Minas Gerais.
Lai, Yi-Peng. 2010. "Gardening Homeland, Deforesting Nation: Re-imagining the Tropics in Michelle Cliff's *No Telephone to Heaven*." *Anglistica* 14, no. 1: 39–51.
Lalla, Barbara. 1996. *Defining Jamaican Fiction: Marronage and the Discourse of Survival*. Tuscaloosa; University of Alabama Press.
Ledent, Bénédicte. 2000. "'Here, There, and Everywhere': Michelle Cliff's (Con)version of Caribbean Identity." In *Writing Women Across Borders and Categories*, ed. M. Ghosh-Schellhorn. Münster: LIT Verlag, 76–90.
Lima, Maria Helena. 1993. "Revolutionary Developments: Michelle Cliff's *No Telephone to Heaven* and Merle Collins's *Angel*." *Ariel: A Review of International English Literature* 24, no. 1: 35–56.
Lionnet, Françoise. 1992. "Of Mangoes and Maroons: Language, History, and the Multicultural Subject of Michelle Cliff's *Abeng*." In *De/Colonizing the Subject: The Politics of Gender in Women's Autobiography*, eds. S. Smith and J. Watson. Minneapolis: University of Minnesota Press, 321–45.
MacDonald-Smythe, Antonia. 2011. *Making Homes in the West/Indies: Constructions of Subjectivity in the Writings of Michelle Cliff and Jamaica Kincaid*. London: Garland Publishing Inc.
Machado Sáez, Elena. 2015. *Market Aesthetics: The Purchase of the Past in Caribbean Diasporic Fiction*. Charlottesville: University of Virginia Press.
Maisier, Veronique. 2012. "Representations of History in Michelle Cliff's and Patrick Chamoiseau's Novels." *Journal of West Indian Literature* 20, no. 1: 51–69.
Martínez-San Miguel, Yolanda. 2014. *Coloniality of Diasporas: Rethinking Intra-Colonial Migrations in a Pan-Caribbean Context*. New York: Palgrave Macmillan.
Mohan, Rajeswari. 2011. "The Excavation of History in Michelle Cliff's Fiction." *Otherness: Essays and Studies* 2, no. 1.
Mordecai, Pamela and Betty Wilson, eds. 1990. *Her True-True Name: An Anthology of Women's Writing from the Caribbean*. Oxford: Heinemann.
Morguson, Alison. 2021. "All the Pieces Matter: Fragmentation-as-Agency in the Novels of Edwidge Danticat, Michelle Cliff, and Shani Mootoo." Unpublished thesis. Indiana University.

Moynagh, Maureen. 1999. "The Ethical Turn in Postcolonial Theory and Narrative. Michelle Cliff's *No Telephone to Heaven.*" *Ariel: A Review of International English Literature* 30, no. 4: 109–33.

Murdoch, H. Adlai. 2010. "Violence and Metaphor: Gender and Postcolonial Identity in *Abeng.*" *Anglistica* 14, no. 1: 31–38.

Nasta, Susheila. 1995. "Setting Up Home in a City of Words: Sam Selvon's London Novels." *Kunapipi* 17, no. 1: 78–95.

O'Callaghan, Evelyn. 1987. "'Vive la Difference!': Political Directions in Short Stories by West Indian Women Writers." Paper presented at 7th Annual Conference on West Indian Literature, University of Puerto Rico.

O'Callaghan, Evelyn. 1993. *Woman Version: Theoretical Approaches to West Indian Fiction by Women.* London and Basingstoke: Macmillan Caribbean.

O'Callaghan, Evelyn. 1998. "Compulsory Heterosexuality and the Textual/Sexual Alternatives in Selected Texts by West Indian Women Writers." In *Caribbean Portraits: Essays on Gender Ideologies and Identities*, ed. C. Barrow. Kingston: Ian Randle Publishers, 294–319.

O'Callaghan, Evelyn and Tim Watson. 2021. *Caribbean Literature in Transition, 1800–1920.* Cambridge: Cambridge University Press.

Odintz, Jenny. 2014. "Creating Female Community: Repetition and Renewal in the Novels of Nicole Brossard, Michelle Cliff, Maryse Condé, and Giséle Pineau." Unpublished dissertation. University of Oregon.

O'Driscoll, Sally. 1995. "Michelle Cliff and the Authority of Identity." *Journal of the Midwest Modern Language Association* 28, no. 1: 56–70.

Ortiz, Fernando. 1940. "Los Factores Humanos de la Cubanidad." *Revista Bimestre Cubana* 21: 167.

Paravisini-Gebert, Lizabeth. 2008. *Literature of the Caribbean.* London: Greenwood Press.

Pećić, Zoran. 2013. *Queer Narratives of the Caribbean Diaspora.* London: Palgrave Macmillan.

Penier, Izabella. 2014. "Postcolonial Nation and Matrilineal Myth: Social Construction of Maternity in Michelle Cliff's 'Clare Savage' Novels." *Alicante Journal of English Studies* 27: 163–78.

Petta, Marissa. 2012. "Dismembering the Master Narrative: Michelle Cliff's Attempt to Rewrite Jamaican History in *Abeng.*" English Senior Seminar Papers, St. John Fisher University, paper 7: 1–26.

Phillips, Glenn O. 1980. "The Caribbean Collection at the Moorland-Springarn Research Center, Howard University." *Latin American Research Review* 15, no. 2: 162–78.

Pollock, Mary. 2003. "Positioned for Resistance: Identity and Action in Michelle Cliff's *Free Enterprise.*" In *Sharpened Edge: Women of Color, Resistance, and Writing*, ed. S. Athey. Westport, CT, and London: Praeger, 203–18.

Potocki, Beata. 2013. "'Apocalypso': Visions of Cosmopolitanism in Michelle Cliff's Fiction." *Global South* 7, no. 2: 62–86.

Prieto, Eric. 2013. *Literature, Geography, and the Postmodern Poetics of Place.* Hampshire: Palgrave Macmillan.

Raiskin, Judith. 1993. "The Art of History: An Interview with Michelle Cliff." *Kenyon Review* 15, no. 1: 57–71.

Raiskin, Judith. 1994. "Inverts and Hybrids: Lesbian Rewritings of Sexual and Racial Identities." In *The Lesbian Postmodern*, ed. L. Doan. New York: Columbia University Press, 156–72.

Raiskin, Judith. 1996. *Snow on the Cane Field. Women's Writing and Creole Subjectivity*. Minneapolis: University of Minnesota Press.

Ramchand, Kenneth. 1970. *The West Indian Novel and Its Background*. London: Faber and Faber.

Ramchand, Kenneth. 1976. *An Introduction to the Study of West Indian Literature*. Middlesex: Thomas Nelson and Sons Ltd.

Ramchand, Kenneth and Cecil Gray, eds. 1971. *West Indian Poetry*. London: Longman.

Renk, Kathleen J. 1999. *Caribbean Shadows and Victorian Ghosts: Women's Writing and Decolonization*. Charlottesville and London: University Press of Virginia.

Richards, Constance S. 2005. "Nationalism and the Development of Identity in Postcolonial Fiction: Zoë Wicomb and Michelle Cliff." *Research in African Literatures* 36, no. 1: 20–33.

Robinson-Walcott, Kim. 2003. "Claiming an Identity We Thought They Despised: Contemporary White West Indian Writers and Their Negotiation of Race." *Small Axe* 7, no. 2: 93–110.

Rody, Caroline. 2001. *The Daughter's Return: African-American and Caribbean Women's Fictions of History*. New York: Oxford University Press.

Sani, Ruta Mara. 1972. "A Bibliographical Survey of the West Indian Novel." Unpublished thesis. Western Michigan University.

Sarnelli, Laura. 2010. "'Eroto-Histories' and Counter-Memories of Violence in Contemporary Caribbean Women Writers. *Anglistica* 14, no. 1: 99–113.

Schröder, Nicole. 2006. *Spaces and Places in Motion: Spatial Concepts in Contemporary American Literature*. Bonn: Gunter Narr Verlag Tübingen.

Schwartz, Meryl F. 1993. "An Interview with Michelle Cliff." *Contemporary Literature* 34, no. 4: 595–619.

Schwartz, Meryl F. 1996. "Imagined Communities in the Novels of Michelle Cliff." In *Homemaking: Women Writers and the Politics and Poetics of Home*, eds. C. Wiley and F. R. Barnes. New York: Garland, 287–311.

Sethuraman, Ramchandran. 1997. "Evidence-cum-Witness: Subaltern History, Violence, and the (De)Formation of Nation in Michelle Cliff's *No Telephone to Heaven*." *Modern Fiction Studies* 43, no. 1: 249–87.

Seymour, A. J. 1966. "The Novel in the British Caribbean." *Bim* 11, no. 42: 83–85.

Shea, Renee Hausmann. 1994. "Michelle Cliff." *Belles Lettres* 9, no. 3: 32.

Silvera, Makeda, ed. 1992. *Piece of My Heart: A Lesbian of Colour Anthology*. Toronto: Sister Vision Press, 14–26.

Smith, Jennifer J. 2009. "Birthed and Buried: Matrilineal History in Michelle Cliff's *No Telephone to Heaven*." *Meridians: Feminism, Race, Transnationalism* 9, no. 1: 141–62.

Smith, Sidonie. 1998. "Memory, Narrative and the Discourses of Identity in *Abeng* and *No Telephone to Heaven*." In *Postcolonialism and Autobiography*, eds. A. Hornung and E. Ruhe. Amsterdam-Atlanta: Rodopi Brill, 37–59.

Springer, Jennifer Thorington. 2007. "Reconfigurations of Caribbean History: Michelle Cliff's Rebel Women." *Meridians: Feminism, Race, Transnationalism* 7, no. 2: 43–60.

Stecher, Lucía and Elsa Maxwell. 2013. "Michelle Cliff's *Into the Interior* and the Trope of the Solitary Female Immigrant." *Callaloo* 36, no. 3: 811–21.

Stephens, Melissa R. 2013. "Imagining Resistance and Solidarity in the Neoliberal Age of U.S. Imperialism, Black Feminism, and Caribbean Diaspora." Unpublished thesis. University of Alberta.

Stewart, Charles, ed. 2007. *Creolization: History, Ethnography, Theory*. California: Left Coast Press.

Stitt, Jocelyn Fenton. 2007. "Gendered Legacies of Romantic Nationalism in the Works of Michelle Cliff." *Small Axe: A Journal of Criticism* 11, no. 3: 52–72.

Strongman, Roberto. 2007. "Postmodern Developments in Michelle Cliff's *No Telephone to Heaven* and Esmeralda Santiago's *When I Was Puerto Rican*." *Journal of Caribbean Literatures* 4, no. 3: 97–104.

Thomassen, Bjørn. 2014. *Liminality and the Modern: Living Through the In-Between*. Surrey: Ashgate.

Tinsley, Omise'eke Natasha. 2010. *Thiefing Sugar. Eroticism Between Women in Caribbean Literature*. Durham: Duke University Press.

Toland-Dix, Shirley. 2004. "Re-Negotiating Racial Identity: The Challenge of Migration and Return in Michelle Cliff's *No Telephone to Heaven*." *Studies in the Literary Imagination* 37, no. 2: 37–54.

Trewick, Lilleth. 2003. "Resistance through Liminality: A Study of Michelle Cliff's *Abeng* and *No Telephone to Heaven*." Unpublished dissertation. Florida Atlantic University.

Turner, Victor W. 1969. *The Ritual Process: Structure and Anti-Structure*. Middlesex: Penguin.

Valens, Keja. 2013. *Desire Between Women in Caribbean Literature*. New York: Palgrave Macmillan.

van Gennep, Arnold. 1960. *The Rites of Passage*. London: University of Chicago Press.

Vella, Lianne. 2013. "Narratives of Becoming: Hybrid Identity and the Coming of Age Genre in Caribbean Women's Literature." Unpublished thesis. University of Birmingham.

Walker, Lisa. 2001. *Looking Like What You Are: Sexual Style, Race, and Lesbian Identity*. New York and London: New York University Press.

Walters, Wendy. 1998. "Michelle Cliff's *No Telephone to Heaven*: Diasporic Displacement and the Feminization of the Landscape." In *Borders, Exiles, Diasporas*, eds. E. Barkin and M. D. Shelton. Stanford: Stanford University Press, 217–33.

Walters, Wendy. 2005. *At Home in Diaspora: Black International Writing*. Minneapolis: University of Minnesota Press.

Walters, Wendy. 2008. "'Object into Subject': Michelle Cliff, John Ruskin, and the Terrors of Visual Art." *American Literature* 80, no. 3: 501–26.

Wekker, Gloria. 2006. *The Politics of Passion: Women's Sexual Culture in the Afro-Surinamese Diaspora*. New York: Columbia University Press.

Wilson, Elizabeth. 1981. "'Claiming an Identity They Taught Me to Despise': Alienation and the Caribbean Woman: From Mayotte Capécia to Michelle Cliff." Unpublished lecture. Department of French, University of the West Indies, Mona, Kingston, Jamaica.

Woodbury Tease, Amy. 2007. "Writing the Wound: Michelle Cliff's *No Telephone to Heaven*." In *Come Weep with Me: Loss and Mourning in the Writings of Caribbean Women Writers*, ed. J. C. Harte. Newcastle upon Tyne: Cambridge Scholars Publishing, 92–109.

Xiuxia, Zheng. 2008. "Female Bonding and Identity Formation in the Female Caribbean Bildungsroman." Unpublished thesis. University of Singapore.

Young, Robert. 1995. *Colonial Desire: Hybridity in Theory, Culture and Race*. New York: Putnam.

Zabus, Chantal. 2014. "'Cyaan Live Split': Under-Dressing, Over-Performing, Transgendering, and the Uses of Camouflage in Michelle Cliff's *No Telephone to Heaven*." In *The Cross-Dressed Caribbean: Writing, Politics, Sexualities*, eds. M. C. Fumagalli, B. Ledent, and R. del Valle Alcalá. Charlottesville: University of Virginia Press, 57–73.

Index

Abdulaal, Lamiaa Hassan Ibrahim, 72, 131n8
Abeng, 5, 9, 11, 18, 22, 26–28, 36–37, 40–45, 47–48, 50, 52, 56–57, 62–63, 65–66, 72, 74, 76, 86, 88, 89–90, 95, 98–99, 101–3, 105, 108, 110–11, 115, 117, 129nn3–4, 133n2, 134n4
Adams, Clover, 73, 131n9
Addante, Martha, 26, 111, 119
Adjarian, M. M., 119
Aegerter, Lindsay Pentolfe, 107
Agbor, Sarah Anyang, 12
Agosto, Noraida, 22, 24, 26, 27–28, 44, 51, 67, 71–72, 75, 106, 109, 111, 113, 116–19, 123
Aguiar, Marian, 25
Alcocer, Rudyard, 6, 29, 31
Alexander, M. Jacqui, 31, 128n3
"American Time, American Light," 97
"Among the Christian Diabolists," 69
Anim-Addo, Joan, 12
Anthony, Michael, 11, 15
"Apocalypso," 132n3, 133n3
Arnold, A. James, 127n1

Babín, María Teresa, 15
Backes, Nancy, 111
Bailey, Amy, 9
Balderston, Daniel, 11
Barnes, Fiona R., 3, 88
Baytop, Adrianne, 9–10, 14
"Belling the Lamb," 24, 35
"Below the Waterline," 104–5
Benítez-Rojo, Antonio, 7
Beriault, Janie, 3
Berlant, Lauren, 56
Bhabha, Homi K., 30

Birkle, Carmen, 3, 131n7
Bodies of Water, 5, 21, 28, 48, 53–54, 65, 66, 70, 82, 92, 96, 97, 99, 127n2
"Bodies of Water," 70, 97, 127n2
Boehmer, Elleke, 31
Booker, M. Keith, 110
Bost, Suzanne, 18, 21–22, 24, 26, 44, 102
Boyce Davies, Carole, 14
Brah, Avtar, 31
Branca, Nicole, 23, 74, 111, 131n10
Breeze, Jean "Binta," 13
Brodber, Erna, 13
Brontë, Charlotte, 20, 45
Brown, John, 9, 17, 69–70, 73
Brown, Lloyd, 14
Buffong, Jean, 12
Buonaiuto, Claudia, 20, 133n5
"Burning Bush," 21, 54
Butler, Judith, 117

"Caliban's Daughter: The Tempest and the Teapot," 64, 134n5
Campbell, George, 15
Carosone, Michael, 110
Cartelli, Thomas, 118
Carter, Martin, 15
Carvalheiro, José, 30
Césaire, Aimé, 10
Chancy, Myriam J. A., 115, 123, 128n2
Chassot, Joanne, 16, 18–19, 26–28, 75, 91, 108–9, 115, 119, 124, 127n2, 132n13, 135n10
Chin, Timothy, 31, 109, 122
Christian, Barbara, 13
Claiming an Identity They Taught Me to Despise, 5, 28, 47

"Clare Savage as a Crossroads Character," 65
Cloud, Christine, 107
Cohen, Robin, 29
"Colonial Girl: And What Would It Be Like," 98
"Columba," 54, 65, 96
Condé, Maryse, 13
Coombes, Annie, E., 31
Costa, Jeanine Luciana Lino, 62
"Crocodilopolis," 25, 74, 93, 97, 104
Croisy, Sophie, 42, 75
Cudjoe, Selwyn, 12
Cummings, Ronald, 8, 13
Curry, Ginette, 80

Dabydeen, David, 7–8, 14–16
Dagbovie, Silka Alaine, 26, 64–65
Dalleo, Raphael, 6
Dance, Darryl, 14
Dash, J. Michael, 7, 127n1
de Lisser, Herbert, 8–11
Derrick, Arthur, 7
Dickens, Charles, 44, 110
Diedrich, Lisa, 71
Donahue, Jennifer, 23, 74, 84, 88, 134n3
Donnell, Alison, 8–10, 12–15, 29, 32, 128n3
"Down the Shore," 57

"Ecce Homo," 127n2, 132n12
Edgell, Zee, 16
Edmondson, Belinda, 19–20, 26, 42, 60–61, 71, 80, 106, 111, 118, 129n4
Eldmair, Barbara, 23, 64
"Election Day 1984," 48
Elia, Nada, 26, 64, 98, 117–20, 135n9
Emery, Mary Lou, 118
Enszer, Julie R., 48
Everything Is Now, 5, 24–25, 28, 49, 59, 64, 74, 82, 93–94, 97, 104, 123, 128n2, 132n12, 133n5
"Everything Is Now," 94–95

Fanon, Frantz, 10
Feng, Pin-chia, 113
Ferré, Rosario, 13

"Ferry, The," 97
Flores, Juan, 29
Ford, Na'Imah Hanan, 129n6
François, Irline, 118
Free Enterprise, 5, 9, 17, 22, 28, 52, 58, 66–67, 69, 72–73, 76–78, 87, 93–94, 97–98, 123, 131n4, 131n9

Gairola, Rahul K., 109
Gifford, William Tell, 4, 18, 27–28, 39, 43, 81, 114, 117
Gikandi, Simon, 26, 88
Gilroy, Beryl, 12
Gilroy, Paul, 7
Glave, Thomas, 128n3
Glissant, Édouard, 29
Gomes, Albert, 9
Gonzalez, Mike, 11
Goodison, Lorna, 13
Gourdine, Angeletta K. M., 3, 56, 108, 119
Greene, Sue N., 13
Grimes, William, 23, 129n5

"Hanged Man, A," 66, 82, 97
Harris, Wilson, 11
Hashimoto, Tomohiro, 23
"History as Fiction, Fiction as History," 71
Hodge, Merle, 12
Holt Peterson, Kirsten, 14
Hoving, Isabel, 4–5, 16–17, 23, 25–26, 47, 75, 88
Hudson, Lynn M., 71
Hyatt, Quincey Michelle, 19, 135n8

Ilmonen, Kaisa, 4, 20, 23–24, 26–28, 36, 44, 46–47, 56, 64–66, 70, 73–74, 81, 88, 95, 100–102, 106, 110, 113, 115–20, 123–24, 130n4, 133n1, 134n5, 135n7, 135n11
Into the Interior, 5, 22, 28, 55, 58, 69, 92, 94, 104, 124, 132n3

James, C. L. R., 7, 9–11
James, Louis, 6, 10
Johannmeyer, Anke, 23, 26
Johnson, Amryl, 12

Johnson, Erica L., 26
Johnson, Lemuel, 50
Jordan, June, 13
"Journey into Speech, A," 36, 46
"Joy of Cooking, The," 55, 58
Juraga, Dubravka, 110

Kamau Brathwaite, Edward, 11, 16
Kaplan, Caren, 61, 80
Kekeh-Dika, Andrée-Anne, 73, 131n7
Kempadoo, Kamala, 31–32
Keulen, Margarete, 84
Kilinski, April Conley, 23
Kincaid, Jamaica, 13
King, Bruce, 10, 12, 15
King, Rosamond, 8, 32, 112, 128n3
Knutson, Lin, 50, 86–87, 121
Krise, Thomas W., 127n1
Kwesi Johnson, Linton, 16

Lacerda, Irene Nicácio, 22, 72, 85, 115–16, 118, 121
Lai, Yi-Peng, 4
Lalla, Barbara, 62, 102
Lamming, George, 10–11, 15–16
Land of Look Behind, The, 4–5, 6, 19–20, 28, 35–36, 46–47, 51, 56, 60–61, 75, 77–78, 84–85, 88, 107–8, 132n1, 133n6 (chap. 3), 133n2 (chap. 4)
Lawson Welsh, Sarah, 8–10, 12–14, 29
Ledent, Bénédicte, 68
Lima, Maria Helena, 64–65, 111
Lionnet, Françoise, 17, 26, 36–37, 63, 71, 90, 124
Lorde, Audre, 13
"Lost Nation Road," 94
Lovelace, Earl, 16

MacDonald-Smythe, Antonia, 26, 61, 71, 74, 118–19, 124, 131n11
Machado Sáez, Elena, 17, 22, 58, 69, 72
Mais, Roger, 11, 15
Maisier, Veronique, 42
Manley, Edna, 9
"Marooned," 58, 105

Marshall, Paule, 16
Marson, Una, 9
Martínez-San Miguel, Yolanda, 37, 42, 74, 112, 118, 134n6, 135n7
Maxwell, Elsa, 92
McFarlane, Basil, 86
McKay, Claude, 10–11, 15
Mendes, Alfred H., 9–10
Méndez Blázquez, Eva María, 21
Miller, Yvette E., 14
Mittelholzer, Edgar, 11, 15
Mohan, Rajeswari, 70
Mordecai, Pamela, 13–14, 16–18, 31
Morejón, Nancy, 13
Morguson, Alison, 101
Morris, Melvyn, 13
Morrison, Toni, 94
Moynagh, Maureen, 111–12
"Muleskin Honeyskin," 82
Murdoch, H. Adlai, 24, 105
"My Grandmother's Eyes," 49, 59–60, 64, 123

Naipaul, V. S., 11, 15–16
Nasta, Susheila, 10
Nichols, Grace, 13, 16
"Night Nursery," 55
No Telephone to Heaven, 3, 5, 8, 10–11, 16, 18, 22–23, 26–28, 40–45, 48–51, 63, 65–66, 72–73, 76, 78, 80–81, 85, 87, 91–92, 95, 97, 101, 104, 110–12, 116, 118, 122, 129n4, 130n5, 133n4, 134n6, 136n13

"Obsolete Geography," 133n6
O'Callaghan, Evelyn, 12, 29, 123, 127n1
Odintz, Jenny, 115
O'Driscoll, Sally, 18, 26
Ortiz, Fernando, 30

Paravisini-Gebert, Lizabeth, 5, 119
Pećić, Zoran, 32
Penier, Izabella, 17–18, 23, 130n6
Petta, Marissa, 89–90
Phillips, Glenn O., 11
"Points of Departure," 58
Pollock, Mary, 65, 73

Potocki, Beata, 118, 132n3
Prieto, Eric, 83
Prince, Mary, 8

Raiskin, Judith, 19–20, 26, 37, 56, 60–61, 64, 79, 112, 117–19, 136n13
Ramchand, Kenneth, 8–9, 12
Redcam, Tom, 8
Reid, V. S., 15
Renk, Kathleen J., 91, 120
Rhys, Jean, 12, 16, 20, 129n4
Rich, Adrienne, 5, 48
Richards, Constance S., 112
Riley, Joan, 12
Robinson-Walcott, Kim, 23
Rodriguez-Luis, Julio, 127n1
Rody, Caroline, 20, 49, 56
Roemer, Astrid, 13
Rutherford, Anna, 14

Sani, Ruta Mara, 8–10
Sarnelli, Laura, 106, 109, 118–19, 135n7
Savory Fido, Elaine, 12, 14
Schipper, Mineke, 14
Schröder, Nicole, 70, 74, 76, 90
Schwartz, Meryl F., 17, 36, 51, 109, 113, 116, 127n2
Schwarz-Bart, Simone, 13
"Screen Memory," 53–54
Selvon, Sam, 11, 15–16
Senior, Olive, 13, 16
Sethuraman, Ramchandran, 52, 70–72, 79, 80, 117, 130n5
Seymour, A. J., 7
Shakespeare, William, 134n5
Shea, Renee Hausmann, 70–71, 131n9
Silvera, Makeda, 128n3
Sinister Wisdom, 48
Smith, Jennifer J., 50, 118, 129n6, 135n7
Smith, Sidonie, 42, 128n2, 129n4
Springer, Jennifer Thorington, 4, 89, 106
"Stan's Speed Shop," 54
Steady, Filomena, 14
Stecher, Lucía, 92
Stephens, Melissa R., 50, 63

Stewart, Charles, 29
Stitt, Jocelyn Fenton, 42, 118, 136n12
Store of a Million Items, The, 5, 28, 54, 57, 78, 82, 94, 123
"Store of a Million Items, The," 78, 82
Strongman, Roberto, 61, 80, 122

Tatum, Charles, 14
Thomassen, Bjørn, 83
Tinsley, Omise'eke Natasha, 128n3
Toland-Dix, Shirley, 56, 81, 84
"Transactions," 123
Trewick, Lilleth, 5–6, 16, 19, 83–84, 116, 121
Turner, J. M. W., 52, 87
Turner, Victor W., 83, 132n2

Valens, Keja, 32, 128n3
van Gennep, Arnold, 132n2
Vella, Lianne, 26, 50, 88, 116
"Visit to the Secret Annex, A," 35

Walcott, Derek, 11, 15, 51, 132n1
Walker, Lisa, 129n4
Walters, Wendy, 62, 74, 84, 87, 90, 98
Watson, Tim, 29, 127n1
Wekker, Gloria, 31
Wilson, Betty, 13–14, 16–18, 31
Wilson, Elizabeth, 20, 74
Wilson-Tagoe, Nana, 7–8, 14–16
"Within the Veil," 4
"Woman Who Plays Trumpet Is Deported, A," 92–93, 133n4
Woodbury Tease, Amy, 50, 51–52, 120

Xiuxia, Zheng, 42, 46

Young, Robert, 30

Zabus, Chantal, 116

About the Author

Photo courtesy of the author

Ian Kinane is Reader in Popular Literature and Culture at the University of Roehampton, London. His books include *Ian Fleming and the Politics of Ambivalence* (Bloomsbury, 2021), *Isn't It Ironic?: Irony in Contemporary Popular Culture* (Routledge, 2021), *Didactics and the Modern Robinsonade* (Liverpool University Press, 2019), *Theorising Literary Islands: The Island Trope in Contemporary Robinsonade Narratives* (Rowman & Littlefield, 2016), and *Landscapes of Liminality: Between Place and Space* (Rowman & Littlefield, 2016).

www.ingramcontent.com/pod-product-compliance
Lightning Source LLC
Chambersburg PA
CBHW020417230426
43663CB00007BA/1205